Also by James W. Finegan

All Courses Great and Small:
A Golfer's Pilgrimage to England and Wales

Blasted Heaths and Blessed Greens:
A Golfer's Pilgrimage to the Courses of Scotland

Ireland

0 km 50
0 miles 50

Ballyliffin G.C.
Ballycastle G.C.
Rosapenna G.C.
Portsalon G.C.
Royal Portrush G.C.
Castlerock G.C.
Portstewart G.C.
Narin & Portnoo G.C.
DONEGAL
DERRY
ANTRIM
DONEGAL
★ Donegal
TYRONE
Belfast
Donegal G.C.
County Sligo G.C.
Bundoran G.C.
Enniscrone G.C.
LEITRIM
FERMANAGH
Carne G.C.
Sligo ★
SLIGO
MONAGHAN
Royal
County
Down
G.C.
Enniscoe House
CAVAN
LOUTH
MAYO
ROSCOMMON
LONGFORD
Seapoint
G.C.
Westport G.C.
MEATH
County
Louth G.C.
WESTMEATH
Mullingar G.C.
Connamara G.C.
Glasson G. & C.C.
★ Dublin
Galway ★
OFFALY
K-Club
KILDARE
Galway Bay G. & C.C.
GALWAY
Druid's Glen
Lahinch G.C.
LAOIS
WICKLOW
Dromoland Castle
Carlow G.C.
European Club
CLARE
Shannon G.C.
★ Limerick
CARLOW
Ballybunion
G.C.
Adare Manor
TIPPERARY
Mount Juliet
LIMERICK
KILKENNY
Tralee G.C.
WEXFORD
Ceann Sibeal G.C.
Waterford ★
Dooks
G.C.
Killarney
G.& F.C.
Cork
Tramore G.C.
Waterford Castle
KERRY
Beaufort
G.C.
Dunloe G.C.
Cork G.C.
WATERFORD
CORK
Harbor Point
G.C.
Fota Island G.C.
Waterville G.L.
Old Head
of Kinsale G.L.

DUBLIN AREA
The Island G.C.
Portmarnock G.C.
The Links Portmarnock
Royal Dublin G.C.
Luttrelstown
Castle G.C.
★ Dublin
Dublin
Bay

Jeffrey L. Ward 1995

Emerald Fairways
and
Foam-Flecked Seas

A Golfer's Pilgrimage to
the Courses of Ireland

JAMES W. FINEGAN

SIMON & SCHUSTER PAPERBACKS
NEW YORK   LONDON   TORONTO   SYDNEY

SIMON & SCHUSTER PAPERBACKS
Rockefeller Center
1230 Avenue of the Americas
NewYork, NY 10020

Copyright © 1996, 2007 by Aberdovey, Inc.

First Simon & Schuster paperback edition 2007

SIMON & SCHUSTER PAPERBACKS and colophon are registered
trademarks of Simon & Schuster, Inc.

For information about special discounts for bulk purchases,
please contact Simon & Schuster Special Sales at
1-800-456-6798 or business@simonandschuster.com.

Designed by Brian Mulligan
Map design by Jeff Ward

Manufactured in the United States of America

10 9 8 7 6 5 4 3 2

Library of Congress Cataloging-in-Publication Data
    Finegan, James W.
    Emerald fairways and foam-flecked seas: a golfer's pilgrimage to the
    courses of Ireland / James W. Finegan.
        p. cm.
    1. Golf courses—Ireland—Guidebooks. 2. Ireland—Guidebooks. I. Title.
    GV975.F56   1996
    796.352'06'8417—dc20   95–46092
                                                       CIP

ISBN-13: 978-0-684-81846-7
ISBN-10:   0-684-81846-9
ISBN-13: 978-1-4165-3298-9 (Pbk)
ISBN-10:   1-4165-3298-6 (Pbk)

For my extraordinary wife,
a nongolfer who has found great pleasure
in exploring Ireland with me.

Contents

10   Contents

Introduction

From the beginning, the phrase "golf in Ireland" has always meant golf throughout the entire Irish land mass—Northern Ireland as well as what is now the Republic—and this book follows that basic principle. The game has ignored the border, and so will we.

You may be surprised, as I once was, to learn that, for all practical purposes, the game in Ireland is about the same age as it is in the United States. America's first club, the St. Andrews Golf Club in Yonkers, New York, was formed in 1888. Ireland's oldest golf club, Royal Belfast, preceded it by just seven years. In both lands golf was played during the 1700s in a couple of places, but soon died out and would not gain a permanent foothold till late in the nineteenth century. The fact is that, for much of the first 400 years of its existence, the game was confined to Scotland.

But once it did take root in Ireland, golf flourished. This is actually a very small land—only minimally larger than Scotland and not so big as the state of Maine—yet today it contains some 335 courses, about 155 of which have just nine holes. In this book we will take a good look at 50 of the 180 that are 18-hole layouts and a rather cursory look at half a dozen of the nines.

If you believe that man doth not live by golf alone (some insist that this precept, on the face of it, is untenable) and that accommodations, dining, and sight-seeing also have to be top-notch, I'm optimistic that you will value the information provided on these subjects. I suspect that most readers would take as much pleasure as my wife and I do in such natural wonders as the Giant's Causeway and the Burren (a 100-square-mile rock garden!), to say nothing of the lonely beauty of Connemara or the grandeur of Connor Pass, especially when these attractions are often virtually next door to where you're playing. Heretical as it may sound, to be on the road in Ireland is almost as satisfying as to be on the course.

You will also find that I incline to spend considerable ink on places to stay. More than 30 different accommodations—everything from a modest B&B such as Mrs. McGivenney's Rushmere House in Tramore to the bona fide palace that is Straffan House at the Kildare Golf and Country Club—are described, sometimes in detail. We dearly love the Irish country-house hotels, and I am delighted to have the opportunity to share our experiences at a number of them. The times we have spent at Enniscoe House and Caragh Lodge and Mount Juliet and Mornington House and Adare Manor, to name only a handful, are among the most cherished memories of our many visits to Ireland, which go back to 1968. Not incidentally, the cooking in these houses is so consistently excellent that I'm afraid my restaurant list is a paltry thing indeed; we almost always dine right where we are spending the night. You'll hardly go wrong doing the same.

Some Practical Advice

This book is intended to be useful in three ways. First, the armchair traveler with an interest in knowing more about Ireland's golf clubs and courses will enjoy it; I've even included information on the country's most storied golfers—Christy O'Connor and Joe Carr, for example, and John Burke and Cecil Ewing, none of whom is a household name here in America—and its outstanding golf course architects, like Eddie Hackett, Christy O'Connor, Jr., Pat Ruddy, and Tom Craddock. Second, and rather more important, the book serves as a planning guide for the golfer who wants to lay out his or her own golf holiday itinerary. And lastly, it can function as a traveling companion, portable enough to pop into a suitcase and have at hand for ready reference throughout the trip.

An appendix contains the addresses and phone numbers of the clubs, courses, and hotels dealt with in the text. This information will be useful for those who intend to make their own reservations for starting times and for accommodations. From May through October, the six months when the weather is best, tee times can actually be more difficult to pin down than hotel

rooms. This is particularly true in the case of the more celebrated courses: Ballybunion, Lahinch, Portmarnock, Killarney,
Tralee. I suggest you pick up the phone and call; since so many
courses now have starting times seven days a week, you might
as well learn straight off whether the date and time you have in
mind are feasible. A phone call enables you to plan accordingly.
You also have the opportunity to find out in this conversation
the green fee, the deposit that may be required, the availability
of caddies or pull carts (ride-in golf carts as we know them are
still extremely uncommon in Ireland), and any restrictions on
women's play. Once you have this information and have
arranged a starting time, you may well want to write a con-
firming note to the secretary. This kind of courtesy is often appreciated, for despite their "open-door" policy, most of the
clubs at which you wish to play are private. In a manner of
speaking.

The accessibility of golf courses in Ireland—and, indeed, in
Scotland and the rest of the United Kingdom—is markedly
different from what we are used to in the United States. Without a member as your host, it is not possible to play at Oakmont or Winged Foot or Seminole. Not so in Ireland; even the
royal clubs—Dublin, Portrush, County Down—welcome the
visiting stranger. Why? Because the green fees paid by out-
siders are a major source of club revenue, sometimes *the* major
source. It is these tariffs, now steadily climbing, that make the
members' dues so modest, on average a mere 10 to 15 percent
of what Americans pay annually to belong to a first-rate golf or
country club. There is, of course, a *quid pro quo*: the Irish courses
are frequently crowded with nonmembers. Perhaps it is in Ire-

land—and in Britain—that we find the true meaning of the term "semiprivate."

I know of no Irish golf club that does not welcome women, though at Portmarnock, for example, they are not permitted to play on Saturdays. At Royal Dublin there are no women members, but wives of members and women visitors do play the course regularly. You should be aware that both men and women visitors may not be accepted at a number of clubs on weekends. That's when you'll want to be spending the night at Adare Manor or Mount Juliet or the K-Club, all of which have their own superb courses.

As for the green fees in Ireland, they were once a negligible factor in a vacation budget. Twenty years ago you paid a pound to play a round, maybe a pound and a half if you were tackling Portmarnock or Killarney or Lahinch. In 1995 the weekday green fee at Portmarnock was £40; at Killarney, £28; at Lahinch, £30—and they are not the most expensive. If you weren't staying in the hotel, it was £65 at Mount Juliet and £85 at the K-Club in 1995. In the unlikely event that you would confine yourself to lesser-known courses, your average weekday green fee would be somewhere in the £15 to £18 neighborhood. And though it is not always a matter of getting just what you pay for, that old saw is not far off the mark in Irish golf.

To give you some idea of the cost of accommodations; a room for two, in season and generally with full Irish breakfast, service, and taxes included, can range in 1996 anywhere from about 35 Irish pounds per night (say, Rushmere House, Tramore) to £265 per night at the K-Club. The middle ground is nicely occupied by the Hidden Ireland country-house hotels and by the Blue Book group, where you will surely be having dinner as well. At Mornington House (Hidden Ireland), for instance, the all-inclusive tariff for two—bed, breakfast, dinner with wine—would be very like £110. At Coopershill House, a Blue Book accommodation, the cost would be more like £145.

One final note: some clubs—I think specifically of Royal Portrush and Royal County Down—state as a matter of policy that visitors must have a current handicap card and/or a letter of introduction with handicap confirmation from the club professional. Only rarely is a golfer actually asked to produce either of these documents, but it is prudent to carry them with you.

The Lure of Seaside Golf

The principal reason for the powerful appeal of golf in Ireland is its panoply of extraordinary links courses. I can tell you that this single fact accounts for my wife's accompanying me, time after time, to Ireland. She has never struck a golf ball, yet she long ago discovered that golf courses, especially those in the splendid duneland, are among the most beautiful places in the world.

Now make no mistake about it, there are today some very fine inland courses in Ireland—Adare Manor, the K-Club, both of the Killarney eighteens, Druid's Glen, Carlow, Mount Juliet—but they are unlikely to compel us to cross an ocean. Not so in the case of Ballybunion and Lahinch, of Royal County Down and Royal Portrush, of Portmarnock and Portstewart, of

Waterville and the Island, of the European Club and Baltray—
any one of them is worth a journey to the ends of the earth.

And so you will find the emphasis here on seaside golf, the
earliest and the most natural form of the game. Of the 50
courses that are examined rather comprehensively, 31 of them
are links, laid out on the sand-based soil that serves as a buffer
between the sea and the arable land at a remove from the salt
water.

Over tens of thousands of years this linksland evolved as the
sea gradually receded, leaving behind sandy wastes which the
winds fashioned into dunes, knolls, hollows, and gullies. Gradually grass, fertilized by the droppings of the gulls, began to
grow in the hollows. It was a thick, close-growing mixture
with stiff, erect blades—the key features of true links turf.

As it happened, nature did not endow the links with trees.
Oh, from time to time a solitary, wind-warped excuse for a tree
will surface, but by and large the great links, which often display a lot of gorse and heather, are treeless, offering a severe,
desolate kind of beauty. Encroaching limbs and claustrophobic
foliage have no place on a pure links. There is an enticing spaciousness, an exhilarating sense of openness and freedom about
the great majority of seaside courses that is rarely found in inland golf.

Linksland that can be transformed into golf courses is a
scarce commodity today. Special planning permission is required. The environmentalists have earmarked virtually all
linksland as having "scientific interest," so we can't expect to
see many true seaside courses created in the years to come. Still,

we can be grateful not only for those Ireland has long possessed, but for the new ones—at Ballyliffin and Brittas Bay (the European Club) and Carne and Portmarnock (the Links Portmarnock)—that have been fashioned in the last three or four years. What an addition they make to the treasure trove!

A Boom in Course Construction

It is difficult to keep up with all the new courses coming on stream in Ireland today. Of the 50 courses covered in this book, a good half of them were built after 1972, and 16 of these 26 opened for play in the past five years. Included among the newcomers are the Arnold Palmer/Ed Seay course at the K-Club, Jack Nicklaus's Mount Juliet, the Robert Trent Jones eighteen at Adare Manor, and Druid's Glen, designed by the Irish team of Pat Ruddy and Tom Craddock. These also happen to be, in my judgment, the four best inland courses in Ireland.

Helping to account for the dramatic increase in golf courses throughout the Republic—perhaps we will soon see something of the kind in Northern Ireland as well—is the availability of European Economic Community grants to developers. The Irish economy has long been dependent on tourist spending. Today the government is convinced that golf can help attract a lot more of that money and, what is more, attract it to areas of the country that have never been noted for their sight-seeing appeal. The outstanding new courses at Carne, in remote northwest Mayo, and at Glasson, outside Athlone, in the oft-ignored "midlands," reflect this thinking. For the golfer, it is development money well spent.

In Praise of the White Markers

For very like 40 years I was what is generally considered a good club player. My handicap moved between 1 and 4, and I won a handful of club championships and a couple of senior club championships. I was always a short hitter, and today I'm an unreliable 8 who thinks that a 210-yard drive—on the flat and in the calm—is not to be disdained.

I mention these things so you will have some idea whose hands you're in as you roam through Ireland. With me, you play from the white tees. Too often, it seems, descriptions of golf holes find the author back on the blues, tackling a course that stretches to more than 7,000 yards, a layout with seven or eight par fours ranging from 415 to 455 yards and a couple of par fives in the 580 neighborhood. Unless I'm badly mistaken, many readers of this book will be more comfortable swinging from the regular markers—overall course length averaging maybe 6,250 yards—with a fellow who pulls out a 5-iron when the shot to the green is 150 yards and a 3-wood when it's 195 yards. Besides, it's difficult for a visitor to get permission to use the back tees (often called the medal tees) in Ireland. They are generally reserved for members in competitions.

The Simple Scheme of It

I've organized this book as though you and I had the luxury of carving about two months out of our lives to play these 50 courses one after another. Each chapter finds us traveling on-ward to a new territory, which may have only two courses on my list or could have five or six. We take them as they fall on the map, with little regard for their pedigree.

In the end we will have encountered almost all of the fabled "40 shades of green," played the great majority of Ireland's finest courses, learned a little about the men who designed them and those who gained fame on them, taken in some of the sights, savored our stays in those marvelous country-house hotels, and made the acquaintance of a number of interesting people.

Our pilgrimage commences in the West, at Lahinch, the very model of links golf, carries us clockwise almost full circle around the entire land, and concludes at the incomparable Ballybunion. The emerald fairways await us; let us begin.

—James W. Finegan
July 1995

Emerald Fairways
and
Foam-Flecked Seas

Chapter One

Orbiting Shannon

The first stroke I ever played in Ireland was my drive on the opening hole at Lahinch more than 20 years ago. I urge you to follow in my footsteps, for as the ball leaves the clubface to wing over this restless and hummocky and tumbling terrain and land on the upslope of a great sandhill, the flag straining on its stick higher yet on a perfect plateau of green, you will know without being told that here is links golf—the reason you have crossed an ocean—in its purest and most joyous form.

Lahinch seems to me the ideal introduction to the game in Ireland, and not just because of its wonderful golf holes.

There is the plain little town itself, which has been called the St. Andrews of Ireland. In truth, Lahinch is even more single-minded in its pursuit of the game than is the ancient royal burgh, for Lahinch has no university, no historical monuments, no handsome blocks of seventeenth- and eighteenth-century houses. It has the two eighteens, a handful of small hotels and B&Bs, some tweed and souvenir shops, several convivial pubs (where the Irish folk music for which County Clare is noted can be enjoyed), and a passion for golf. Even lovely Liscannor Bay, on which the town is set, seems of little moment other than as a backdrop for some of the golf holes. Golf, more often than not, is the opening subject in any conversation here, and though other topics may well be touched upon along the way, the talk will inevitably come full circle back to what really matters, like the blind second shot on Klondyke, or the best line for the drive on 12 (perhaps a little left of the castle is more prudent), or the impact of World War II on the career of the illustrious John Burke. If you play golf, talk golf, or are merely content to listen to golf being discussed, you will be entirely at home here.

The place has another distinct virtue: It is just 30 miles north of Shannon International Airport. There can be few things more rewarding in the life of an American golfer than to make the transatlantic night flight, pick up a rental car at Shannon, and, somehow miraculously refreshed and rejuvenated, tee off not an hour later at Lahinch.

I recall doing just that in 1974, when the predecessor of the present clubhouse was still in use. It was a simple, spartan structure then, the stone-floored changing room unheated and *sans* lockers. You hung your clothes on a wooden peg. Dangling from the peg next to mine were rosary beads. It could only be Ireland!

That day there was a neatly typed little notice at the main entrance to the clubhouse advising the members that the club would be closed Monday out of respect to John Burke, whose funeral was being held then. John Burke was the greatest player in the history of the club and one of the half-dozen greatest in the annals of Irish amateur golf. A big strong fellow with a wide swing arc, he was noted for the phenomenal length he could produce with woods out of deep and clinging rough. He won the Irish Open Amateur in 1947, defeating the up-and-coming Joe Carr at Royal Dublin; the Irish Close Amateur eight times, between 1930 and 1947; the West of Ireland Amateur six times; and the South of Ireland Amateur 11 times (Lahinch was the permanent venue). In 1932 he was named to the Walker Cup team, the first golfer from the Republic to be so honored. I suspect that no one could remember the last time Lahinch had been closed. Only an event of such magnitude as John Burke's passing could have prompted it.

It was a day for encountering notes at Lahinch. In the clubhouse there was one under the broken barometer that said: "see goats." Some four or five goats have for years grazed on the links, and they continue to do so today. They are our guide. We may not have the sense to come in out of the rain, but they do. When the weather turns mean, the goats turn toward the clubhouse—and shelter. So keep an eye out for them and their peregrinations.

Golf was first played at Lahinch in 1892, when members of the Black Watch Regiment, stationed at Limerick, heard of what was rumored to be ideal golfing country in the sandhills by Liscannor Bay. Over they came to see for themselves, and agreed that it was worthy ground. Nor would this mark the only time that Scots would bring the gospel of the game to the benighted Irish heathens.

The club itself was founded a year later. As is almost always the case, the course we play today is an evolutionary product incorporating elements of the original layout (half the holes in the sandhills, half in the much less interesting terrain on the other side of Liscannor Road); of the Old Tom Morris scheme, 1897 (still half and half, but considerable improvement to the holes themselves); of the Charles Gibson design, 1907 (13 holes now in the dunes, five on, if you will, the wrong side of the tracks); of the Alister Mackenzie plan, 1928 (all 18 now in the glorious duneland); and of the current eighteen (basically Mackenzie but with a number of attractive later modifications).

A word or two about Alister Mackenzie, whose fame today rests on such masterpieces as Royal Melbourne, Cypress Point, Augusta National (with Bob Jones), and Crystal Downs (with Perry Maxwell). A Yorkshireman born in 1870, Mackenzie studied medicine at Cambridge, served as a surgeon in the Boer War, then came home to establish a practice in Leeds. He began to dabble in course design during the first decade of the century and gradually gave up medicine to devote full time to golf course architecture. Over the next 20 years, beginning about 1914, he designed, remodeled, or expanded countless courses in England, Ireland, Scotland, Australia, New Zealand, Argentina, and the United States. In 1920 he published a small book titled *Golf Architecture* in which he set down what he judged to be the 13 essential features of an ideal golf course. One of them must endear him forever to the high handicapper: there should be a complete absence of the annoyance caused by having to search for lost balls. The book was widely influential and is considered a classic of the genre today.

Lahinch, par 72, can be stretched to over 6,700 yards, but it is regularly played at about 6,300 yards, with the ladies' markers at 5,500 (par 74). That perfect opening hole, uphill, is followed by a delightful short par 5, spilling downhill past the clubhouse, and then a good 145-yarder with a steep falloff on the left of the raised green. Now comes the strong—and altogether wonderful—410-yard 4th, where the drive must gain a fairway at the top of a high, steep hill, and the long second shot, turning left now, must carry a broad expanse of rough country in order to reach a green defended by low dunes and little sandy pots at the wings. There is not a great quantity of sand at Lahinch, but it is doled out in such meager measures that there are actually 101 bunkers.

Two of golf's most celebrated curios now confront us, consecutively. First comes "Klondyke," the 475-yard 5th. We drive up a narrow, secluded valley formed by high grassy dunes on both sides of the fairway. Nothing unusual in that. What makes this hole unforgettable is the sandhill that abruptly terminates the fairway, looming some 30 feet above us at about 350 yards from the tee. This startling obstruction calls to mind a traffic cop's hand thrust up intimidatingly to make sure you stop. What is now required is a 4- or 5-wood that surmounts this blockade and comes to rest on the far side of it in the expanse of fairway shared by the 18th hole. An item on the back of the scorecard, appropriately printed in red, is worth quoting:

"SPECIAL WARNING re KLONDYKE: 5th HOLE. The Committee of Lahinch Golf Club wish to inform all players that they will not accept liability for accidents at the crossing of the 5th and 18th fairways. It is the responsibility of each in-

dividual golfer to ensure that there is no one on the crossing before he plays over Klondyke."

Well, having safely negotiated the crossing and putted out,
perhaps for a par five, we proceed to the tee of the 6th hole,
which could be said to be even more improbable. A 145-yarder,
the 6th is called "Dell" because the green is tucked away in a
little natural amphitheater between two sandhills, one walling
off the front of the green and one backstopping the rear. Between the two nestles the putting surface, which has considerable breadth but very little depth. There is no sign of a
flagstick, no suggestion of a green. This could fairly claim to be
the blind hole of the world. But the Committee has taken pity
on us; a white marker stone placed on the fronting hill provides
the line (the stone is moved whenever the cup is changed), and
so we launch our 6-iron prayerfully in the general direction,
trusting that if a carom off a steep slope should follow, it will be
more helpful than harmful.

Some have called the hole defective (and worse). That may
be. But, believe it or not, skill does have some role in this low
adventure (beginning with the club choice), and taken in the
right spirit, it is tremendous fun.

With "Klondyke" and "Dell" now behind us, we begin a virtually unbroken skein of marvelous holes that carry us higher
and higher into these majestic and turbulent sandhills, out
along Liscannor Bay, then back to interior ground with nearly
as much feature and fascination as the more dramatic reaches.
We keep expecting the occasional indifferent hole. It is
nowhere to be found. Every hole is inviting, a visual delight in
a wild and woolly landscape culminating at a green so superbly

natural—on a plateau or in a dell, more often than not—that even the most artful bulldozing could never simulate it. Hole after hole is fair and challenging. Of the eight two-shotters (par fours) that remain, five or six of them are classic links holes, and three of them are among my favorites anywhere.

The 375-yard 7th calls for a rising drive to a generous expanse of fairway that, at about 240 yards, comes to a sudden halt when the terrain plunges to a cavernous hollow with a large sand bunker as its floor. This pit is to be avoided like the plague. The second shot, from the safety of the high ground, now sails down through the flanking dunes to a tightly bunkered green set strikingly above the ocean.

The 12th is rather more straightforward but, at 440 yards, a bear. It is also a beauty. Here, from a lofty perch at the cliff edge, we drive at the ruins of the ancient O'Brien Castle in the distance, the sands of the river estuary immediately on our left but far below and just waiting to snare the aggressive hook that gets away. A pretty multiple-arch stone bridge over the river beyond the long green (42 yards, by my pacing) is an appealing element in this composition.

(The Castle, I might point out, is the name given to the second eighteen, several holes of which are routed around this ancient fragment. This is a relief course, designed to handle the overflow from the principal eighteen. Some 5,400 yards long, this par-67 layout is, unfortunately, laid out over dull ground. In no sense is it an acceptable substitute for the Old Course, though the turf itself is generally good.)

As for the final par four I will mention, the 13th, it is 175 yards shorter than the splendid 12th, but it demonstrates convincingly that the game owes little to length. A scant 265 yards, it nonetheless has plenty of bite. The drive is imperiled on the right by a deep hollow that calls for a blind pitch from the long and throttling rough. The fairway slopes off to the left, and the consequences of a pull are less dire. Yet even a straight tee shot that leaves only a little half-wedge is no guarantee of success, for the plateau green, not far above us, is heavily bunkered and double-tiered. The chance of three-putting is uncomfortably real. This is a teasing hole, full of opportunity and, potentially, also of frustration.

Well, it is all here at Lahinch—the spectacular duneland that makes links golf the most natural and most satisfying expression of the game, the magnificent vistas that lend such exhilaration to a round, and, above all, a succession of varied and spirited golf holes that test the top-rank player and still delight, at every turn, even the least accomplished among us.

Alister Mackenzie said, however ingenuously (if not immodestly), that Lahinch might come to be regarded as "the finest

and most popular course that I or, I believe, anyone else ever constructed." For my part, I would simply say I cannot name another course that, day in and day out, I would rather play. For here, in fullest measure, is Bernard Darwin's indispensable ingredient: pleasurable excitement.

Two of Ireland's great natural wonders lie just north of Lahinch, and I encourage you to set aside a little time to see them both. Some 15 minutes drive up the coast are the Cliffs of Moher, which stretch along the sea for almost five miles and range in height from 400 to 600 feet. A variety of seabirds, including puffins, razorbills, and kittiwakes, can be observed there, particularly in nesting season. The best view is to be had from O'Brien's Tower (not to be confused with the O'Brien Castle), approached by a track that leads away to the left off the main road. On a day when the wind gusts unexpectedly, you will want to take care.

Some 20 minutes farther north, beyond Lisdoonvarna, lies the Burren. The word *burren* means "great rock" in Gaelic. And surely this is the greatest rock formation any of us is ever likely to encounter—100 square miles of limestone. It is a lunarlike wonderland, a baffling and eerie plateau of gray stone seeming to stretch away limitlessly and containing within its bounds prehistoric graves and ring forts and ancient Celtic crosses. It is a favorite stamping ground of geologists and botanists. In its natural rock gardens grow an extraordinary assortment of flowers, among them orchids and blue spring gentians, white anemones and yellow primroses.

In the very heart of the Burren, near the bottom of Corkscrew Hill on the road to Ballyvaughn, is an excellent small hotel in the Irish country-house tradition. Its name is Gregans Castle, and if it is not at all castellated in appearance, you will not be disappointed in the welcoming atmosphere, the creature comforts, the gardens, and the views across this unique wilderness to Galway Bay. There are 18 bedrooms and 4 suites. The emphasis is on comfort but not at the expense of style. Laura Ashley fabrics (florals and paisleys), period furniture, an occasional family heirloom—all contribute to a sense of warmth and well-being. Peat fires in the public rooms are a gracious touch.

The cooking is of a high order. Since the hotel is only four miles from the sea, the menu always offers a number of seafood dishes. As a reminder, a patch of Galway Bay is clearly visible in the distance from the dining room. The wine list, while not extensive, is a good one.

Peter and Moir Haden, who own and operate Gregans Castle, make an excellent team. There is about him an unmistakable sense of professionalism and crisp efficiency—you know the hotel will be well run—while she is quite outgoing, eager to help make sure that your stay in this remote and starkly beautiful spot is enjoyable. She mentioned that they frequently host golfers playing as far away as Ballybunion, a good hour and a half to two hours south. I was not surprised.

Gregans does not look like a castle, but Dromoland certainly does. With its battlements and crenellations and turrets and towers, its impregnable gray stone walls and its air of antiquity, it matches most people's dreams of what a castle should be. Located in Newmarket-on-Fergus, less than 15 minutes from Shannon Airport, it is ideally situated for touring golfers, who find it a convenient stopping place the day they arrive in Ireland and the day before they leave. Then, too, Dromoland Castle is a hotel with its own 18-hole course.

Despite staying at Dromoland on three prior occasions, it was not until 1995 that I ventured out onto what always looked to me to be a pretty but innocuous layout that surely could provide nothing more than a pleasant walk in the park. I was wrong. Pretty it assuredly is, but the walk is often a trudge and the test can be stern.

The long, curving driveway that takes you to and from the hotel cuts right across the course. What you see from the car is an expanse of rolling land, a complete absence of rough, a green or two almost indistinguishable from the fairway and with neither character nor defenses, and some sturdy old trees that obviously aren't going to get in any golfer's way. In short, the place for a family fivesome before or after tea.

Ah, 'tis but a snare and a delusion!

Against a par of 71, the course measures about 6,200 yards for men, 5,400 for ladies. The turf, a meadowy mixture, provides a minimum of run. The opening hole measures 390 yards and plays 460 yards—uphill every step of the way, doglegging smoothly right. The 2nd, 520 yards downhill, plays only 470 yards, but woods are tight on the right, the fairway slopes steeply left, and the green is on a shelf. Since the 3rd hole is your basic 230-yard straightaway par three, a perfect driver is all that's called for. Two perfect drivers will not get you home on the rising 450-yard par-four 4th, where bunkers right and left patrol the crowned green. The 5th looks just like the 4th, but since it's a mere 410 yards, your inclination is to consider it a breather. At 560 yards, the 6th is decidedly not a breather, but it does lead to the 7th, a 140-yarder played from a vertiginously high tee in the trees down to a very narrow green backdropped first by Lough Dromoland and, on the far side of the water, by Dromoland Castle itself. It is one of the exquisite vistas in the world of inland golf. The first nine concludes with the fine 390-yard 8th, a wooded roller coaster of a hole, and the falling 220-yard 9th.

The second half is more than 400 yards shorter, and it is easier—what wouldn't be?—but it, too, is hilly and, if anything, there is more variety and the greens are jauntier. The modest river Rine pops up a couple of times, the lake itself comes into play on the 10th, 11th, and 18th, and there are some attractive distant views to the Shannon estuary.

Put it all together and, despite the very light bunkering, the even lighter rough, and the deceptively easy look of things, this eighteen at Dromoland Castle is hardly dismissable. As for the architect, I could learn nothing about him but his name, B. E. Wiggington.

I was introduced to a husky 18-year-old member of the hotel's room service staff, a 2-handicapper who knew this course and the other courses in this neck of the woods well. After reviewing with him several of the outstanding holes here, I asked him which of the two, Dromoland Castle or Lahinch, would be more difficult from the regular tees on a pretty day and with a wind between 10 and 15 mph.

He did not have to mull his response. "Oh," he said instantly, "Dromoland would be harder."

Dromoland Castle, which dates in part to the sixteenth century, was long the ancestral seat of the O'Briens, the most powerful clan in County Clare and directly descended from Brian

Boru, High King of Ireland in the tenth century. Impressive reminders of the castle's historic past can be found everywhere: in the wood and stone carvings, the paneling, the old portraits and landscapes and still lifes, and the romantically beguiling gardens and grounds. There is a total of 75 guest rooms and suites, many overlooking the lake. All accommodations are quite comfortable; some are luxurious to the point of opulence.

The public rooms manage the difficult trick of being both stately and warm. There is nothing hushed about the atmosphere at Dromoland, and the guests, many of them American, obviously do not feel constrained. They are having a good time here.

The dining room struck us as particularly beautiful—mahogany paneling below the chair rail, blue and gold antique velvet wall covering above, three large crystal chandeliers, a marble fireplace that suggests the ecclesiastical Gothic leanings of this particular room, irresistible views of the lake from every table. And the cooking fully holds up its end of the bargain. It inclines to be fancy: dodine of guinea fowl with foie gras; a salad of veal sweetbreads with bacon and croutons; braised fillet of sole in a champagne sauce laced with squid ink; iced chocolate and coffee soufflé with calypso sauce. It need scarcely be added that the wine list is extensive.

One of the special appeals of dinner at Dromoland Castle is the singer/harpist, whose repertoire goes far beyond the obligatory "Danny Boy" to include unfamiliar and often moving Irish folk ballads. She is the ideal complement to the room, the food, and the view.

Some 500 yards past the terminal at Shannon Airport lies the Shannon Golf Club. The course, designed by John D. Harris, who laid out the second eighteen at Lahinch, opened 30 years ago. Par is 72. It can play as long as 6,870 yards, and from the regular tees it is almost 6,300 yards. I wish I could be more enthusiastic about this course, a rather level parkland design with many attractive trees, deciduous as well as evergreen, but I'm afraid that too much of it is rather ordinary. Still, the turf is uniformly excellent, and you can be confident of a warm welcome in the clubhouse.

Perhaps 20 minutes south of Limerick, on the N21, and no more than 40 minutes south of Shannon, lies the picturesque village of Adare. It stands on the river Maigue and is noted for its thatched-roof cottages, its great oak trees, and its ancient ruins. Among the village restaurants, the Mustard Seed has a reputation that goes well beyond County Limerick for contemporary interpretation of classical dishes. Three pubs— Sean Collins, Lena's Bar, and Bill Chawke's Lounge Bar—offer traditional Irish music.

For more than 90 years Adare had just nine holes of golf, at the Adare Manor Golf Club. This was a rather compact layout, so much so that it was the only nine-hole course I can think of with just eight fairways: the first hole and the last hole "shared." Within the past few years, the course was extended to eighteen. I confess that I have not played the new holes, which, like the original nine, are routed through pretty parkland. I suspect that there is more challenge here than we might at first expect.

Next door, however, is all the challenge a golfer could ever want. At Adare Manor itself, which is to say within the grounds of what was for centuries the demesne of the Earls of Dunraven, Robert Trent Jones has laid out a course to rank among the three or four finest inland courses in Ireland and among the top 15 here overall. What's more, it is the center-piece of a truly great hotel and resort which, in addition to golf, offers indoor swimming, horseback riding, clay pigeon shoot-ing, fox hunting, and fishing ("Excellent piscatorial conditions are available on the river Maigue, which meanders through the grounds and yields plump salmon and trout catches.")

Also within the grounds are many of the historic ruins that draw visitors to Adare, including a fourteenth-century Augus-tinian priory, a fifteenth-century Franciscan friary, and Desmond Castle, which dates to the twelfth century. The castle remains are composed of a keep within a moated inner ward, two great halls, a kitchen, bakery, and stables. The friary has well-preserved cloisters, with a very old yew tree in the center of the enclosure.

The aerial view of the hotel that adorns its color brochure suggests nothing so much as a 500-year-old French chateau—gray stone great house perched on the riverbank and fronted by formal gardens, its countless chimneys and gables giving promise of rich architectural adornment within. In fact, this splendid dwelling, built by the Second Earl of Dunraven, was not begun until 1832. In 1988, after an immensely detailed restoration—to say nothing of the installation of much in the way of plumbing—it opened as a luxury hotel.

The elaborate decoration is a miracle of carved stonework—arches, gargoyles, chimneys, bays, window embrasures, etc.—and of carved plasterwork (the numerous gracefully patterned ceilings). There are 365 leaded glass windows. The interior spaces were conceived on a grand scale; one of the most renowned is the Gallery, which is 132 feet long and 26 1/2 feet high and is lined on either side with seventeenth-century Flemish choir stalls.

The private rooms scarcely pale in comparison with the public rooms. The accommodation we occupied (#406) on a visit in the spring of 1995 was spacious, high-ceilinged, impeccably appointed with pieces that called up both the eighteenth and nineteenth centuries, and possessed of idyllic views. It also provided two fireplaces—there are more than 50 in the manor—one in the bedroom (ebony and tile), one in the bathroom (charcoal gray marble). Over each hung a Venetian-glass mirror.

This bathroom was very grand indeed, 15 feet by 12 feet and with a softly vaulted ceiling. In addition to all the expected fixtures, it boasted a handsome dark iron chandelier, a striped satin armchair, and a broad Chippendale-style low chest of drawers beneath a generous window giving on the formal gardens and the golf course, that view complete with a short stretch of the river Maigue. From time to time, you have relished breakfast in bed; this is the only place I can think of where "breakfast in bath" might be even more tempting.

As at Dromoland, so at Adare: the food is superlative. The table d'hote menu has good variety—five starters, six entrées, nine desserts. I am recalling with particular pleasure a carrot and ginger soup; panfried medallions of monkfish accompanied by a stew of broad beans, tomatoes, and garlic potatoes; and a poached pear in a burgundy syrup and with a pear sorbet. The wine list is all that it should be.

Of even more importance to some of us, so is the golf course. It roams over 230 acres of the 840-acre estate. Some of the holes are framed by mature trees; others play over more open ground.

This is very gently rolling parkland, and I doubt that the overall elevation change is more than 25 feet. The manor house itself hoves into view on a number of occasions during the round, not just at the beginning and end. In addition to the river and a sneaky little tributary, there are two ponds and a 14-acre lake that contribute enormously to the aesthetic charms—and not simply from a visual standpoint. Again and again—on 5, 11, 15, 16, and 18—we actually hear the water rushing over weirs. Perhaps it will even drown out the sound of our gnashing teeth. For this course, despite its serene beauty—or rather, in large part *because* of it—is a punisher, surely one of the half-dozen most difficult courses in Ireland. That is true whether this par 72 is played at 5,400 yards, 6,200 yards, 6,600, or 7,100.

Ten holes are menaced by water—10 holes and no fewer than 15 shots. Sometimes the danger is remote; more often it is boldly confrontational. We waste no time in having to face up to it, for the green on the sharply doglegging 380-yard 1st taunts us from just a few paces beyond a stream. This is a risk we might accept with a certain sangfroid along about the 7th or 8th, but not on the opening hole. That same stream, I hasten to add, reappears uneasily close to the right side of the following green, where our approach will again be played from more than 150 yards out.

There is respite on the next three holes—respite from water, that is—but now there are the fanciful bunkers, almost all of them large and some of them deep, and the fanciful greens, almost all of them large and replete with intriguing cup positions, that maintain the tension. It quickly becomes clear that unless we place our approach in the proper sector of the green, we will be three-putting consistently. It may be the only consistent aspect of our game.

The 7th is an especially intimidating par five, even though it measures only 495 yards from the regular markers. Each shot is imperiled, on the right, by the curving shore of the lake. Here is an exemplary "cape" hole, inviting us on the drive to cut off as much of the water as we dare and, if we've been successfully aggressive, to fly in the face of sweet reason again on the long second shot in the hope of setting up a birdie. The hole can, of course, be played timorously out to the left from tee to green.

If no hole at Adare is less than good, as is certainly the case, the last four constitute a sparkling finish. On the 15th, only 350 yards long, both tee and green are sited at the river's edge, and the fairway never gets far from it. A large tree on the left, some 50 yards short of the green, eliminates the possibility of deliberately taking the water on the right out of play. The 16th hole, 160 yards, plays fully across a pond to a heavily bunkered green. There is no reason to get wet unless we focus exclusively on avoiding the sand. The 17th, a charming two-shotter of 375 yards through the trees and over lightly rising and falling ground, is no card-wrecker, but the three-leaved green is difficult both to hit and to putt.

Which brings us to the home hole, a daunting piece of business indeed. It is 510 yards long. For some 440 yards the river all but abuts the left edge of the fairway. It then swings right and sweeps across in front of the green, which is located just below the manor house itself. A couple of substantial trees in the right side of the fairway (you know Trent Jones was thinking of the 18th at Pebble Beach) force our second shot left, thus heightening the threat of the water. Admittedly, the third shot, over the river, is not long, but we must be up, and the green, cunningly, is not deep. It is a great hole—beautiful, fraught with danger but entirely fair, making no untoward demands on the swing yet requiring control of it and of our nerves and our thinking at every juncture. The 18th at Adare is a perfect summation of all that has gone before it.

Robert Trent Jones was well into his 80s when he undertook to fashion Adare. It was his second Irish design, following the Cashen Course at Ballybunion, which opened in 1984 and will be discussed in the final chapter of this book. I am certain that Jones, the preeminent figure in golf course architecture during the second half of the 20th century and the creator of such outstanding courses as The Dunes, Mauna Kea, Spyglass Hill, Peach Tree (with Robert Tyre Jones, Jr.), Point O' Woods, Metedeconk National, and Nueva Andalucia's Las Brisas Course (near Marbella, Spain), to name only a handful, must be pleased with his work at Adare. There can be observed here no diminution of his remarkable gifts. It is a course fully worthy of its magnificent home.

Chapter Two

Galway Bay
and Connemara

The very name is provocative: Galway Bay Golf and Country Club. Not Galway Bay Golf Club. Not even Galway Bay Country Club. Golf and Country Club. Clearly, we are in for something out of the ordinary.

The drive north from Adare, first on the N21 to Limerick, where we pick up the N18, then across the stone-fenced pastures of County Clare—Ennis and Gort the principal towns along the way as we stick with the N18—has now taken us into County Galway and out on the Renville Peninsula to this quite imposing new facility. It may well be worthy of its name, for here we find a million-pound clubhouse, a Christy O'Connor, Jr., championship-style eighteen, luxury holiday homes for sale, and a whimsical signpost beside an even more whimsical practice putting green.

The green, adjacent to a stone-banked artificial pond, is divided into two parts by a sliver of a stream. A couple of tiny bridges, also of stone, connect the halves. It is all quite amusing, with the arched miniature crossways calling to mind the fabled bridge that spans the Swilcan Burn on the 18th hole of the Old Course at St. Andrews.

As for the black and white signpost, attached to it are five "arrows," each pointing in a different direction: to the 1st tee, to the 18th green, to the 19th hole, to the housing village, and to "NEW YORK—3,071 miles." Ah, the Irish are droll.

But there is, perhaps, more here than mere drollery. For as that "New York" arrow suggests, the inspiration for this establishment is the American country club, with all the appropriate trappings. The club's promotional literature refers to the course as "the unique American-style layout," and to the "large golf academy with American-style practice area." The resplendent multilevel clubhouse would look very much at home in any upscale suburban setting stateside. Sleek and spacious and spiffy—was that really Muzak in the locker room?—it is set on a rise, with expansive window walls and a flagstone terrace assuring memorable views of the course and of Galway Bay. Galway City is eight miles away, across the water.

Christy O'Connor, Jr., the Galway native who designed the course, is a veteran of the European tour. Some Americans will remember him as the player who struck a splendid 2-iron across the water to the 18th green at the Belfry in 1987, assuring the European team of victory in the Ryder Cup. He speaks of the course as "of championship standard but, in my opinion, a fair test of golf." The "but" is curious, as though *championship* and *fair* were generally inimical. Still, he is right. It could well host an important competition, and it is in no sense excessive or capricious. At Galway Bay you get exactly what your swing merits.

Par is 72 (the traditional mix of 10 par fours, 4 par fives, 4 par threes), and since there are four sets of tees, the course can be played at 5,550 yards, 6,300 yards, 6,700, or 7,100. It is quite open—there are relatively few trees—and it is pleasantly rolling. One gets the impression that earth has been moved here, but not mountains.

Bunkering is a major element in this layout's defenses. There are 90 sand bunkers, and there is an attractive variety to their shapes and sizes. No green is sand-free. There is strategic bunkering in the landing area of every drive except the one on the 3rd hole, and happily, these hazards are never harshly penal.

The waters of Galway Bay wash three sides of the club property, but this is not links golf. There are no sandhills. The terrain neither tumbles nor undulates, and the turf is not of a seaside type or texture. The feeling of the course underfoot is meadowland, and since it has an excellent watering system, it is unlikely ever to play firm and fast.

But the sea is almost always in view and the wind is almost always a factor and often a ferocious force, so exposed are the holes. There are half a dozen artificial water hazards, and they are by no means merely decorative, menacing the shot to the green on the 480-yard 6th and the drives on the 7th, 8th, 9th, and 12th. "The *natural* water hazard," O'Connor points out, "is the Atlantic Ocean."

Indeed the sea is there, along the full length of three of the par fives and one par four, admonishing the slicer as it froths over the rocky strand. It backdrops the tee on three of the one-shotters as well as the green on the 12th, where our second must traverse a man-made lake. However, more often than not, the ocean is at too respectful a remove—which is not to suggest that a genuine banana ball won't drown. It will. But never are we forced to carry an inlet and never does the beach truly border the fairway, except for a short stretch of the 16th. I should point out that on the shoreline behind the 16th tee, the remains of a number of small circular stone huts dating back some 700 years can be seen. Between the 2nd and 10th greens is the Rathnapours ring fort ("the fort of little potatoes"). And Leadmine Hill, the site of a fifteenth-century copper and lead mine, forms a spectacular backcloth for the par-three 13th.

This is a very good golf course in a setting of extravagant beauty. It still has a little maturing to do (it opened in 1993 amid colorful festivities that included fireworks over the bay, an ecumenical blessing by the Bishop of Galway and the Church of Ireland's Rector of Galway, and skydivers descending on the clubhouse from 5,000 feet to bestow bouquets on the female dignitaries present), but it should have considerable appeal for those seeking an American-type golf experience (golf carts are available). For some Americans, it could be a bit too much like home.

Perhaps 11 or 12 miles north of the Galway Bay Golf and Country Club, and about 7 miles from Galway City, lies the village of Moycullen and, a mile off the N59, Moycullen House. It is the home of Philip and Marie Casburn and it is one of 35 houses that make up the Hidden Ireland group. This is an association of owners of distinctive homes, spotted throughout the country, where overnight guests are welcomed. Both dinner and breakfast are served. Each house has architectural character and merit, and the owners are eager to share their way of life with people who can appreciate these things. To phone or write for full information, see the Appendix.

Surrounded by 30 acres of woodlands, rhododendrons, and azaleas atop a high hill, Moycullen House commands the surrounding countryside and affords a distant view of Lough Corrib. Of the five guest rooms, which are simply but comfortably furnished, only one has a private bath. Guests have use of a private sitting room, which, like the dining room and most of the bedrooms, has a period fireplace. A log or peat fire, except in high summer, seems to be burning somewhere most of the time.

The house was designed in the "arts and crafts" style—it has great oak doors with their original iron locks and latches—and was built in the early 1900s by a Scottish lord who came to the west of Ireland for sporting holidays. The trout and salmon fishing hereabouts, whether in sea or lough or stream, is outstanding.

Marie Casburn is an accomplished cook (veal kidneys flambé is one of her favorite starters) and Phil Casburn is very knowledgeable about golf. He sells seaweed, kelp, to golf clubs all over Ireland; among his 50 or so customers for this organic fertilizer are Connemara, Portmarnock, and Westport. "I'm afraid," he says ruefully with a nod toward the extensive millwork, "that the income from our guests would not even keep us in paint around here."

Down in the village of Moycullen, on the main road, is an atmospheric pub called the Ferryman Lounge. Some nights—often Sundays—there is music. When we were last there, a two-man Irish combo called Oklahoma (don't ask!) was offering every type of native music from dirges to jigs. Wonderful stuff—wonderful place for a nightcap.

A little more than an hour and a half from Moycullen, on a spit of land jutting into the Atlantic Ocean at the far western edge of County Galway, is the Connemara Golf Club, at Bally-conneeley. You will not begrudge a moment of this drive.

Head for Oughterard first, then Maam Cross. Nearly 30 years ago, on our first visit to Ireland (a nongolfing trip) and in a futile search for the Connemara cottage from which my mother's mother emigrated to America in the 1890s, my wife and I found ourselves in Maam Cross. At this lonely crossroads of the N59 and the R336 there were a post office and Mrs. Pea-cock's Tavern. Hoping to get lunch, we went into the bar and were shown to the dining room by a girl of about 17. She was eager to oblige us, but her resources were limited. Thus began one of the memorable culinary adventures of our life.

Though seven or eight tables were set in this unadorned, high-ceilinged room, there were no other customers. The temperature in that room on this blustery day in early May could not have been 55. Harriet and I shivered invol-untarily, our eyes darting about for a source of heat in a room that had no fireplace. High on one wall we spotted a little electric heater. Our young waitress was not unmindful of our concern.

"Why don't you sit right there?" she said, pointing to a table for two directly beneath the heater. "I'll switch it on and it will warm you up in no time."

She did as promised, disappeared, then quickly returned.

"We're havin' the mutton today," she said.

"The mutton?" I asked, hoping to encourage her to continue with the bill of fare.

"That's what we're havin'," she said.

"I don't think I've ever had mutton," Harriet said.

"Well," I said, "neither have I. It's like lamb. That is, it's sheep, which, of course, is just lamb grown up."

"There's . . . ah . . . nothing else?" Harriet asked the girl.

"No," she replied, simply but not stubbornly. "That's what we're havin'. It's very good. We had some Yanks come through last week. They had the mutton and they loved it."

Doubtless, I groaned inwardly, the *same* mutton.

"Do you have anything to start with?" Harriet asked. "Maybe some soup?"

"Oh, yes, yes, soup. To be sure. We're havin' the oxtail soup."

"Oxtail soup?" I said. "I don't think I've ever had that either."

"Oh, it's very good, very filling," she assured us.

"Well," I said with forced jocularity, "if you're havin' the oxtail soup, I guess we're havin' the oxtail soup."

The girl smiled politely and started to go, but Harriet, desperate now to establish a safety net of some kind, said, "Do you think we might have a salad? Any green vegetables, maybe with a slice of tomato, will do. Anything at all."

"I'm afraid there's no salad. We're havin' mashed potatoes and turnips."

The oxtail soup was, to understate the case, strong. It looked like a gravy and it tasted as though it had been wrung out of the tail of the toughest, meanest, leatheriest, oldest ox in Connemara. We each took a sip. It was lukewarm and vile.

"*They* may be havin' the oxtail soup," Harriet said, "but *I'm* not."

When the girl came to take our soup plates, she was surprised that we had not eaten. I lamely explained that we chose not to fill up on soup for fear that we'd not be able to do justice to the main course.

The mutton was revolting. It was so powerful that it made the oxtail soup seem sissy by comparison. It was also very well done, like a cedar shingle on an 80-year-old roof, and it was smothered in an aggressively greasy gravy. As for the mashed potatoes and the turnips, each was presented in the shape of a perfect igloo, and the only way I know to achieve this is with an ice cream scoop. The mashed potatoes were an Oxford gray, and one jab with a fork made it clear that they were implacably lumpy. The turnips, despite being overcooked to a fare-thee-well, somehow managed to be equally lumpy.

Harried ordered a beer and I asked for a cup of tea. There was black bread, but neither of us had strength enough to lift it, let alone chew it.

The girl brought the beer and the tea. We gulped the beverages down.

"We've got to get out of here," Harriet said.

"I know, but what can we say?"

"Just say we've got to get out of here."

"Look, we come in here and ask for something to eat and they oblige us and then we turn our noses up at the food and just leave. I feel awful about this."

"So do I," Harriet retorted, "but not for the same reason."

I asked the waitress for the bill. "But you've hardly touched your dinner," she said.

"I guess we weren't as hungry as we thought," Harriet said, feigning regret convincingly.

"Yes, yes, that's it," I chimed in, seizing what I regarded as a brilliant inspiration on my wife's part. "I guess we weren't as hungry as we thought."

"Well," the girl said apologetically, "I'm afraid I've no choice but to charge you for two dinners. It comes to one pound three."

"Is that all?" I responded guiltily. "That doesn't sound like nearly enough. If I thought for one minute that you were lowering the price because we—"

"One pound three it is. Including service." I mentally made the translation to dollars—$2.76—quickly pulled some money from my wallet, handed her the required amount, and added five shillings.

"That's too much," she protested. "Much too much. I said one pound three. You've given me one pound eight."

"Well," I said, "the other is your tip."

"But the service is in the one pound three," she insisted. "I told you that."

"I understand," I said, "but I want you to have the other five shillings."

"It's too much."

"Nonsense. You deserve it."

"How could I? You didn't eat but a mouthful."

We had risen and were now edging toward the door.

"Goodbye," Harriet said. "And thank you."

"You're welcome," the girl said, "but it's too much."

In the car now and backing out of the parking area, we felt, absurdly, as though we'd been lucky to escape with our lives. Then we started to laugh uncontrollably.

Mrs. Peacock's has expanded over the years since. Today, in addition to the bar and the restaurant, there are several guest rooms, a service station, and a large shop offering souvenirs (trinkets made of Connemara's green marble are a good buy), gifts, and men's and women's clothing. Also a thatched roof cottage there is supposed to function as a kind of museum commemorating the making of John Ford's *The Quiet Man,* which starred John Wayne, Maureen O'Hara, and Barry Fitzgerald, and which was filmed in this area. The ties between that popular movie and this dark little shelter are, at best, ephemeral, though there is a color print of the cottage with a note across the bottom signed by Miss O'Hara and wishing the people involved in making the movie "all the best."

As for the food at Mrs. Peacock's today, we have not sampled it. But surely it must have improved, as has the cooking all over Ireland during the past 30 years. The threat of a bad meal, regardless of where one wanders, has, it seems to us, been largely eliminated.

Beyond Maam Cross we plunge into the very heart of Connemara. This is not Ireland of the "40 shades of green." Much of it has a tawny tint, or a buff-brown, prompting someone with a poetic touch to speak of this unpeopled landscape as "the golden silence of Connemara." The drive uncovers a tapestry of lonely beauty, what with the pond-pocked bogs and the rippling rises, sometimes heather-clad, the sharply soaring Maamturk Mountains, the boulders, the limestone meadows, the bleak moors, the absence—near total—of trees, and the absence—near total—of man. All of this under a canopy of shifting cloudscapes that, with astonishing rapidity, tender, then withdraw, then restore the promise of a pretty day.

The sturdy Connemara ponies catch our eye from time to time, running wild and free. But it is the sheep who constitute the hazard to safe driving. Be alert for them to appropriate the smooth and sinuous two-lane road that carries on to Recess (*Straith Salach* in Gaelic) and then to Clifden. When they sashay defiantly down the middle of the paving, they present no problem, for we see them and we have no choice but to be patient. But when what looks for all the world like yet another of the hundreds of limestone boulders beside the road suddenly rises and steps in front of the car, then there is danger and a shrieking of brakes and tires that does violence to the stillness of this remote and barren land.

At Clifden, the unofficial capital of Connemara, we head south. On our right for much of this last leg of the drive is Mannin Bay, with its occasional good bathing beach (this is not to suggest that the water is *ever* warm enough even to splash about in); and a mile or two inland is the point at which the first airplane to cross the Atlantic Ocean, piloted by Sir John Alcock, landed in 1919 after a nonstop flight of 16 1/2 hours that began in St. John's, Newfoundland.

The game at Ballyconneeley is serious—6,800 yards of it from the regular tees, almost 7,300 yards from the championship markers. There are also gold markers, which, on the scorecard, are called "Winter Tees." The gold course is 6,400 yards long. I suspect that even in high summer the great majority of golfers at the Connemara Golf Club play from the winter tees; otherwise, the round would be an endless slog. The ladies' markers provide a course of 5,600 yards.

Eddie Hackett, about whom I will have more to say in the next chapter, designed the course. It opened in 1973. The contemporary-style clubhouse, set on a modest rise, affords lovely water views. The ocean, however, never gets within a hundred yards of the golf holes. It is often in sight, particularly from the high ground on the second nine, but it is never in play.

Connemara is a wide-open par-72 layout that seems to have been designed—as were many courses in the 1970s—with the big hitter in mind. The fairways and greens are generous, the bunkering is light in the tee-shot landing area, and though the rough can be strangling, there is little excuse for visiting it. The most distinctive feature of this rugged terrain is the plethora of great gray boulders and rock outcroppings. There is a stern, flinty look to this links that is shared by no other course I know. The hospitality here is confined strictly to the clubhouse, chief among the charms of this comfortable haven being the marvelous homemade bran-raisin muffins.

The first nine is distinctly the lesser of the two, for it is routed over ground that is sometimes flat and featureless. But there are good holes here, like the opener itself, a medium-length par four that doglegs sharply left as it rises softly to a well-bunkered green on a little knob. Also very testing are the 190-yard 6th, with steep falloffs at the elusive green, and the 420-yard 8th, where, even if we should manage to reach the somewhat ill-defined green with our long second shot, the likelihood of three-putting on this improbably contoured surface is very real.

The second nine, where par is 37 and three of the last five holes are par fives, is a triumph. It is hilly, the ground often tumbling and pitching. The wonderful uphill 12th, 440 yards culminating in a plateau green, feels like 500 yards. The one-shot 13th—a surprising pond is tucked in a hollow on the right—plays from a pulpit tee to a broad green. It is delightful, but it is also 210 yards long. At the noble 14th, with a sweeping view of the links and the Twelve Ben Mountains and the Atlantic Ocean from its lofty tee, the 510 yards does not give us pause, but the plateau green beckoning from the far side of a deep dip makes club selection on the pitch a dicey matter. The 15th, *only* 385 yards, calls for a medium-to-long iron that must climb to another carefully sited plateau green, this one with a steep bank at the front. At the 410-yard 16th water rears its head in a curious—and lethal—fashion: on the left, to snare the pulled and anemic second shot, are two "water bunkers" some 50 yards short of the green, and a third perhaps 20 yards off the putting surface. Both 17 and 18, which are 515 and 520 yards respectively, play from elevated tees. On the former the green is neatly cocked up in the sandhills, and on the home hole a ditch crossing the fairway abut 60 yards short of the green imperils the gambling fairway wood that does not quite come off, while the green, on a low bluff, will tolerate no weakness whatsoever, for here the underhit pitch automatically retreats down the face of the slope into a bunker at the base.

This is big golf at Ballyconneeley, big and fine on what I have come to think of as a beloved rockpile. The course is a perfect reflection of the austere beauty that is the world of Connemara, primeval in feeling, stark and treeless and mercilessly exposed to the elements.

Clifden, some nine miles north of Ballyconneeley, is an agreeable if undistinguished market town, with considerable bustle, thanks to tourists, who find it a good spot from which to explore the western part of Connemara, and shopkeepers, who find the tourists a good target for wearables, particularly the handsome Connemara tweeds (some of which, I have it on good authority, are actually woven in Connemara). Though Clifden is situated above an inlet of Ardbear Bay, there is little hint of the nearby sea.

Only about a mile outside the town, and just off the Ballyconneeley Road, is an attractive B&B called Mallmore House. Set in 35 acres, this Georgian-style house overlooks the sea. Most of the six bedrooms, all of which are spacious, are on the ground floor, have their own private bathrooms, and enjoy lovely views. The peat-burning fireplace makes the living room a convivial spot and helps to enhance the old-world charm of the place. The Hardmans are excellent hosts.

At the other end of the price scale—and on the far side of Connemara, near the village of Cong—stands Ashford Castle. If you are of a mind to splurge, this, like Dromoland Castle and Adare Manor, is another opportunity to do it. It is a nineteenth-

century storybook baronial pile sited between the gentle Cong
River and idyllic Lough Corrib. And even the most sophisticated traveler has to acknowledge the opulence of Ashford. It is
the embodiment of the stately luxury implicit in the designa-
tion "castle hotel," the elements falling into place almost by
rote: richly carved dark woodwork, including paneled ceilings
and intricate balustrades; imposing fireplaces and glittering
crystal chandeliers; acres of leather seating, much of it tufted;
huge and splendid porcelain urns and vases and wall-mounted
platters; sideboards and tables in scale and ornament of royal
pedigree; occasional suits of armor; numerous period pictures,
both portraits and landscapes, some of them original canvases,
others reproductions. You will not be surprised to learn that
Ronald and Nancy Reagan stayed here on a state visit in 1984,
nor that Ashford Castle is the property of the same firm that
owns Dromoland Castle

The accommodation we occupied here six or seven years ago
overlooked the gardens and the lake and consisted of a vast bedroom (27 feet long, 13 feet wide, 16 feet high) with a graceful
light-brown Sienna marble fireplace and a vast bathroom (22
feet long, 6 1/2 feet wide, 16 feet high) with a vaulted ceiling
and heated towel racks.

There are two dining rooms, the George V and the Con-
naught (both the names of highly regarded hotels, an odd
touch), and the excellent cooking ranges from continental to
nouvelle French. We still talk about a delectable salmon and
wild sorrel soup.

There is also golf at Ashford Castle, nine holes that Eddie
Hackett designed in 1984. Laid out over what was once the

deer park of the estate, the course offers one very hard hole (the 390-yard 3rd, doglegging 90 degrees left and climbing sharply to a blind green); two very good holes, both par fours (on the 2nd we play across a gentle valley to a plateau green; on the 5th a large old oak constricts the landing area for the drive, and the green is beyond a steep rise); one extremely pretty hole (another plateau green, this one in a glade on the 136-yard 4th); and only one rather negligible hole (the 161-yard 9th, a slightly falling shot to an open green that does, however, have the ravishing Lough Corrib as its backcloth). The course is a rolling and perfectly mowed lawn—no rough to speak of, little definition between holes at times, very few bunkers—punctuated by tees and greens and trees. It measures 3,000 yards against a par of 35, and if it is scarcely serious, it is also not a joke. If you are staying at the hotel, it is yours—*free*—for the playing. And depending on the time of day, it may well be yours alone.

It proved irresistible to Tom Watson and Lee Trevino in July of 1994. They had stopped in Ireland for a few days prior to going on to Scotland for the British Open at Turnberry. Golf was not the reason for their decision to stay at Ashford Castle, but when they learned of the presence of this nine right there on their doorstep, nothing would do but they give it a go. No caddies were available. A minor inconvenience. Placing their bags on pull carts, off they went, the two legends, Watson and Trevino, like a couple of kids let out of school early, grinning and "towing the trolley." Nothing was going to stand in their way when it came to adding some sporty fun to the delights of Ashford Castle.

Chapter Three

A Great New Course
and a Great Old
House

Now that we've reached the far west, we're going to stay there, heading north out of Clifden on the N59 through Leenane and sticking with it as it enters County Mayo and winds its way through the Sheffry Hills, crossing the Eriff River and continuing up to Westport.

England's Frederick W. and Martin Hawtree, a father and son team who represented the second and third generations of golf course architects (Frederick George Hawtree, Fred W.'s father and Martin's grandfather, was the founder of this dynasty), laid out the course at Westport in 1972 together with A.H.F. Jiggens, also a partner in the firm of Hawtree and Son. Though most of this organization's work was done in the British Isles, there are a number of Hawtree courses in continental Europe and in South Africa. In two instances, North Carolina's Mount Mitchell Golf Club and New Jersey's Links Golf Club, the Hawtrees carried out American commissions.

Like Ballyconneeley, Westport is long, 6,600 yards from the medal tees, almost 7,000 from all the way back. The Irish Amateur Close Championship (no nonIrish need apply) has been contested twice on this par-73 course. The first six holes at Westport, running to and fro on an open meadow and finishing at the clubhouse, are a disappointment, but with the 7th the game is on, and a thoroughly enjoyable game it is, thanks to an attractive mix of holes—three short holes (two of them not so short at 200 yards); four long holes, including the spectacular 515-yard 15th, where our drive from an elevated tee must traverse a finger of Westport Bay; and five par fours, three of them averaging 435 yards. On the 11th tee we take dead aim at Ireland's "holy mountain," Croagh Patrick, from the summit of which St. Patrick is believed to have banished all the reptiles from the land. There is some niggling doubt as to the truth of this pious tale, but there can be no doubt about the excellence of this golf hole, which climbs, doglegs right in the landing area of the tee shot, and at 420 yards requires two strong hits if we are to reach the skillfully bunkered green in regulation. Now, at long last on a course that is inland in turf and feeling, we have gained the heights that offer a striking panorama of water and mountains and meadows. It is all extraordinarily beautiful, and no matter how many times we encounter a vista of this nature on the courses of Ireland we can never simply take it in stride.

The home hole, at 500 yards and with a characteristically spacious fairway, gives us a chance to improve our figures. The mooing of the cattle in the stone-walled meadow along the right side of the fairway will not distract us. Nor shall we be unnerved by the "Valley of Sin" in the left forepart of the vast putting surface, nor by the critical gaze of the players who have already finished and are now comfortably settled in the handsome glass-walled clubhouse behind the green. A four is not beyond our dreams, though it may tax our ability.

I remember spending some time in Westport itself several years ago. We had a pleasant lunch in the bar of the Railway Hotel—cheerful and roomy, with lots of dark-stained wood— and then went window-shopping. Westport is a charmer, and not by accident. An architect—some say James Wyatt, others speculate that it was a Frenchman—laid out the town for Peter Browne, 2nd earl of Altamont. The Carrowbeg River flows through the very heart of it, its banks stone-framed so that the narrow stream suggests a canal. Pretty old limestone bridges arch over the Carrowbeg from time to time, and tree-lined malls flank it. Ireland is not full of towns with such style, to say nothing of elegance.

Just outside town is Westport House, a superb Georgian mansion set on a cove of Clew Bay. The tour is not guided. Some of the old furnishings are worn and shabby, but there is a homey reality about it all that is quite engaging. There are several notable moments: the magnificent neoclassical plasterwork in the dining room by James Wyatt; a Holy Family by Rubens at the top of the grand marble staircase; and two portraits by Joshua Reynolds in the Long Gallery. It is in this noble hall that, after examining a raft of stiff and stately figures and, in the process, becoming a bit bored, we suddenly come, at the far end, upon three color snapshots of the present owner's young children. An endearing touch by the "curator."

Since Westport House is the seat of the Marquess of Sligo, whose family has occupied it for over two hundred years, there is inevitably a lot of anecdotage connected with it. The 2nd Marquess, it turns out, allowed nothing to stand in his way when it came to decorating the mansion. He spent four months in an English jail for bribing British seamen in time of war to bring his ship, loaded with antiquities, from Greece to Westport.

That same entrepreneurial spirit continues to run in the family. A shop in the basement offers knicknacks at high prices. Also on the grounds—and mercifully out of sight of the great house—are a children's zoo, a pitch 'n' putt course, tennis courts, a playground, a "slippery dip," a caravan park, a campground, a bar, a restaurant, and heaven knows what else. The promotional leaflet boasts of "over 1,000,000 visitors welcomed" to "Ireland's Number One Attraction." And, you will be heartened to learn, "For family parties—adults and only the first two children pay—you can bring in six children for the price of two!!!" The 2nd Marquess would have applauded.

We head due north now, skirting island-dotted Clew Bay, through Newport and Mulrany and, once again on the ever-useful N59, through Castlehill and Ballycrory on up to Bangor. Here we take the R313 west, out to Belmullet. Just beyond this village is the Carne Golf Course, which opened in 1993 and which I am inclined to go rather far out on a limb for by calling it the single most remote *great* course in the entire British Isles.

Few, I suspect, will question the remoteness of this spot, for we have now found our way to land's end in the little-populated northwest corner of County Mayo. I said to Eamon Mangan, my companion for the round at Carne, that I had a sense of having gone as far west—as far toward America—as it was possible to go in Ireland.

"Do you know," he replied, "when John Kennedy was elected president, we lit bonfires here in Belmullet that night, celebrating with you, signaling across the sea—as though the light from the bonfires could be seen on American shores? How thrilled we were here. Oh, we felt so close to you! I was just a boy, but I know I shall never forget that night."

The explanation for the construction of this golf course, far from any place of size or substance, is a simple one: to promote tourism. Government funding was an essential ingredient in the project. Eamon Mangan, co-owner with his brother of a furniture store and adjacent pub in Belmullet, is a shareholder in the nonprofit organization that built the course and that aims to add a trailer park, vacation chalets, and a hotel on this 240-acre site. Now in his late 40s, Eamon is also the man who, day in and day out, supervised the building of this extraordinary links over a period of almost four years. He had no experience whatsoever in this sort of thing, but his mentor was the course's architect, Eddie Hackett.

Eddie Hackett was born in Dublin in 1910. For more than 40 years he worked as a golf professional, beginning as an assistant at Royal Dublin and later serving as head professional at Portmarnock. He apprenticed in golf course design under Henry Cotton and Fred W. Hawtree. Hackett laid out his first course in 1964. Over the next 30 years he designed some 30 courses, many of them nine-holers, and remodeled or expanded at least 120 others. He never worked outside Ireland, but within the confines of the Irish land mass he has played an impressive role in the expansion of the game. He has long been renowned—and admired—for the modesty of his fees. Making lots of money never interested him; it was enough to make a living. Giving his countrymen a worthwhile place to play—that was the motivating force in his long and fruitful career. "Eddie has been involved in this project for eight years now," Eamon said to me, "and he has not pocketed as much as 10,000 pounds all told for his services."

At Carne the man who designed Waterville (with John Mulcahy) and Ballyconneeley and Enniscrone and Murvagh was offered the best tract of linksland that had ever come his way, and he seized upon it, at age 77, with the passion and delight of someone half his age.

"The first time he saw this land," Eamon said, "he walked over it, up and down these giant sandhills, through the hollows and the dells, out to the sea and back to where the clubhouse would be built—there was nothing here then, absolutely nothing, just this virgin duneland—and when he had finished and made all his mental notes—I never saw him jot anything down—we suggested that we drive into town, have a cup of tea, and get him on the road for home. He said no, that what he wanted to do was go over the ground again, all of it. He was enthralled at the possibilities and he wanted to make sure that he had it all there, in his mind's eye. So, at 77, off he went again into the sandhills, with us traipsing along at his side. You had to believe it was going to be a wonderful course."

And so it is. From the 1st tee to the 18th green, it is all that one could ever yearn for. With the exception of Ballybunion and perhaps County Down, no dunescape in Ireland is more majestic than this wild stretch along the Atlantic coast of Mayo. And Eddie Hackett has made the most of it, routing his holes imaginatively—indeed, audaciously—in order to take full advantage of this tumultuous terrain and to challenge the player to his fullest. Hackett does not believe that he has created a monster, but he was at pains to make it testing: "One of my priorities has to be to protect par against the assault of the fine players."

The opening hole, 385 yards from the white tees—the course, a par 72, can be played at 5,200 yards, 5,750 yards, 6,300, and 6,700—proclaims boisterously the thrills that lie in store. From an elevated tee we hit across a valley to the far hillside, the heaving fairway slanting softly to the right. The second shot is blind. We must walk forward to reconnoiter it, then come back to play up over the crest and down to a beautifully sited green with a steep little falloff on the right. No miracle is required to make a par, but both swings must be sound; indeed, so must our alignment. There is neither sand nor water. It is all perfectly natural.

Surely it was the green sites that dictated the routing of the holes at Carne. Having spotted a plateau or a dell just crying out to be used as target and putting surface, the architect must then have traced his way back—175 yards or 410 yards or 530 yards—to a potential teeing ground. Such a methodology, selecting the finish first and then seeking to determine the start, can produce some superlative holes, some surprising holes, and, if the topography is particularly churning, some holes that might be considered excessive. The 11th and 12th here, two very short par fours, probably fall into that last category for many people. Both play invitingly from lofty tees with dazzling sea views. Both are doglegs, the 11th definitely right, the 12th emphatically left. We lash away off the high tee, troop down the long slope to our ball in the lowlands, and now cast about for a green. Ah, there it is, around the corner of a pyramidal dune and high above us—almost vertically above us in the case of the 12th—on a shelf that functions marvelously as a place to cut a hole and insert a flagstick. On a single 320-yard hole (in this case on two such holes in a row), we have gone far down, turned a corner, and climbed far up. I believe that Darwin would have called it "jolly."

Golf amidst great sandhills, especially if the architect is reluctant to move ground to accommodate a more conventional flow, is often filled with unpredictable moments, to say nothing of stirring challenges.

"Once Eddie had laid out the holes," Eamon said as we wound our way along a dune-framed valley on the first nine, "and put the routing plan on paper, then detailed the size and contours of the greens, and once I'd agreed to take on the job of construction supervisor under his guidance, he got out here only rarely. His big worry was the bulldozer operator. Again and again he warned me to keep a close eye on that fellow. 'Stay right with him,' he would say, 'otherwise he'll flatten it all out for you and ruin it. It's in his nature to want to level things. You'll see, but you must not let him.'

"The bulldozer operator was not my only worry. Many

times over the months, the locals who were on the dole were brought in to work on the construction. They were paid 20 percent more than the dole would have provided them. I had to be alert all the time with them as well, and for the same reason. Many of them had a farming background and they had that same instinct to want to flatten the land and get rid of all the wonderful natural ripples and hillocks and dips.

"Every once in a while Eddie would shape up a few low mounds around a green, and sometimes the two of us would be dissatisfied with the look of them, the artificial appearance. So then I would just turn over this sandy soil and let it sit there for a week, maybe two, while the wind worked its magic, fashioning it into mounds that looked for all the world as though they must have been created by nature."

Late in the round Eamon asked me if I'd noticed how few man-made hazards there were. I said yes, but that I'd not been keeping a count. "There are just eighteen sand bunkers, plus those two water traps—they're almost a Hackett trademark— back at the beginning, which you noticed on three and four. Well, that's all there are. We're very proud of this. Eddie calls it a tribute to the character of the land he was given to work with. The great sandhills themselves and the natural configurations of this terrain—the pitching and the tumbling and the undulating—they are the course's defenses."

If you ever play the remarkable old course at Machrie, on Scotland's island of Islay, you will experience a similarly natural links routed through towering sandhills. There are only six bunkers on that worthy ground.

The finish at Carne, like so much that has gone before, is

spectacular. The 17th is one of the strongest and finest par fours in my experience. From a tee high in the sandhills, the drive on this 440-yarder calls for a long forced-carry over a ravine to the opposing slope, where the hole doglegs right and rises to a green set perfectly in the dunes. Just short of the green on the right is a steep falloff into a cavernous hollow. The 18th, 525 yards, swings left steadily all the way over a dune-framed roller coaster of a fairway that culminates in a deep swale just short of the green. You may be able to see the flag on your pitch from the bottom of this dip, but you will not be able to see the vast putting surface.

I make no apology for loving Carne. If it errs at all, it errs in the right direction: on the side of exuberance. It is a no-holds-barred celebration of the joy of golf, the test and the surprise and the sport and the sheer delight of the game, in a setting of colossal sandhills. We are all in Eddie Hackett's— and Eamon Mangan's—debt.

From Belmullet we retrace our steps to Bangor, where the N59 awaits to carry us to Crossmolina. One stretch of the drive finds the road unwinding in a series of gentle curves right beside the pretty river Owenmore. A few sheep graze here, and a whitewashed cottage pops up from time to time. For the most part we are traveling through bogland, the cut peat itself sometimes stacked near the road. It is a landscape of rusts and browns, with low mountains in the distance framing much of the scene. Our goal is not a golf course—that will have to wait till tomorrow—but Enniscoe House, where even a three-night stay would seem distressingly short.

Two miles south of Crossmolina on the road to Pontoon and Castlebar, a sign on your left and a pink pebbledash gatehouse signal the entrance. It is a long, winding, gently rolling run from here to the main house, first through trees and then across meadows, all of it on a harshly pocked and rutted one-lane driveway.

Nothing quite prepares you for your first sighting of the manor, a masonry structure painted a sizzling pink. Susan Kellett will assure you that pink is the color it was painted when it was built, a little more than 200 years ago. Of traditional Georgian design and symmetry, it is acknowledged to be "the last great house of North Mayo," and has recently been declared a Heritage House of Ireland. Set in its own park surrounded by mature woodland through which a path runs down to Lough Conn, the place has its own jetty, and two of the islands, one with a fifteenth-century castle in ruins, belong to the 150-acre estate.

Mrs. Kellett is a descendant of the family that settled this land in the 1660s. She owns and runs Enniscoe House, which, like Moycullen House, is a member of the Hidden Ireland group. The stately rooms, the family portraits, the antiques and heirlooms, the oval staircase hall and fan-glazed dome surrounded by plasterwork foliage and medallions of classical figures, the open fires, the pervasive sense of more leisurely times—in truth, it is all so extraordinary that no mere wandering golfer deserves any of it (though, of course, his non-golfing wife merits it all).

Susan Kellett makes you feel at home. "It can be rather gloomy here," she says, "unless we have guests." She is an ex-

cellent cook, though inclined to be modest about her culinary
skills. "This is country-house cooking, not fine restaurant
cooking. I couldn't do the elaborate sauces, nor the elaborate
presentation." What she can do, for instance, is sliced breast of
pigeon with bacon, mushrooms, and parsley in a very light
vinaigrette and mustard sauce; and Lough Conn trout, smoked
on the premises and served in a cream sauce with dill; and an
almond meringue cooked in sugar and caramelized. The wine
list is not ambitious, but you will find something on it to your
taste, perhaps even the house red, which, on our last visit, was
a delicious and inexpensive claret.

The larger bedrooms—there are only six in total, each with
its own bath—look away over the park to the lake. The principal pieces in the room we occupied on our first visit were a
magnificent Sheraton canopied four-poster bed and an equally
magnificent Irish Chippendale tall chest of drawers, which
came from Mrs. Kellett's mother's ancestral home, Heathfield,
in nearby Ballycastle. The makings of a fire are always freshly
laid on the marble-framed hearth here. We like to strike a

match shortly before turning in. There is nowhere that the day comes to a close more graciously than it does at Enniscoe House.

A 30-minute drive north, and just over the line into County Sligo, lies the Enniscrone Golf Club. We are again in Eddie Hackett's hands, and if this links does not quite measure up to Carne, it is wonderful seaside golf nonetheless. Or at least it is once you reach the 3rd tee.

The round begins with two par fives of flabbergasting dullness. Blame it, if you will, on the location of the red brick clubhouse. This attractive contemporary structure sits on a stretch of flat and uninteresting land. Getting away from it in style and out into the true seaside golfing country was the problem the golf architect faced. He did not solve it with so much as a suggestion of flair. Even the two greens are mere extensions of the level fairways.

That having been said, Enniscrone, which opened for play in 1975, is first-rate by even the strictest standards, the holes ranging from good to great. Par is 72, with the course measuring almost 6,600 yards from the competition tees, about 6,000 yards from the regular markers, some 5,500 for the ladies. Each of the four one-shotters is superb. On the 170-yard 8th, for instance, with the green tightly framed in the dunes above and only the top half of the flagstick showing, a grassy hollow some 12 to 15 feet deep, invisible as we stand on the tee, lurks to swallow any shot the least bit pushed and underhit. The 13th, with the green cocked up even more defiantly in the dunes, measures 202 yards and plays 225, unless there should be a wind off the sea barreling down the chute at us, in which case it must play 275 yards. Surely it is one of the half-dozen finest long par threes in Irish golf.

Of the many outstanding par fours, the tandem of 9 and 10 may be the most memorable. Both are short, about 340 yards. On the 9th we play from a remote scrap of turf perched perhaps 15 feet above the beach and now, our back to the water, face a long uphill forced-carry over broken ground dense with the long rough grasses. The solid drive lands in contorted terrain where a level lie is unlikely. Our second shot, perhaps calling for a 6- or 7-iron, is then hit slightly uphill across a deep swale, the broad shelf of green backstopped by a high and steep sand-hill. From tee to cup, it is thrilling, natural, right.

Considerably higher than the 9th green, the 10th tee, at very nearly the peak of this range of sandhills, overlooks the entire world of Enniscrone: the Ox Mountains; the miles of unspoiled beach that bound this peninsula; Killala Bay, its color—now steel gray, then foam green, then cobalt—at the mercy of the ever-shifting skyscape as the bay itself blends into the limitless Atlantic. On a truly fine day we can see as far north as distant Donegal, perhaps glimpsing—or are we imagining it?—a mountain near Mackras Head, just south of Killybegs. As for this 10th hole, it is hard to put one's mind to it, but if we can and in so doing produce a strong, straight drive, then perhaps a birdie may await as we plunge almost vertically over riotously tumbling terrain, our short approach to a gathering green set dell-like in the dunes.

It was on our first visit to Enniscrone that we got a lesson in high-finance, Irish style. As we drove slowly down the main street of the nearby village of Kilglass, I lowered the window to ask a woman on her way home from the market whether there was a bank here, as I wanted to exchange dollars for pounds.

"What's today?" she asked.

"Tuesday," I replied.

"Ah, noo, nooo, the travelin' bank comes through here on Thursday."

Chapter Four

Two Poets:
William Butler Yeats
and Christy O'Connor

You will be inclined not to believe it, but here we are, heading east through County Sligo, and once again we find ourselves on the N59, of happy memory down in County Galway and out in County Mayo. This all-purpose two-laner is carrying us from quite near Enniscrone through Templeboy and Skreen to Balisodare, where we pick up the N17 and proceed on a northerly heading to Sligo Town. On the far side of this pleasant county seat lies Rosses Point, home of the County Sligo Golf Club. This spin through rolling verdant pastureland—we do not glimpse the sea till the very end—takes just under an hour, and it brings us to one of the most cherished places in Irish golf.

The game has been played at Rosses Point, as the County Sligo Golf Club is universally known, since 1894. The course we enjoy today, however, is largely the work of Harry Colt and John Alison, who extensively revamped the original links in 1922.

Eddie Hackett made minor revisions some 60 years later. It was immediately after Colt and Alison completed their assignment that the West of Ireland Championship was played here for the first time. The championship has been held here more than 30 times since. Cecil Ewing, one of Ireland's four or five greatest amateurs, was born within a few paces of the links in 1910, and here he learned the game. A giant of a man with massive forearms, Ewing was noted for his ability to hit low and forcing long irons through even the most violent winds. A counterpart of John Burke at Lahinch, he won the West of Ireland ten times between 1930 and 1950, the Irish Open Amateur twice, and the Irish Close Amateur twice. Six times, between 1936 and 1955, he was chosen for the Walker Cup team. In the 1938 match his victory over New York's Ray Billows in the singles was one of the key elements in the only British and Irish triumph between 1922, the year of the inaugural Walker Cup Match, and 1971. Cecil Ewing's enduring eminence and the influence of the County Sligo Golf Club itself had much to do with the spread of the game in the west of Ireland.

It could be reasonably claimed that no golf course is more splendidly situated than Rosses Point, on the heights between Drumcliff Bay and Sligo Bay, with wondrous views in every direction. This is the countryside made famous by the poetry of William Butler Yeats. To the north is Lissadell and to the south Knocknarea, both inspirations for his verse. And lording it over the entire scene is flat-topped Ben Bulben. It is all here and all in full view with every step we take—sea, strand, mountains, meadows, even the very roofs of Sligo Town in the distance. From the knobby tee of the par-four 9th, it is possible on a fine day to see five counties—Sligo, Donegal, Roscommon, Leitrim, and Mayo.

Now be assured that golf holes do not play second fiddle to the setting, for this is a championship test, as you will soon discover whether you play from the medal tees (just under 6,400 yards) or from the blue markers (just over 6,600 yards).

The first four holes and the 18th are on the clubhouse side of the mighty hill that is the central topographical feature of the links. The other 13 holes, beginning with the 5th, which dives from a pinnacle tee, are, as we commence the round, out of sight in the lower stretches of the course that are closer to the sea. It is there that we find undulating fairways and modest dunes covered with wild grasses.

There is an appealing variety to the holes themselves and to their routing. Many holes parallel the shore, but a nearly equal number do not, so we joust with the omnipresent—indeed, one sometimes thinks, omnipotent—wind from every conceivable direction: fore, aft, cross, quartering. Fortunately, the layout is not heavily bunkered.

Surprising in the case of a course so wonderfully natural, Rosses Point has virtually no blind shots. Almost always the task is plain to see. However, on several occasions—the 425-yard 7th, 415-yard 8th, 180-yard 13th, 435-yard 14th—that task is complicated by streams uncomfortably close to the greens. The 17th—425 yards from the white markers, 457 yards from the blues—is one of the most indomitable two-shotters you are ever likely to play. It climbs steadily through framing sandhills, doglegging left, the fairway narrowing the higher we go. Our drive must be kept left if we are to have any chance of getting home in two. But the bold tee shot with even a shade too much draw disappears into a deep ravine, while the one played cautiously out to the right automatically converts the hole into a three-shotter.

After the game you will want to have lunch, or at least a drink, in the very spruce clubhouse, which affords some of the most arrestingly beautiful views in all of Ireland. A pause here will give you the opportunity to recapture a few of your favorite moments on this glourious eighteen.

I must point out that cheek by jowl with the clubhouse is Yeats Country Hotel. It is both serviceable and convenient, and its very name forces us to concede that it is not great golf but great poetry that gives this corner of Ireland world renown. Even the scorecard pays homage to Yeats: The 9th hole, called "Cast a Cold Eye," aims toward Drumcliff and serves to remind us that we should pay a visit to the church there, where Yeats's grandfather served as rector and where the poet is buried. To visit his grave is to see firsthand that Yeats's wish for a final resting place "under bare Ben Bulben's head" was granted. The uncompromising last lines of "Under Ben Bulben" were, at his direction, inscribed on his headstone:

> Cast a cold eye
> On life, on death.
> Horseman, pass by!

On a considerably less somber note, you may also want to visit Lissadell (open May through September), where Yeats was a guest at the manor house near the turn of the century. It is one of the best surviving examples of the Irish country estates that Yeats referred to as "the great gray houses."

Better still, however, is to spend a night or two in another of the great gray houses, Coopershill, a superb eighteenth-century limestone manor that welcomes guests.

Coopershill House, not 20 minutes south of Sligo Town and just off the Dublin Road (N4), stands on high ground at the center of a 500-acre estate of farm and woodland. A lovely little river winds its way through the property. Separation from the outside world seems complete; wildlife is abundant and undisturbed.

If you have stayed at Enniscoe House, you will be struck by the similarities between it and Coopershill (once you have put out of your mind the hot pink that bathes the Lough Conn manor). The two houses are much the same size and shape (each has six guest rooms). They are both Georgian, with Coopershill, built in 1774, some 20 years older. Each is stately, possessing antique-filled rooms that have retained their original regal dimensions. And both are owned and operated by landed gentry, who, as it happens, are rather good friends. The hospitable Brian and Lindy O'Hara are the sixth generation of O'Haras to call Coopershill home. Their children are the seventh.

Fires are generally burning in the sitting room and the dining room. As at Enniscoe House, each family unit eats at its own table. Ancestral portraits—nine of them—decorate the walls, candles provide all the light that is necessary, and two massive eighteenth-century walnut sideboards function as the serving tables. The food measures up to the setting: pickled mushrooms in a light curry sauce, hot tomato and orange soup, filet of beef

in a Dijon mustard sauce, a simple green salad and several vegetables fresh from the kitchen garden, choice of half a dozen Irish
cheeses, meringues with fresh fruit salad and cream. We drank
the house red, a nice bordeaux, then ended the evening beside
the fire in the sitting room with coffee and homemade fudge. A
delightful repast.

Back on a persistently northerly heading now, which calls for
retracing our steps through Sligo Town and following the N15
for less than half an hour up the coast to Bundoran, a popular
seaside resort. Here the Great Northern Hotel owns the golf
course adjacent to it and leases it to the Bundoran Golf Club,
which, as was the case at Rosses Point, was formed in 1894.

The eighteen here is routed over a cramped piece of land that
looks to me to be somewhat less than 90 acres—no wonder the
tees at 14 and 17 are protected by screens and our shot on the
128-yard 3rd has to be hit over the corner of the 2nd green. The
course we play today was designed in 1901 by 25-year-old C. S.
Butchart, a native of Carnoustie and the same man who, some
25 years later, became the head professional at the palatial
Westchester Biltmore Country Club (the word "Biltmore" was
subsequently dropped from the name of this suburban New
York City enclave); Butchart went on to produce, almost as an
avocation, handmade woods that were particularly prized.
Harry Vardon revised Bundoran in 1908.

By and large, the holes have little distinction. But though it
is lightly bunkered and less than 6,200 yards at full stretch—
par is 69, with five short holes and only two long ones—it is
not easy. Some of the hills are steep, the powerful ocean winds

rampage across the links unimpeded, the rough grows high and lush in summer, and the greens then become hard and fiery fast.

More than half the holes have a prosaic parkland feeling. Not till we reach the green on the 390-yard 8th do we appreciate the nearness of the sea and of a long golden beach, both of which are in view from the high ground of 9, 10, 11, 12, and 13. The 13th, a downhill one-shotter of 230 yards that often plays into the wind, was the scene of one of Christy O'Connor's legendary exploits when he was the professional at Bundoran during the 1950s.

O'Connor, who played in 10 consecutive Ryder Cup Matches between 1955 and 1973, was renowned for his shotmaking wizardry. Whatever it took, he could find a way to get the ball on the green. One day, in a four-ball with three members, he hit his shot onto the 13th green. So did one of the others. This chap asked the great man what club he had used. A 3-iron, Christy told him.

"I went with a 4-iron," the follow volunteered.

O'Connor promptly pulled 10 golf balls out of his bag and dropped them on the tee. Beginning with the 1-iron and working his way down to the pitching wedge, he proceeded to hit the 10 balls onto the green, 230 yards away, each one with a different club.

Bundoran is not a course we make a point of playing. There is little of a visual nature that is appealing, perhaps even less in the way of memorable holes or shots. Still, it is not dismissable, probably because we would, however grudgingly, be proud to make an acceptable score here. One of the members told me that a big amateur tournament is held in this part of Ireland every year. Called the Northwest Challenge and sponsored by a major brewer, it is played on three courses: Rosses Point, Murvagh, and Bundoran. "Time and again," he claimed, "the highest scores are at Bundoran."

Less than half an hour north on the coast road lies the Donegal Golf Club, at Murvagh, some five miles south of Donegal Town. It is easy to miss the club's sign, on your left, if you are driving briskly up the N15. A very long lane, only one-car wide, leads back to the spacious clubhouse, which was built in a contemporary style and with a lot of glass in order to take advantage of links—but not water—views.

The course, which opened in 1977, is a creature of the ubiquitous Eddie Hackett. As at Enniscrone, he had trouble getting away from the clubhouse. The opening hole is a bland 525-yarder over flattish ground to an open green. It represents our best chance at a birdie, but comes so early in the round, when we are scarcely limber, that I'm afraid we rarely take advantage of the opportunity. The 2nd hole is played over equally uninspiring ground—we are working our way out toward the sandhills and the sea—but, at 415 yards, tending very lightly uphill and into the breeze, it is a tartar. Three and four—the 185-yard 3rd, thanks to some cunning mounding and a knobby green, has considerable interest—continue to carry us farther out on the Murvagh Peninsula, and it is at the 5th that we enter the country of the majestic sandhills. Indeed, the four holes beginning here are as fine a stretch as any golfer needs. The 190-yard 5th requires nothing less than a perfect shot to hit and hold the narrow and perilously sited plateau green with its steep falloff in the dunes. The 6th and 8th, 520 and 550 yards, respectively, boast summit tees above the broad beach that are sovereign in their command of Donegal Bay and unnerving as exposed platforms from which to launch drives into the wild dunescape below, where the long rough grasses mantling the sandhills wait to ensnare the errant stroke. On the 7th, 380 yards, our drive soars away from yet another high tee to float far down into the turbulent lower ground, leaving us still a medium iron from a sloping lie to a green cloistered in the dunes. Yes, this is marvelous golf, and there is more to come, perhaps never again to be quite so spellbinding but still challenging and grand much of the way.

There is an alluring naturalness to the links at Murvagh, a truly elemental quality, together with a haunting remoteness—a barrier of dense woodlands cuts this rugged, sandy peninsula off from the world—all of it adding up to a beguiling haven of seaside golf.

Because there are multiple tees, the course can be set up to play at any length from 5,800 to 7,300 yards. At the high figure, Murvagh is one of the three or four longest courses in the British Isles. Most of us will find it more than we can handle at 6,600 yards, even against a par of 73 (there are five par fives). The greens frequently shrug off the long approach shot, and only deft chipping will save the day.

The last time I played Murvagh, in 1993, it was shortly after the "All-Ireland Clergy Competition." The club steward told me that 300 men of the cloth had turned out and that Bundoran was used as well.

"Mostly ordinary parish priests," I ventured, "but maybe some monsignors?"

"And higher," he said.

I asked about the name of the tournament. Did "All-Ireland" mean Northern Ireland as well?

"Of course," he smiled. "The troubles have never been allowed to get in the way of the game."

About four miles north of Murvagh, and on the same side of the N15 as the golf club, lies St. Ernan's House. This hotel is situated on its own small wooded tidal island in Donegal Bay. Access is by means of a 200-yard-long causeway, and you all but blink in disbelief at your first sight of this graceful early nineteenth-century house, perched on a rise above its mirror-like reflection in the water.

Merely arriving at St. Ernan's House is a treat. You leave your car down on the stone-banked quay (an informal parking area some 10 or 12 feet above the water), walk through an opening in a fieldstone wall and up glass-canopied steps, enter a sunny little flower-filled conservatory that functions as a kind of vestibule, then proceed into the richly paneled reception area. Here you are very likely to be greeted by Brian O'Dowd, who, together with his wife, Carmel (she is an accomplished cook), owns and operates this lovely little hotel.

St. Ernan's House was built in 1826 by one John Hamilton and remained in his family for nearly 160 years. In 1983 it was converted into a hotel with 13 guest rooms, and it manages to retain the personality of a private country home. There is little of a commercial flavor here. As you would expect, each room is furnished individually. The one we occupied, #9, a spacious corner room with views over the bay and the causeway, was homey (the old mahogany wardrobe and the chest of drawers both giving off a suggestion of lemon oil) and quite comfortable, though scarcely what would be called chic. There is no sign of an interior decorator's practiced hand.

The dining room, with its brown marble fireplace and its elaborately draped windows overlooking the water, is somewhat more formal than the other public spaces. A four-course prix-fixe dinner is served. I recall one evening when Harriet, who has a penchant for seafood, chose the prawn cocktail, the crab bisque, and the trout in a white wine sauce. Thank heaven there was no such thing as a fish dessert.

I also recall—it may have been that same evening—that after coffee by the fire in the sitting room we felt an inclination to stretch our legs before turning in. So we walked down the glass-covered flagstone steps to the parking quay. A calm that rarely seems to bless our hours on the links had descended on this corner of Donegal. We stood in silence for a moment or two beside the stone wall above the inlet. A half-moon in the clear sky cast the subtlest glow on the placid surface of the water. We were unwilling to let go of yet another good day.

Chapter Five

A Vote for Myrtle Beach

Donegal Town, with a population of about 2,000, is situated at a point where the river Eske flows into Donegal Bay, but its main square, called the Diamond, enjoys no view of water. Nor, despite dating back nearly 400 years, does the Diamond have any aura of antiquity; the low commercial buildings that frame it are, for the most part, late nineteenth- and early twentieth-century structures of no architectural merit. There are a couple of small hotels and pubs and a variety of shops, including one or two with antiques and secondhand books. At the center of the green is a 22-foot-high granite obelisk in memory of the Four Masters. In the early seventeenth-century four Irish Franciscan brothers stationed in a nearby monastery that is now in ruins compiled a history of the world that came to be known as the "Annals of the Four Masters." Not far from the monastery is Donegal Castle, on the estuary. The great square tower dates to 1505. Roughly a century later, Sir Basil Brooke, who laid out the Diamond, added substantially to the castle. A fine and graceful Jacobean structure, it is very much worth a visit.

If you head west out of Donegal Town on the N56 toward Killybegs, through Dunkineely, you will, in a matter of minutes, find yourself at Bruckless House. Set in 19 acres bordering Bruckless Bay and surrounded by a spacious informal garden (rhododendrons and azaleas predominate) and mature hardwoods, this is an attractive eighteenth-century dwelling with a traditional cobbled farmyard. Irish draft horses and Connemara ponies are bred here (obviously, not all Connemara ponies are running wild and free!), and if you have one of the front rooms, you will often see these animals, to say nothing of sheep, grazing in the meadow that runs down to the shore. Bruckless House has a total of five guest rooms, only two of them with private bath.

The afternoon that we arrived, Clive Evans—he and his wife Joan are the proprietors—helped me up to our room with the luggage but immediately excused himself in order to drive over to a neighbor's place and attend to a sick horse.

Bruckless House is comfortable, though both hot water and ice cubes can be in short supply, and the Evanses have no license to sell whiskey, wine, or beer. The rooms are simply decorated and uncluttered. The Evanses spent 20 years in Hong Kong— Clive Evans was an officer in the British colonial police—and the furnishings, particularly in the living room and dining room, reflect this to some degree. In the living room, where a log and/or peat fire burns much of the time, there is a handsome four-panel Chinese screen and an equally handsome ebony Chinese cabinet with pearl inlays.

Both mornings at Bruckless House we had breakfast with a German family from Krefeld, outside Dusseldorf. The mother and father spoke excellent English. The teenage daughter, who was studying English in school, was not so fluent. But perhaps her knowledge of American history would turn out to be a bit more accurate.

When the parents learned that my wife and I are from Philadelphia, they beamed. "Philadelphia!" he exclaimed. "That is remarkable! Philadelphia was founded by Mennonites from Krefeld. What a coincidence! I can hardly believe it!"

Harriet and I were dumbfounded.

"I think there's some confusion," I said as tentatively as possible. "You see, Philadelphia was founded by a group of English Quakers led by William Penn."

"No," he replied firmly, "that cannot be the case. It was Mennonites from the town we live in, from Krefeld, who founded your great city. That is why today in Krefeld there is a Philadelphia Platz and a Philadelphia Strasse."

"Well," I said, "I'm just amazed that I've never heard of any German Mennonites in connection with the establishment of Philadelphia. You see, we've spent our whole lives there, always believing that it was William Penn who founded Philadelphia. He was given a very large land grant by the king of England late in the seventeenth century. As I'm sure you know, Pennsylvania was named after him. And Philadelphia was its first city. Penn named it Philadelphia, which is Greek for the city of brotherly love."

"I believe," he said with an air of finality, "that if you look into the matter a little more closely when you return you will find that Philadelphia was really founded by Mennonites from Krefeld."

Whoever said travel is broadening knew what he was talking about.

It was Clive Evans who told me about the Narin and Portnoo Golf Club. I had never heard of it.

"I'm not a golfer," he said, "so I'm no judge of these things, but they tell me it's quite nice."

Let it be said at once that Portnoo, as it is popularly referred to, is more than "quite nice." It is actually quite wonderful.

The drive from Bruckless House, on the N56, to Portnoo takes half an hour, a little longer if you stop in Ardara at any of the woolen-wear outlets with their Donegal tweeds. Portnoo is a little seaside resort strung out charmingly on the gentle hills above Gweebara Bay. It has two attractions: the golf course and the beach.

The first glimpse of the golf club, a bird's eye view, is not reassuring, for the clubhouse, nestling in the sandhills, is all but surrounded by trailers. Call them "caravans," if you will, the effect of such an armada is nonetheless tacky.

The small clubhouse, on the other hand, is bright and cheerful and tastefully decorated. And the L-shaped bar makes it immediately clear that the Irish have got their priorities straight: the long leg of the "L" is used for selling drinks, the short leg for selling golf equipment. There is no pro shop.

I've been unable to learn who laid out the course, but I do know that it opened for play in 1930. A look at the scorecard suggests a scarcity of acreage: total length of 5,865 yards, par of 69. A look at the opening shot confirms this. The drive on the

320-yard 1st is played over the adjacent 18th green. And then we are off on an adventure that gains in intensity as we move into the round. Routed through massive sandhills and over fiercely undulating ground, this is an altogether natural course—surely very little earth was ever moved here—and an out-and-in design, with the 9th green as far from the clubhouse as it is possible to get. The course also serves as grazing ground: surrounding each green is a strand of low-voltage electrical wire about 18 inches above the ground in order to keep the cattle off the putting surfaces.

There are six par threes, ranging from good to great, and three par fives (chance to make up some ground here). A skein of nine holes from the 5th through the 13th is of such challenge and drama and sport and unpredictability—and immense satisfaction—that I could scarcely credit my senses. The jottings on my scorecard provide some idea of the golf awaiting at Portnoo. The 383-yard 5th: "Splendid—fairway climbs over wildly heaving ground through draw to plateau green in dunes." The 144-yard 8th: "Exhilarating—from pinnacle tee to equally high shelf and straight out to sea." The 325-yard 9th: "Drive floats forever down to hummocky fairway, then short pitch to tiny knob of green at land's end high above rocky shore." The 200-yard 11th: "Tee reveals entire world of Portnoo, endless golden beach far below, green atop a wind-whipped sandy ridge." The 190-yard 13th: "Terrorizing shot across abyss of broken ground to green sequestered in dunes."

By the time we have completed the first 13 holes we have already played five par threes. Then, in succession, come two par fives. There is a very simple explanation for the apparent imbalances: these are the holes that fall most naturally on this marvelous stretch of linksland, and the architect was sensitive enough to take them as he found them.

After the round on our first visit, we had a sandwich and a drink in the clubhouse. The steward told us that the club has about 350 members, that almost all of the trailer owners belong to the club, that touring golfers find their way here from America, Canada, the Continent, even Japan, and that in high summer every hole is covered from daybreak to dark every day. We also learned that the amateur course record, a 64, shot in 1979, belongs to a local priest, Father Brendan McBride, who, as it happens, also served as president of the club for a time in the late 1980s. Parochial duties would seem not to be too pressing in this Donegal village.

I mentioned the electrical wire protecting each green. "Why do the cows have free run of the links?" I asked.

"Because," the steward replied, "it is the farmers who own this land, not the club."

As we were preparing to leave, I thanked him for his hospitality and once more voiced my high opinion of the course. "No one needs better golf than Portnoo," I concluded.

"Aye, yes, it is quite good, quite good," he agreed, but I thought there was a certain restraint in his response. Then he added, "You know, just a few weeks ago a group of us from here went over to the States to play, to play at Myrtle Beach. Ah, don't they have wonderful golf there! I loved it!"

Back on the N56 now, we are heading north, much of the time along the coast, with its high cliffs and secluded coves and rocky islands, its fiords and fishing villages and sandy beaches. Rosapenna is our goal, via Gweebarra Bridge and Gweedore and Creslough and Carrigart. A brief detour permits a visit to Glenveagh Castle, which Philadelphian Henry McIlhenny (doubtless a descendant of Mennonites from Krefeld) deeded to Ireland about 15 years ago. It is strikingly sited on a rocky promontory and has gardens, particularly the rhododendron section, even more splendid than the great house itself.

The golf course at Rosapenna is owned by the Rosapenna Hotel, which serves as the clubhouse. I'm not likely to forget our initial visit to Rosapenna, for we arrived at the first tee to find a ladies' clinic in full sway (not swing, *sway*). A dozen beginners were attempting to hit the golf ball—six of them practice-swinging vigorously preparatory to teeing off, three others approximately 150 yards down the fairway (playing, approximately, their fourth or fifth shot), and three more approaching the green. All were under the tutelage of the professional and his assistant, the assistant wielding a videocam in order to record, for now and forever, these highly imaginative golf swings. I had no choice but to forego the pleasure of this opening hole (300 yards uphill to a breezy plateau green), bypass this unnerving exhibition, and hasten directly to the 2nd tee. Desperate men do desperate deeds.

On the 2nd hole an American couple from St. Paul, both about 70 years old, invited me to join them. They had visited Ireland once before, but for sight-seeing only. This time they had come for the golf, but, to our surprise, not for the shrines. They had no desire to battle the sandhills and the winds and the crowds at Ballybunion or Lahinch or Tralee or Portmarnock, and had actually been seeking out such unknown inland courses as Athlone, Birr, and Longford, which they felt would be more suitable to their game. Both appeared to have handicaps in the low 20s. So similar were their abilities, in fact, that they vied with each other at match play with no strokes given, though Mrs. Keyes did get a slight advantage by playing from the ladies' markers. She kept the score and seemed rather more intent on their little competition than did her husband, who, on a couple of occasions, was uncertain whether he had accumulated a 5 or a 6. But Mrs. Keyes always knew and was pleased to guide his recapitulation. Harriet and I were not surprised to see her win the match, and rather handily at that, by 3 and 2.

Len Keyes was a retired lawyer. "Well, semiretired," he said. "I still handle a few clients." He volunteered that Warren Burger had been a partner in the same firm and was a lifelong friend. "He was a very good attorney," Len confided, "but I think we were all a little surprised, including Warren, when he was chosen for the Supreme Court."

My playing companions were not on a tight schedule. They would be in Ireland for the biggest part of a month and were simply roaming wherever their fancy took them. Confident that they could always find a room for a night in a B&B, they made no reservations. If a place looked nice, they just knocked on the door.

Rosapenna, it turned out, was their first taste of seaside golf. They were by turns astonished and charmed. And well they might have been, for there are few more irresistible places to play. What's more, there are few courses with a more impressive pedigree: Old Tom Morris, James Braid, Harry Vardon, Harry Colt, and C. H. Morrison all had a hand in shaping Rosapenna.

The first nine is traditional links golf as we work our way out through the low dune-framed valley beneath the ridge of sand-hills bordering Sheephaven Bay. Undulating fairways, tees on convenient hillocks, generous greens on plateaus or in dells, the occasional frighteningly deep sandpit, the occasional shallow bunker in the very heart of the fairway, the great gashes in the faces of sandhills, the long rough grasses to throttle the off-line stroke—it is all here. There are no trees, no ponds. We are once again at Lahinch and Murvagh and Portnoo, seaside golf of supreme naturalness and demanding a complete arsenal of shots.

The second nine—more specifically, the final eight—stands in sharp contrast. Here, again and again and again, it is spec-tacular golf, literally golf as spectacle, that we savor. Having turned our back now on the dunescape and left the low ground, we play up and down and over and around a single great hill. On the 11th we drive across a road, then head steeply up the hill we will come to know so well. Long enough on the card, 427 yards, it is punishingly long to play. The 12th continues this near-vertical ascent, but this time the measured mileage, 342 yards, makes the hole manageable. Now, at the summit, we stand upon the 13th tee, the ruins of Rosapenna House a few yards off to the right, and we prepare to launch a tee shot that will plunge blindly—and seemingly endlessly—down the fairway. The hole swings easily right in the landing area, and now that we have reached our drive the green is in full view, perched high above Mulroy Bay. Heady stuff. Potent stuff. And because of the precipitously falling nature of the drive, playable stuff as well, even though this two-shotter is 455 yards long.

And now that we have come down, we must climb back up. And so we do, thanks to a short one-shotter followed by a very strong par four, bending left and rising as it dares us to bite off a sizable chunk of the rough in the elbow of the dogleg if we are to have any hope of reaching the green in two on this 418-yarder.

The three holes that take us home are more of the crowning glory that is Rosapenna, with 17 in particular laying it all out for us, an arresting 360-degree panorama of town and water, meadow and mountain. Rosapenna, staggering in its beauty, endearing in its naturalness, is the only course I can think of that is ringed by water and ringed by mountains. And lest the enchantment of the setting threaten to overshadow the shot values of the course, please know that this is first-class golf. Though it measures only 6,270 yards from the back tees (5,550 from the ladies' markers), there are, on this par 70 layout, no fewer than six two-shotters in the 400-yards-plus category.

Len and Donna Keyes did not join us in the hotel for a sandwich. "We've got to find a place to sleep tonight," he said cheerfully as we parted in the car park.

We would spend the night at Rathmullan House, another of those handsome Georgian mansions, this one less than an hour away, on Lough Swilly, one of the great fiords that indent the Donegal coast. Here we occupied Room #4, a spacious, sunny corner accommodation looking down over the gardens and through the ancient elm and oak trees to the sandy shore of the lough and across to distant Buncrana and the mountains back-dropping it.

The bathroom was vast and contained an old tub on feet and a separate stall shower. The bed, an old-fashioned double, was not vast. But if you can overlook this circumstance—or manage to get a room with twin beds and the same ravishing view—you will find yourself downright delighted to be here. Bob and Robin Wheeler are thoughtful hosts, the open fires in the public rooms seem to burn all the time (there were four blazing—two in sitting rooms, one in the cellar bar, one in the drawing room—when we went into dinner both nights in mid-April), the period furniture and paintings and crystal chandeliers give the interiors character and style, and dining in the Arabian-tent-design restaurant, with its long arched windows giving on the lake, is thoroughly rewarding. The cooking is both excellent and imaginative: rabbit and guinea fowl terrine with an apple and horseradish sauce, timbale of smoked salmon and avocado mousse, baked fillets of rainbow trout filled with cream cheese and leeks and served in a lemon butter sauce, roast loin of pork stuffed with apricot and herbs and served on a purée of apple and apricot, pineapple and kiwi *en cage* with hazelnut parfait.

Just a couple of miles up the coast is the little Otway Golf Club, which has a nine-hole course that looks to have been shoehorned into about 35 acres of dipsy-doodle land along the lake. Could be fun, from what I observed.

"Observe" was also all I managed to do at Portsalon, some 15 miles north of Rathmullan House on Lough Swilly, where the course is laid out amidst beautiful mountain and sea-lough scenery and where the game has been played since 1891. The course today—there have been many changes over the years, and there is no record as to who effected these changes—measures 5,878 yards against a par of 69. About half of the holes are routed through duneland, the other half over rather meadowy ground. There is a sportiness and unpredictability to much of it. The three one-shotters on the outbound nine are quite good: the steeply dropping 196-yard 2nd; the even longer 5th, 208 yards and rising across desertlike wasteland; and the 174-yard 8th, where the minuscule green, encased in a dell-like framing of low dunes, would be difficult to hit in a dead calm from half that distance. The 13th, at 431 yards, is by far the longest par four; called "Matterhorn," it has a strange pointed rock outcropping, reminiscent of that famous peak, which must be cleared on the second shot. The finish is stiff, with both 17 (a dogleg left 526-yarder that crosses a stream) and the 405-yard 18th (here a burn just short of the green must be carried) playing into the prevailing breeze.

I confess that on the only occasion when my wife and I were in this neck of the woods I simply did not have the time to play Portsalon. That was my misfortune. It looks to me to be the kind of lively little course that is the essence of enjoyable holiday golf.

The northernmost golf in Ireland is at County Donegal's Ballyliffin, an hour and a quarter drive from Rathmullan House and far out on the Inishowen Peninsula. However remote, this is an ideal setting for the game, framed as it is by almost ominously dark hills, on the one hand, and the brilliance of a sweeping bay, on the other. Astonishingly, there are now two eighteens here, the second one not even a year old as this book is published.

Let's look at the Old Course, if that is what it's to be called, first. John Redmond, one of the most authoritative commentators on Irish clubs and courses, calls it "underrated." Matthew Harris, one of Britain's foremost golf photographers, says it is the finest golf course he has ever seen. Indeed, it was Harris's assessment that spurred me to seek out Ballyliffin, up there on this extremity, not 10 miles from Malin Head itself. I had never heard of Ballyliffin till I stumbled upon the Harris pronunciamento.

Well, I can report that it is not the finest course I've ever seen. Nor is it among the hundred or, for that matter, two hundred finest courses I've ever seen. But it is good and it is fun, and if you approach it expecting to encounter some testing shots and some worthy holes in a duneland setting of undeniable grandeur—the sandhills stretch away as far as the eye can see—you will be glad you made the trip, or trek. But this eighteen is not Enniscrone or Murvagh or Connemara, not to mention Ballybunion, Rosses Point, or Waterville.

The back tees boost the length to just over 6,500 yards, but members play the course at about 6,150 yards. Par is 72. My companions for the game were John Geoghegan, the club's captain, and Cormac McDonough, a recent past captain. They were a study in both similarities and contrasts. Both were about 60, of average build and a little less than average height, and could be expected to break 80 on a relatively calm day. But John had a flat swing and hit a low hard draw, while Cormac had a very upright swing and hit a power fade. When it came to making a living, Cormac was a banker and John worked for a company that makes women's blouses. "I'm in the rag trade," he told me with a laugh, and I was surprised to hear him use what I have always assumed to be an American expression. I was also amused at the sound of this 7th Avenue phrase with an Irish lilt to it.

When Cormac learned that I am a Philadelphian, he said, rather as though it were the most natural thing in the world, "Ah, that's where my father was born, on Broad Street. But the family turned around some years later—he was nine—and moved back to Ireland, in 1913. I guess not all the emigrants were happy in the States. He will be ninety in June."

Six holes, including half of the 10 par fours (6, 8, 10, 11, 15) and the 113-yard 9th (a little nothing if ever there was one), are dismissible, though pleasant enough. The two best holes on the first nine are the smoothly uphill 2nd, 497 yards, and the climbing par-three 5th, where a long iron must be hit precisely to find a plateau green ringed by dunes.

The second nine, better and stronger than the first, is routed nearer the shore. The 13th and 14th, both played from high tees, are outstanding, the former a par five of 485 yards culminating in a green on a knob in the sandhills, the latter a splendid and sweeping dogleg left of 370 yards through the dunes. The 18th, at 556 yards and curving left, plays between low dunes on the right and high dunes on the left to a prettily sited green near the clubhouse.

I almost wrote that the 18th "plays along level ground between, etc." That would have been an egregious gaffe, for there is no level ground on the older eighteen at Ballyliffin. Therein lies the course's singularity and a large measure of its appeal. Stances and lies constitute the principal challenge to scoring here—not out-of-bounds threats (there are none to speak of), not water (there is none), not impertinently convoluted greens, not harshly penal bunkers (there are few bunkers of any description). Yes, there is rough, and it is long and snarly, but the fairways are, on the whole, quite generous.

However, so fantastically rippling are these fairways, so unimaginably wavy and undulating, so rife with wrinkles and furrows, so akin to an endless scrub-board, that a truly flat stance or a truly flat lie—to say nothing of the two in tandem!—is the rarest commodity at Ballyliffin. Most of us are simply not equipped to digest an endless diet of tilts. This eighteen, whatever the blandness of a number of holes, is nevertheless a remarkable experience.

Eddie Hackett is responsible for the most recent revisions to the course, which first opened for play little more than 30 years ago and appears to have been laid out by one or two members of the Greens Committee. Pat Ruddy and Tom Craddock designed the second 18, which, smack beside its older sister, opened in 1995.

Craddock won the Irish Open Amateur in 1958, and the following year the Irish Close. In 1967 and 1969 he competed in the Walker Cup Match. Ruddy is one of the foremost Irish golf journalists and golf promoters. The two had teamed up several years earlier to lay out the highly regarded St. Margaret's course, a couple of miles from the Dublin airport. On his own,

Ruddy had designed and built the European Club links in County Wicklow.

They were called in by Ballyliffin's Development Committee in 1992, not to lay out a new eighteen, but simply to upgrade the existing links. When Ruddy learned that the club owned a total of 360 acres of duneland, he suggested that the first thing Ballyliffin ought to do is build a second eighteen.

"Look up the map of your property in the government offices," he told the committee, "and you will find that the bureaucrats of the European Community have drawn a red line around it, earmarking it as an area of scientific interest. Golf course construction is still exempt from planning laws. That's not going to last much longer. Soon it will be impossible to build a golf links here. But if you act right now, you will get in under the wire."

The club, though far from rich, did not hesitate, and within months the project to build a second eighteen in this sleepy little village got under way. Less than a year later the Irish government enacted a law making planning permission a requisite for golf course development.

The game on the new 18 starts and ends at the simple clubhouse, but 14 of the holes are routed through the high duneland north of the original course. Here the scenery is more stirring and the golfing terrain offers more feature and elevation change.

Par is 72 (three long holes, three short holes, a dozen par fours). Total yardage for the ladies is 5,650. The men play a hefty 6,700 yards. From the tiger tees, the course measures almost 7,100 yards, with the second nine, par 37, totaling 3,800 (only one of the half-dozen two-shotters here is as short as 400 yards).

The linchpin of the links is a mountainous sandhill that looms over the entire property. The first two holes, a pair of sturdy par fours, 380 and 400 yards, respectively, work their way out across the plain that contains most of the original eighteen. The architects have often called for steep revetted bunker faces, and fronting the elevated green at the 2nd hole is a particularly cavernous—and implacable—example of the genre. The members were dubious about their chances of ever completing the round if this type of torture chamber were to crop up often, so a "committee" accompanied Ruddy and Craddock out to review the problem. Several of the group dropped balls into the pit and, as feared, were unable to extricate them. With only a 9-iron in hand, however, Ruddy, "popped it out, no bother." Then Craddock, a right-hander, partially embedded his ball in the face of the hazard, stood up to it left-handed with his partner's 9-iron turned over on its back, and proceeded to explode the ball to within a foot of the hole. The discussion ended, the "committee" retreated.

Holes 3, 4, 5, and 6 tack their way up one side of the huge sandhill. By this time, the player, without any onerous climbing, has reached the crest and now essays the thrilling 7th, a 165-yarder that plunges about 120 feet to a target green that appears to be a little larger than a scorecard.

This experience is replicated on the second nine, on the other side of the great sandhill, with holes 12 and 13 ascending to the pinnacle, and 14, the 140-yard cousin of 7, falling forever to a lovely green on a platform near the base of the hill. The 7th and 14th are already much talked of as "the terrible twins." In truth, they are doubly noteworthy, for it is impossible to think of one without the other.

Among the other especially outstanding holes are two of the par fives. The 4th, only 470 yards, is routed through a deep, dune-framed valley. A huge bunker on the right menaces the drive. A crossbunker on the second shot complicates our depth perception. Backdropping the green is Glasheddy Rock, out in the Atlantic, and we are reminded of playing a shot at Turberry against the silhouette of Ailsa Craig. Just short of the green is a swale 20 feet deep. On this heaving and tumbling links, it looks entirely natural, but it is actually the creation of a bull-dozer. Ground has been moved here on the new course—something that may never have happened on the original links—but sparingly.

The 13th, 520 yards, is a marvelous roller-coaster ride through another valley in the dunes. The fairway is wide to accept the drive but then, funnel-like, becomes progressively narrower, rising as it nears the green. Messrs. Ruddy and Craddock appear to have drawn their inspiration from the great 15th at Pine Valley.

It is a very good layout, this second eighteen, and it has already become the principal magnet for attracting visitors to this outpost. A couple of plain and comfortable small hotels, a church, a post office, two grocery stores, and a scattering of cottages make up this community of some 500 souls. And now it offers a pair of linksland courses, one of them unique because of its humpy terrain, the other, less idiosyncratic, notable because of its arresting holes and consistently high shot values. What an extraordinary place this Ballyliffin is!

But then, the same might be said of County Donegal taken as a whole, beginning with Murvagh in the south and including Narin and Portnoo, Rosapenna, Portsalon, and this veritable hotbed of the game, Ballyliffin.

Chapter 6

The Curtain
Is Lifted

From 1969, when violence first erupted in Belfast and Londonderry, till September 1994, when a then uneasy truce was finally declared, Northern Ireland saw few American golfers. Those who did make it a point to get up there—I went for the first time in 1980—generally confined their games to the great seaside courses at Newcastle and Portrush, both towns at a considerable remove from the unrest of the two major cities. We were confident that no harm would come to nomadic golfers, and if that attitude may have struck our families and friends as a bit foolhardy, the record proved us right: no tourist was ever killed in Northern Ireland by the random violence that scarred this quarter of a century.

It might be well to mention that Northern Ireland, familiarly known as Ulster, occupies roughly one-sixth of the Irish land mass. It is scarcely 85 miles from top to bottom, and very little wider. Despite British hegemony over the six counties of

Northern Ireland, golf has been administered throughout the island since 1891 by the Golfing Union of Ireland, which has its headquarters in Dublin. Competitions have always embraced the players from both sides of the border. In its own small way, the game has served as a unifying force.

There are about 80 golf courses in Ulster—seaside, parkland, meadowland, woodland, many of them admittedly modest nine-hole layouts—and among them are several that are indisputably among the greatest in the world. In this chapter we'll take a look at five courses in the province, all of them at the sea.

The drive from either Ballyliffin or Rathmullan House to Castlerock takes nearly two hours. Here, on the County Londonderry coast, where the Bann River enters the Atlantic Ocean, the Castlerock Golf Club was founded in 1901. The initial nine was laid out by "Mr. J. Coburn the Greenkeeper of Portrush." In 1908, Ben Sayers, of North Berwick, Scotland, extended the course to 18 holes. An outstanding clubmaker who was also one of the top players of his time (he competed in every British Open from 1880 to 1923 and on a couple of occasions came tantalizingly close to claiming the old claret jug), the colorful 5-foot, 3-inch Sayers had trained as an acrobat before turning to golf as his livelihood. For many years he would celebrate the holing of a lengthy or tricky putt by doing a series of cartwheels or handsprings across the green.

In 1925 Harry Colt introduced several changes to the Castlerock links, and Eddie Hackett effected even more extensive revisions in the 1960s. Over the years several Irish championships, both amateur and professional, have been held here.

The entire course fits neatly between the railway and the river and the sea. Par is 73—five long holes, four short holes, and nine two-shotters. The course can be stretched to 6,700 yards, but it is generally played at about 6,250. Many of the holes are routed through inviting duneland. An equal number occupy less attractive ground.

Often cited as a feature hole is the 4th, a 200-yarder on the more meadowy ground near the railway. With a boundary tight on the right and a little stream not far from the left side of the green, the only haven here is the putting surface itself. The 7th, 8th, and 9th return to the seaside terrain. A superb 400-yarder, the 7th ripples along over very uneven ground before rising to a green beautifully sited in the dunes. From a high tee, the grand 8th doglegs right, with dunes on that side in the landing area, then climbs to a perfect shelf of green. At the exacting 9th, a sand-free 190-yarder that plays into the prevailing breeze and often calls for at least a 3-wood, an old quarry looms to the left of the green.

The second nine is much like the first, with some holes cradled in the rumpled duneland, others out in the open. The round finishes with a flourish. From its lofty tee on a ridge, the 485-yard 17th affords beautiful views across the Bann estuary to our next stop, the links at Portstewart. After a falling tee shot, we tack our way past mounds and hollows and sandhills, careful at the end to avoid the lone bunker, just off the right front of the raised green. On the last hole, 340 yards long, the drive is again downhill, but this time it is blind (there is not a handful of blind shots in the entire round). Jutting into the fairway from the right is a formidable sandhill. We must stay well left of it or the second shot—uphill to a plateau green with a steep drop on the left—will also be blind. A little local knowledge goes a long way here.

You will notice in the course of the round some golf holes near the sea that you never do get to play. They look stimulating. They are at least that, their narrow fairways weaving through the dunes toward small greens on plateaus or in dells. You may also sense that there are very few players—perhaps none at all—on them. This is the Bann Nine, a thoroughgoing charmer that, if you can spare an hour and a half, should not be missed. Laid out by England's Frank Pennink in 1986 to serve as a relief nine, the holes incline to be quite short—three of the par fours, for instance, are between 250 and 260 yards, and the one par five is only 447—but the fairways and the greens are cunning targets, and some genuine shotmaking is called for. The club's secretary told me that the nine gets some play from women and children, but that fully 80 percent of the men have never tried it.

The clubhouse was also constructed within the last 10 years, and you will want to have lunch upstairs in the bar or the dining room and enjoy the attractive views over the links to the sea. I remember that when we visited the club in the spring of 1994 I had difficulty striking up a conversation with the bartender. A strapping young man in his late 20s, he seemed either shy or standoffish. At no time did he smile. Between Harriet and me, we managed to pry out of him that he was a member of the club, that he played to a 4 handicap, and that he believed Castlerock to be the best of the courses in County Londonderry. Asked whether he had ever been to America, he said he had not but was hoping to get there one day. When I paid the bill, he handed me the change and then, to my surprise, fished out from under the bar a glass beer mug with the Castlerock Golf Club logo on it in blue. He awkwardly thrust it into my hand. "Here," he said simply, "so you'll remember us."

As the crow flies, it looks to be only a stout par four across the water to Portstewart from Castlerock. But the drive takes a good 15 minutes, so jagged is the coastline.

Portstewart Golf Club celebrated its centenary in 1994. The club was fortunate—indeed, given the nature of his vocation, it could fairly be said that Portstewart was blessed—in having for its secretary during more than 25 years at the beginning of the century a retired Baptist minister from nearby Coleraine, the Reverend P. H. Blackie. A man of energy and conviction, he was a big individual with a powerful voice, who, though generally kind and courteous, could also be unbending where the rules were concerned. On one occasion during a tournament he intercepted a lady competitor making haste for the clubhouse. He asked her why she was leaving the field of battle. That good woman, now covered in the embarrassment characteristic of those more genteel days, explained that she was forced to answer a call of nature. Firmly, the Reverend Blackie barred her way, enlightening her as to the Rule of Golf prohibiting players from entering the clubhouse during a competition and advising her that she should "go at once to the bunkers, madam, to the bunkers!"

Shortly after the Reverend Blackie took office, the club, seeking ground for expansion, moved to the west end of town, at Strand Head. The course that we play today is located here, but it is quite different from the one that Portstewart members and guests enjoyed for about 80 years. In 1986, the same year in which Castlerock's Bann Nine was laid out, Portstewart decided to build seven holes in the adjacent hilly and virgin duneland called "Thistly Hollow" and to incorporate these new holes into what is now the principal layout here. The result of that decision was the creation of one of the great seaside courses of Ireland.

The man charged with designing the new holes was Des Giffin, the Greens Convener (what we would call "Chairman of the Golf Committee"). Like George Crump at Pine Valley and Hugh Wilson at Merion and Henry Clay Fownes at Oakmont, Des Giffin had no experience in golf course design. But he had imagination and taste, a sense of what constituted a good golf hole, and a respect for the natural contours of the land. He wrote in the club history of "the sprawling wasteland of steep ridges and valleys, often covered with impenetrable sea buckthorn. . . . As a child I had spent many happy hours playing through this magnificent wilderness and I knew the ground well. As far as possible I tried to work with the land rather than against it, and although some drastic changes were necessary . . . I hope that the course, with its elevated tees and sudden, unexpected vistas of sea, river, and mountain, allows the golfer to take as much satisfaction from the natural beauty with which he is surrounded as from the test of golf with which he is presented."

Par is 72. The course can be played as short as 5,800 yards and as long as 6,780 yards. In between, there are tees at 6,100 and 6,500. There is also an unusual stretch of four holes on the second nine without a par four, as two short holes bracket two long holes.

The greatness of Portstewart is proclaimed on the very first hole—nay, on the first tee. This launching pad is high. Everything our delighted eye embraces lies far below: on our right, the frothing combers of the Atlantic Ocean breaking upon a broad scimitar of golden beach; dead ahead, a cluster of massive sandhills; on our left, the gentler holes along the river Bann. The tee shot on this 410-yarder floats seemingly forever, down to a level landing area where the fairway curves smoothly right to seek a green nestled between huge dunes that are mantled in buckthorn and long grasses. It is an opening hole as sublime and unforgettable as the 1st at Machrihanish. No higher compliment can be paid.

Now we move into the heart of the soaring sandhill country and, for the next seven or eight holes, savor every aspect of seaside golf at its most marvelous: the sequestered holes winding along dune-framed channels, the plateau greens and the pulpit tees, the tumbling fairways and the gathering bunkers, the doglegs that range from subtle to, as on the 8th, pronounced, and, withal, the sheer exhilaration of it. There is even an audacity to this sequence of holes at Portstewart that reminds us of Carne and the new course at Ballybunion and the back nine at Tralee.

The second half finds us turning inland to more-open ground, but if this is a less exuberant canvas, there is still nothing in the least humdrum about it as we play over beautifully undulating ground, often in view of the sweet river Bann. Nor are we likely to forget the double fall-and-rise 17th, a 400-yarder with a singularly intimidating plateau green, precipitous falloffs on every side.

However pressed for time you may be, don't fail to have either lunch or a drink in the clubhouse dining room, which reveals the same breathtaking sweep of sea, strand, sandhills, and distant Inishowen Head (Ballyliffin here) that greeted us at the start of the round. It was here that we chatted with Michael Moss, the club's manager. I was curious about the annual dues.

"Two hundred and fifty pounds," he said. "Which must be close to four hundred dollars. Now I know that's very little by your standards, but our members are not used to spending money in order to play golf. So I have to keep reminding them that they get forty-five holes."

"Forty-five holes?"

"Oh, yes, the eighteen you just played, then the other nine right here—it's made up mostly of holes replaced by the new seven—and then there's another eighteen at the far end of town, where the club first played a hundred years ago. Half of that course runs right along the sea. So considering what two hundred and fifty pounds buys, I don't think it's an excessive subscription."

Among other events, the club has twice hosted the Irish Professional Championship and the Ulster Professional Championship, as well as the 1983 and 1984 Irish Ladies' Open Amateur and the Irish Amateur Close in 1960 and in 1992. In 1951 it was used as a qualifying site for the British Open, when that greatest of all championships was held just 10 minutes away, at Royal Portrush. This marked the only occasion in its nearly 140-year history that the Open was played outside Scotland and England. It could well happen once again, in 2001, and at the same club.

The fourth oldest golf club in Ireland, Royal Portrush was founded in 1888. Its name then was the County Club. In 1895, with the Prince of Wales (later King Edward VII) as its patron, it became the Royal Portrush Golf Club.

Today the club is run by Wilma Erskine, who carries the title of Secretary-Manager. Very much on top of things at this busy club, she has a quick and keen wit.

"As a traveling golfer," I said on our 1994 visit, "I don't know that I can really tell the difference between Ireland and Northern Ireland. I'm sure you can, but I can't."

"You're right I can," she laughed. "The roads are much better here."

It was a pointed reminder that we were in the United Kingdom.

Over the years, more than 50 championships, amateur and professional, men's and women's, have been conducted here, including the Irish Open Amateur (inaugurated at Portrush in 1892), the British Amateur (the redoubtable Joe Carr winning for the third and last time here in 1960), the British Ladies', and, of course, the aforementioned 1951 British Open, which was won by Max Faulkner, five times a Ryder Cupper.

An uninhibited man with a dazzling wardrobe and a powerful swing, Faulkner could be engagingly brash, and never more so than in this championship. After only 36 holes and holding a scant two-stroke lead, he was found to be signing autographs

"Max Faulkner, Open Champion 1951." As it turned out, he was as good as his name, finishing the 72 holes two strokes ahead of runner-up Antonio Cerda.

There is flexibility in setting up the course for men—6,400 to 7,400 yards. But for the ladies, it is an extremely long course, over 6,100 yards, against a par of 76. For decades men's par was 73. Not too long ago, with but a stroke of the pen, the 477-yard 18th, a par five that yielded a number of birdies, became a very long par four.

Over the years a number of men have had a hand in shaping the course, most notably Harry Colt, the first golf course architect who was not also a golf professional. Among his many outstanding designs are Rye, the New Course at Sunningdale, Swinley Forest, and St. Georges Hill, all in southern England. It is Colt to whom we are chiefly indebted for the course we play at Portrush today.

There is promise and attractive variety in the early going. The 370-yard opener is inviting: downhill on the drive, uphill on the second shot to a plateau green. This is followed by a 485-yarder working its way along a secluded allée in the dunes to a green boldly bunkered—the pits at Portrush are to be sedulously avoided!—well out in front, just where the attacking second shot may land. Then comes a good medium-length one-shotter, which is succeeded by nothing less than two of Ireland's best par fours. At the 4th, 440 yards, we drive over a stream to a fairway with a bunker in its left side and a boundary close on the right. There is no sand at the green, just low dunes pinching the entrance and a steep falloff left to carry away our long second, possibly a full-blooded wood, if it should come in hot and hooking.

As for the 5th, 65 yards shorter, it is not so rigorous, but it is equally fine. In fact, it is majestic. The easy climb up to the tee brings us to the highest point of the course. Here it is that the grandeur of Portrush is stamped indelibly in our memory, the entire sweep of the proud links cascading wildly from the high ground through the splendid duneland, curving slashes of emerald fairway in bold relief against the shaggy golden sand-hills, down to the high cliffs above the broad beach. Virtually all of the championship eighteen, called Dunluce, lies exposed to our enraptured gaze. So, too, is most of the less difficult but also outstanding Valley Links (6,273 yards, par 70, home of the club's Ladies' Branch, with its own clubhouse). The golf holes constitute, if you will, the foreground. Beyond, to the east, our eye is caught first by the White Rocks—no mystery as to why this hole is so named—imposing limestone cliffs that lead to Dunluce Castle and then, a little further on, to the Giant's Causeway. On the west, the dark bulk of Inishowen Head rears out of the sea. Straight ahead, backdropping the links and only a few hundred yards offshore, is the long line of the Skerries, a series of low islets that serve as a breakwater. On a clear day, though we cannot see forever, we can indeed make out the coast of Scotland. It is vague, admittedly, almost shapeless, but Machrihanish is there, on the Mull of Kintyre, and we may be forgiven for imagining that we see it.

Is there, on any other golf course, a view to match it, this one from the 5th tee at Portrush? Maybe at Turnberry or Pebble

Beach or Portstewart. Almost certainly at Royal County Down. Is there a view to surpass it? Not in my experience.

Now to play this 375-yarder. There are no bunkers, there is no burn, and the only boundary is over the green, so it is scarcely a hazardous undertaking. But the fairway, flanked by sandhills cloaked in the long rough grasses, is far from generous, and it doglegs, turning right beyond a high dune about 200 yards out. Dare we, from this enticingly lofty perch, swing aggressively in the hope of carrying this sandhill and thus setting up a shortish approach that might produce a birdie? Or is that carry a trifle longer than it looks? And is the reward really worth the risk? A more conservative route, left of the dune, will leave a medium iron, while the gambling tee shot that fails to carry it can cost more than one stroke, so clinging is the tall and tangled rough, and no more forgiving because of the beguiling presence in it of primrose and bluebell.

We are faced with a decision. The wind will help us make it. If it is at our back, the choice is easy. But more often than not, it comes at us from the north, whipping in off the white-flecked sea, sometimes head on, frequently off the port bow. And we are totally exposed to its force and its vagaries, compelled now to launch a shot that, no matter how skillfully struck, must sail, must hang, must float weightlessly as it seeks to find the safe harbor of the fairway below.

Hole in, hole out, Portrush is generally acknowledged to pose the sternest test of driving of any championship course in the British Isles. The fairways incline not only to be narrower than what we have come to expect at the sea, but the curving nature of them (only 1 and 18 play straightaway, tee to green) persistently bedevils us. No small measure of control is required here.

But now, on the nonpareil 5th, we let go with a free and unhurried swing—perhaps on not quite the bravest of lines—and the ball comes to rest reassuringly in the fairway. The distance remaining to the green, itself set strikingly above the beach, is about 155 yards. It is a modestly rising shot over uneven ground. Natural mounds and hollows defend the green. There is a steep falloff on the right, and the pushed iron will bounce down into punitive rough from which a successful recovery is unlikely. Old photographs reveal that there was once a great dune at the left of the green, but it collapsed and fell into the sea some years ago. Today the slope on that side is a gentle one, manageable for the skillful chipper. The overly bold iron could plunge over a sandy precipice to the beach, which often hosts bathers and strollers and sometimes even horsemen. The beach is out of bounds. The net of it all is that a good shot is required to hit the green, but not a perfect one. And since this medium-sized target is double-tiered, the putting is scarcely automatic and can, from above the hole, be unsettling.

The other hole at Portrush that is equally celebrated is the 200-yard 14th, called "Calamity Corner," where our shot must avoid a 75-foot-deep chasm skirting the right side of the green. But it is the 5th that seems to me the perfect distillation of all that is so admirable about Portrush: the premium on good driving but not brawn, the entirely reasonable demands on our iron game, and the marvelous green complexes, where the putting surfaces themselves require thoughtful appraisal and a confident stroke, and missing them generally leaves us facing a delicate little pitch or chip that we just may not be able to bring off. Good judgment—knowing our own limitations—is called for. There is drama but not intimidation. And there is worthy challenge from tee to cup. All of it against a seascape of transcendent beauty. Small wonder that Royal Portrush is regarded as one of the 10 or 12 greatest seaside courses in the world.

More than 80 years ago Bernard Darwin wrote of Portrush in his seminal *The Golf Courses of the British Isles*: "The air is so fine that the temptation to play three rounds [in a day] is very hard to overcome, while I may quote, solely on the authority of a friend, this further testimonial to it, that it has the unique property of enabling one to drink a bottle of champagne every night and feel the better for it."

Well, the air is still that fine. In truth, there may be no more invigorating—make that intoxicating—spot on all the globe to play. And surely, as the champagne allusion suggests, we do indeed come to Royal Portrush in a celebratory mood. However, since the world's oldest distillery, Bushmills, dating back almost 400 years, is no more than a couple of miles away (visitors are welcome), the spirit of choice more often than not will be that prized local brew. A long-honored tradition is the hoisting of the Union Jack over the halfway house near the 10th tee, a sign that "a wee dram" is available to fortify us as we undertake the second part of the ongoing struggle.

This is a particularly beautiful and interesting section of Northern Ireland, one that well rewards even the casual sightseer. The holiday town of Portrush itself, with its splendid situation on a peninsula jutting into the Atlantic, its terraces of brightly painted houses, and its long beaches sweeping away on either side, has been likened to a liner heading out to sea.

Portstewart—sheltered harbor, oceanfront promenade, glorious beach (a road gives cars access to this two-mile-long stretch, which can be driven virtually from end to end)—has always been an especially lovely resort. So lovely, in fact, that its well-bred nineteenth-century residents actually prohibited the building of a railway station for fear of bringing vulgar people to the town.

About seven miles east of Portrush is Northern Ireland's most famous sight, the Giant's Causeway. It is an astonishing complex of some 37,000 basalt columns packed together, their tops forming "stepping stones" that lead away from the shore at the foot of the cliffs and disappear under the sea. Since similar columns can be found on the Scottish island of Staffa, in the Hebrides, the romantic legend persists that the Causeway was a road from Antrim to Staffa built by an Irish giant whose sweetheart lived there.

Other nearby places of interest, all of them on the coast, include Ballintoy, with a population of less than 300 and a pretty white parish church; Ballintoy Harbour, which is reached by a corkscrew road and where jagged volcanic stacks form an archipelago of islets, caves, and rocks for clambering; Whitepark Bay, with its half-moon of perfect beach in a grassy bowl of dunes and cliffs and its tiny hamlet of Portbraddan tucked in a cleft of the cliffs like dice in a box; Cushendum, a secluded beach village of Cornish-style cottages, the whole of it now protected by the National Trust; and Cushendall, an equally picturesque village where three glens meet beneath a flat-topped mountain and where the river Dall enters the sea.

Since Northern Ireland has not been a tourist destination for 25 years, it is not chock-a-block with outstanding places to stay. One very attractive small hotel is in the Coleraine area, less than 30 minutes from the courses we've just been playing. Open only since 1994, Ardtara Country House (the name means "old house on the high hill"), is a nineteenth-century Victorian manor with an extraordinary collection of antiques and with working fireplaces just about everywhere you turn, including all eight of the grand guest rooms (king-size beds). As you may have sensed already, we are fireplace freaks. So when our accommodation, #3, turned out, like the one at Adare Manor, to have two fireplaces—one in the bedroom, one in the bathroom—we were hooked forever. Happily, the cooking at Ardtara is also top-notch, with the emphasis on local produce and seafood. And for those of us who are reluctant to roam too far from the links, there are, in this eight acres of woodlands, a practice tee and putting green.

There is one other golf course up in this part of the country that I want to mention. Ballycastle, less than 20 miles east of Portrush on the Antrim Coast Road, is not great golf. In truth, it's not even serious golf. You do not cross an ocean in order to play it. But if you are in the neighborhood, you might want to take the opportunity. It is the purest holiday golf.

From the back tees it is all of 5,660 yards long. Yet par is not 66 or 67—it is 71. The result is a slew of short par fours, seven of them, ranging from 236 to 310 yards. Our wedge gets a workout, but because of the size and the siting of some of the greens we are not guaranteed of routinely putting for birdies.

Ballycastle has what might be called an identity crisis. The first five holes—the Margy River is on our left here, and in the middle are the remains of a thirteenth-century friary—are routed over grassy meadowland. The next five, plus the 18th, occupy a cramped piece of authentic linksland, with the 6th and the 9th actually bordering the beach. The other seven holes, 11 through 17, run up one side of a great cliff, then across it and down the other side. The game at Ballycastle is lively and unpredictable, and with it comes plenty of chances to gaze down on the charming town itself or across the harbor to Rathlin Island and beyond, to Scotland's Mull of Kintyre.

It is time now to head south to Newcastle, home of Royal County Down. You could make that drive from, say, Portrush in just under two hours. But I urge you to spend some extra time—perhaps another 45 minutes—by following the Antrim Coast Road, the A2, south to Larne. Whether at sea level or high on the headlands, this is one of the glories of motoring: the unfolding splendor of mountains, glens (every one of the nine Glens of Antrim spilling down to the road), and sea, and the remarkable variety of colors—brown moorlands, green glens, white limestone, black basalt, red sandstone, and yellow ochre from iron ore.

At Larne we leave the sea and, via the A8 and the A1, make our way around Belfast (some of the capital in view) on a motorway, then proceed through Hillsborough and Ballynahinch to Newcastle.

It is impossible for Harriet and me to think of Belfast without recalling the six months that our second son, John, then 23 years old, spent there in 1979, working as a counselor with underprivileged children. When he left home for this assignment, I suggested that he take his golf clubs with him and that with any luck he would at least play County Down, some 30 miles south of the city, and perhaps even Portrush. In fact, he did manage to get in both these games. But other than the two rounds, his contact with golf was limited to hitting balls on a big playground in the evening.

"So," he told us later, "I was at least able to hold onto some semblance of a golf swing by practicing occasionally. Although one time that did turn out to be dangerous."

His mother stiffened. "What do you mean, John?" she asked. "What's dangerous about hitting practice balls."

"Well," he said, "it wasn't really dangerous. That was a bad choice of words. It was almost ten o'clock one evening, but still plenty light enough to see the ball—sometimes you think it'll never get dark in Belfast—and I was hitting three-iron shots. Well, I banged out the whole bagful and now it was time to go pick them up. Thinking I might want to hit them back, I carried the club with me. So off I went across the field, and when I was about halfway there, in from the far side of the field and heading straight toward me came two British soldiers. As we got closer I could see that they were carrying machine guns which they had aimed at me. I stopped. I mean I didn't take another step. They were about 50 or 60 yards away. I held the club I was carrying up over my head and called out, 'Don't shoot! My three-iron isn't loaded!' "

I laughed, grateful to have the tension broken.

"My God, John!" Harriet gasped. "They could have . . . "

"Now, Mom," John said, "it wasn't all that tense. So we just kept walking toward each other, and as soon as they could see that it really was a golf club, they put their guns up. I guess we met somewhere near the middle of the field and the three of us just laughed."

"But how did they come to be there?" I asked.

"Oh, they told me. They explained it right away. One of their planes, a British reconnaissance plane flying slowly over the city—you know, just keeping an eye on things—had spotted me and mistaken my three-iron for a rifle. The pilot radioed the nearest soldiers and suggested that somebody get over here fast and find out who I was and what I was up to. So that's how the three of us came to be standing there on a big Belfast playground, me with my three-iron, them with their tommyguns. They were both about my age, and they thought it was all pretty funny."

I recall thinking at the time John recounted this incident what an extraordinary world this had become, when three young men, boys really, all of them far from home, could come together in the middle of a field under such curious circumstances, the threat of violence palpable as MacLeish's "globed fruit," and instantly see the humor in their meeting.

Twice have I been to Royal County Down, magnificently sited on a curve of Dundrum Bay and a short walk from the center of Newcastle. The first time I got a feeling for the club, the second time for the course.

Permit me to explain.

In 1980, on my initial visit to what is generally regarded as Northern Ireland's premier golf club (some would say its most socially conscious golf club), I was one of a group of six Americans. We arrived on a Saturday and were welcomed into the very bosom of the club—which is to say that we joined the party.

Every Saturday, the then-secretary, John Hubbard, explained to us, a number of members assemble upstairs in the lounge/bar, which, from its broad windows, provides views of the links and the bay. There appeared to me to be somewhere between 40 and 50 on hand that Saturday in late May, all of them drinking vigorously (who among them had as few as three whiskeys before lunch?) and talking animatedly (the decibel level was high) for an hour or so. Everyone put his name in the hat to indicate that he was available for the game. Our names were duly deposited. One member, then president of the Congress of Golfing Unions (of England, Scotland, Wales, and Ireland), said, "When we talked about the six visiting Americans coming to play on Saturday, I suggested that we treat them like members, exactly like members, and throw their names in the hat. That way we can spread them out, put one each in a four-ball with three of us—and they won't play so slowly." This prompted laughter.

So did an exchange between one of my traveling companions, a New Yorker, and the secretary.

Said the New Yorker, "I approached your great club with some apprehension, to say nothing of awe."

Replied the urbane Hubbard with a twinkle, "Quite right." Again, considerable laughter.

Whoever had been appointed to handle the hat that Saturday soon withdrew from the hubbub of the big room to sort through the names and, relying on his intimate knowledge of both the players' abilities and the reliability of their handicaps, to establish the four-balls. Some time later he reappeared to post the pairings under the small brass clock on the wall. This was the cause for whooping and groaning and calling about the room to spread the news.

Once the pairings were duly published—and a final drink ordered and downed (often neat)—the gathering moved into the dining room. Four-balls ate together, which enabled them to sort out their better-ball matches. The lunch was no ham-and-cheese-sandwich business. It started with a serve-yourself soup course, the silver tureens awaiting on a large antique sideboard. A waitress brought the entrée—roast leg of lamb that day, with a mint gravy—plus four vegetables, including the obligatory potatoes and cauliflower. Finally, we returned to the sideboard for cheese, which was accompanied by coffee or tea.

Having waded through this nearly two-hour festival of food

and drink and camaraderie, it was now time to head for the tee. In our case, that was the 10th tee, because there were already three groups waiting to hit off the 1st, and one of our four-ball, a 44-year-old Belfast businessman by the name of Brian Strafford, who was slated to become the club's next captain and who was also a member of Royal Belfast, made it clear that we'd better hie around to the 10th tee if we wished to get off promptly and play at a decent pace.

I had no choice but to shoulder my light bag and follow, though in fact this was not at all to my liking. When playing a course for the first time, especially a celebrated one that I wish to remember clearly, I need to play the holes in order. Otherwise, it is difficult to appreciate their true flow and the rhythm of the round. I also find myself having the very devil of a time weeks or months later in distinguishing between the 7th and the 16th or the 3rd and the 12th. And at Newcastle, as Royal County Down is generally called, this turns out to be regrettable, for the two nines are not of equal excellence. The first nine is better than the second.

We had a competitive and enjoyable match, with the low handicapper, who turned out to be me, giving the others three-quarters of the handicap differential. It was a straight 18-hole match—no Nassau—for a pound. Brian Strafford was teamed with John MacKinlay, a 35-year-old Scot from Dornoch who was now teaching school in Belfast. They were single-digit handicappers and long hitters. My partner, a man nearing 70 who had been a member of the club for 51 years and now played off 18, enabled us to collect the modest wager when he hit a lifetime pitch from a patch of heather on the far side of a high, steep mound some 35 yards short of the 425-yard 8th (our 17th) green for a four. This broke the deadlock, and we managed to protect our slim lead on the final hole.

It had been, in every sense, a delightful day, but though I came away with a very real sense of the club, I wondered whether my feel for the great course itself was all that it should be.

Fourteen years passed before I returned, this time with only my wife at my side on a spring day, not atypical, on which there were scarcely a dozen people on the links.

Golf was first played here in 1889, shortly after the club was formed. Old Tom Morris was called in from St. Andrews and commissioned to lay out the course for a sum not to exceed four pounds. There can be little question but that the frugal Irish got their money's worth from the frugal Scot. As you would expect, the Morris design has since been extensively altered, including revisions by Harry Vardon in 1908 and 1919. Nonetheless, the course remains wonderfully natural, and over the years, like Royal Portrush, it has hosted countless Irish and British championships (the latter including both the Amateur and the Ladies') and, in 1968, the Curtis Cup.

What strikes us—in truth, assaults us—are the massive sandhills, the profusion of gorse (overpoweringly golden in spring, impenetrable at any time), and the heady views. Then comes the challenge of playing the course. And that, by and large, is a matter of the bunkers and the bounces and the "blinds."

Half a dozen holes, beginning with the 2nd, entail a blind drive over a dune or a dune ridge to reach the narrow fairway that—we must take it on faith—lies somewhere on the far side. Add to that three or four occasions when the green itself is hidden.

There are 129 bunkers here, almost twice as many as on the average well-bunkered eighteen. These pits, shaggy-lipped (sometimes heather bewhiskered) and deep, are ferocious. The mandate is simple: *if you get in, get out.* To attempt more is to court disaster.

And finally, because this is undulating links terrain, the bounces can be capricious, so the element of luck is present.

Still, the unassailable greatness of seven or eight holes and the extraordinary beauty that surrounds us at every moment more than compensate for the insistent pressure on the swing. Three holes may be taken as typical of the challenge on a course that, even from the so-called forward tees, measures more than 6,500 yards against a par of 71. The 374-yard 2nd hole calls for a blind drive over a ridge, followed by a second shot guided through a cut in another ridge to an adroitly bunkered green on a low plateau. The even finer 5th, 409 yards from a tee elevated in the sandhills, asks us to bite off as much as we dare of a heathery outcrop of hill on the right, around which the hole doglegs enroute to a green framed by low dunes. The equally superb 13th, 422 yards long and routed through the seclusion of a gracefully curving valley all its own, requires a perfectly struck blind second shot over the corner of a high righthand sandhill if we are to gain the refuge of the green. The greens, it should be noted, afford a respite: they incline to be level and are surely the simplest to master of those on the world's truly great courses.

As for the views, in all of golf there are few so celebrated as the one from the 9th tee at County Down, the loftiest point on the course. Far below on this downhill par five, beyond the attractive white clubhouse, are the rooftops of Newcastle. Backdropping the town are the Mountains of Mourne, a faded purple, their tallest peak, Slieve Donard, often wreathed in clouds. Your gaze also encompasses miles and miles of green countryside bordered by the Irish Sea, which changes in color from leaden to cobalt whenever the wind disperses the clouds and the sun takes charge of this heart-stopping panorama.

I said earlier that the second nine does not measure up to the first. In fact, it is the final two holes—for some observers, the final three—that prove disappointing. The first 15 holes are, take them one by one, superlative. I would as soon play them as the first 15 on any course in the world. The 16th, from its lofty tee, is admittedly great fun. But a two-shotter that can be driven—it is only 265 yards long from the championship tees, 236 yards from the forward tees—by players of the first rank is little more than an amusing curio, especially when there is no penalty incurred in failing to hit what is essentially an undefended green.

The 17th—376 yards from the regular markers, 400 from the blues—is straightaway over uninspiring ground, a slightly falling tee shot, a slightly rising second. In the center of the fairway, just out of reach of even a cracking good drive, is a small pond. It looks artificial. How it came to be there—and heaven knows it has been there for decades—one can only spec-

ulate. It has no earthly purpose except to give pause to those
who drive the ball more than 275 yards. For the rest of the
world, it is merely decorative.

The home hole is a level and straightaway 528-yarder over
more of this same featureless ground. It is littered, beginning
about 190 yards from the tee, with 23 pot bunkers, a telling in-
dication that the terrain itself provides little interest or challenge. The problem of getting back to the clubhouse on the
landward side of the sandhills was not solved with style.

But if the climax is distinctly anticlimatic, this should not
dampen our enthusiasm for this great links. In every respect—
shotmaking requirements, turf (springy fescue on a sandy
base), holes of fascination and individuality in perfect harmony
with the landscape, and scenic splendor—Royal County Down
is one of the treasures of the game. Quite understandably, it is
for many knowledgeable and widely traveled golfers their favorite course in all the world.

Next door—in fact, interwoven with the championship
eighteen at times, so that it is possible to proceed, mistakenly,
from one course to the other—is the ladies' course. Only a little over 4,000 yards, against a par of 65, it is still enormously
sporting.

On our 1994 visit, my wife and I had lunch in the pleasant
dining room that the club reserves for visitors. A motherly
silver-haired woman served us. Noting our American accent,
she said that she had six children and that the two youngest,
both unmarried, were soon to leave for the States.

"My daughter is going to San Francisco to work in a pub or
a restaurant. She's told it's a grand city and a great place for

young people trying to make their way. There's not much opportunity in Newcastle, the unemployment being so high and so many on the dole. The boy works right here, on the greenskeeper's crew. He likes it and he has studied agronomy in college, but there are several older men ahead of him for promotion and he's afraid it will take too long to get up the line. So he's leaving in less than a month for the same kind of work in North Carolina. He says there are a lot of golf courses there and they are building new ones all the time."

I assured her that her son was almost certainly making a good move that held every promise of a bright future. Surely it was what my own grandparents must have believed. The Irish immigration to America, begun 150 years ago, continues.

With its three-mile-long beach, its harbor for pleasure craft, and its setting in the lee of the mountains, Newcastle is the principle seaside resort on the County Down coast. There is nothing of a Portofino prettiness about it, nor are any of the wonders of the world here. But the promenade along the seafront has an old-fashioned charm and interest (a fountain in the gardens commemorates Percy French, composer of the famous Irish ballad "Where the Mountains o' Mourne Sweep Down to the Sea"). The little Glen River leads upward from the center of town through Donard Park into the forest. And the Shimna River, with its trout and salmon, flows down through Tollymore Park and enters the sea at the heart of Newcastle.

A couple of miles south of town, and all of 10 minutes drive from Royal County Down, is the excellent Glassdrumman Lodge. It is no more than 12 years old and sits about a mile back from the sea, which it still views, in the foothills of the mountains. The inn's own property is crisscrossed by stone fences separating gardens from pastures.

We occupied a corner bedroom called "Knockree," which had very broad windows (sea, but not mountain, view) and a gas-fueled fireplace (ersatz logs and coals).

The young woman who served as general factotum and who was engaged to marry the chef—the cooking is good enough to earn a listing, but not a star, in the Michelin guide—told us that in high season perhaps 80 percent of their ten accommodations (eight rooms, two suites) are rented to golfers, many of them Americans. I said that I was an American golfer, from Philadelphia.

"Oh," she exclaimed, "then you must know Mr. Scott! Richard Scott. He's from Philadelphia. He's a member at Pine Valley. He was our savior!"

I said I'd known Dick Scott for many years.

"Well, he discovered Glassdrumman—I don't know how, but he did. And he's told all his friends that when they come to Newcastle this is where they must stay. And then they told their friends."

The best advertising is clearly a satisfied customer.

Chapter 7

Side by
Side

A little more than an hour south on the coast—we are back in the Republic now—lies the fishing village of Baltray, with its occasional thatched-roof cottages, a speck on the map just north of the substantial market town of Drogheda. Once beyond Drogheda, there is a growing sense of remoteness as we drive out along the estuary of the river Boyne to the links of the County Louth Golf Club, popularly known as Baltray.

Let it be said at once: Baltray is a great and glorious course, a classic sandhill layout with consistently high shot values, admirable variety, moments of tension and of beauty. What's more, its greens are among the very best—and most creatively contoured—in Ireland.

Golf has been played over this ground since the founding of the club in 1892, but not until Tom Simpson, whose genius can also be observed at Ballybunion, Cruden Bay, and Royal Ab-

131

erdeen, extensively revised Baltray in the mid-1930s did it take its place among the top rank of Irish courses.

From the first shot, the game is on. This strong opener, never shorter than 410 yards and #3 on the stroke index, begins with a drive into sloping and hummocky ground that must avoid a pair of penal bunkers on the left and, a few paces farther on, another pair on the right. The hole then swings easily left, and perhaps a dozen yards short of the green and just beyond a gentle rise, there is a bunker, squarely in the middle of the fairway and blind, to snare the underhit long iron. The green falls off to the right. It all adds up to one of the half-dozen most exacting beginnings (Oakland Hills, Royal St. George's, Aberdovey, Pine Valley, Oakmont) I know of.

Par is 73 (five long holes, four short holes, nine two-shotters), with the course measuring 6,375 yards from the regular tees, 6,750 from the blue markers. Three of the first half-dozen holes—the 2nd, 3rd, and 6th—are par fives, all playing to different points of the compass over undulating ground. The 3rd, 520 yards, is a bunker-free jewel whose fairway is squeezed almost to extinction short of the green, intimidating the big hitter who dreams of reaching the green with a very long blind second shot over a dune ridge. For the rest of us, the pitch across violently broken ground to the tiny, hidden green is thrill enough.

The two par threes on the outbound nine, both in the medium-iron range, find us on lofty platforms totally exposed to the wind as we play across swales to plateau greens defended by gathering bunkers and by steep falloffs in the sandhills. The rough here is often a combination of bracken and long marram grass, and the presence in it of wild golden daisies and flowering pink broom makes it not one whit less hostile.

A cluster of par fours on the inbound nine—12, 13, 14—weaves through the tossing duneland beneath the range of high sandhills along the Irish Sea. They are the quintessence of links golf. The first two, both well over 400 yards, call for a long second shot fired through a gap in the dunes. The teasing pitch on the 322-yard 14th to a small plateau green partially concealed in the dunes is as unsettling as that on the 14th at Muirfield Village or the 5th at Little Island, down in Cork. It is on the dune-top tee of this 14th that we take a deep breath as our gaze embraces the broad golden beach, the gray-green sea, and, if the day be fine, the noble Mountains of Mourne themselves, the backdrop for our game only 24 hours earlier, some 40 miles away up the coast at Newcastle.

The final stretch includes two more very good par threes and, to wind things up, a shortish par five with nine bunkers to direct the way and a last chance to snare the birdie that may have eluded us throughout the round. Curiously, there is nearly 300 yards between the 18th green and the clubhouse, room enough for a true 19th hole on a very spacious course that sprawls over some 200 acres.

Though the club has never hosted a professional tournament with an international field, a fact that probably accounts for its lack of renown beyond Irish shores, it has produced two of Ireland's most outstanding women amateurs: Clarrie Tiernan, the first Irishwoman to be selected for the Curtis Cup team (1938), and the legendary Philomena Garvey, six-time Curtis Cupper (between 1948 and 1960), 1957 British Ladies' champion (and runner-up for that crown on four occasions), and 15-time Irish Ladies' champion. Baltray has twice been the venue for the Irish Close Amateur, and it is annually the site for the East of Ireland Amateur Championship, which Joe Carr (nine-time Walker Cupper and three-time British Amateur champion) managed to carry off 12 times. Some 25 years after his last victory here in the East of Ireland, according to a story related by Donald Steel in his masterful *Classic Golf Links of Great Britain and Ireland,* Carr had a young caddie on his bag in a social game at Baltray who was ignorant of his player's renown. The great man was struggling. So much so that the caddie asked, "Ever played here before?"

"Yes," replied Carr, "as a matter of fact, I have."

"Did yer ever play in the East of Ireland Championship?"

"Yes," said Carr.

"And did yer ever do any good?" insisted the boy.

"I won it twelve times," came the answer from Carr with a modest nonchalance, thinking he might have the last word.

"Well," concluded the boy, "the standard must have been much worse in your day."

On my first visit to Baltray I chatted briefly with Paddy McGuirk, an excellent player who won the 1973 Carrolls International Tournament and some years afterward succeeded his father as head professional at County Louth. We spoke of Philomena Garvey and Joe Carr, and he said that a few years ago Arnold Palmer and Lee Trevino had played Christy O'Connor, Jr., and Des Smyth in an exhibition match there. "Palmer and Trevino seemed quite taken with the links."

When Paddy realized I was a golf writer, he urged me not to tout Baltray. "We've already got all the play we can handle," he said, "including some Americans and—would you believe it?—Australians. When they come over and they're playing at Portmarnock and then going up to Newcastle, don't they want to stop here for a game. We're right on the way, much too convenient."

He also provided an explanation for the crowded courses of today that went a little beyond the golf boom. "Aye, golfers are getting out more often today, playing more rounds than they used to, because they have more leisure. And the golfing societies, there are a lot more of them, and their outings tie up a course. But there's another side of it that I've noticed. A man who could afford it—a man who'd made his pile or was making it—used to belong to two or three clubs and spread his play among them. There's a lot less of that today. Even rich men will belong to only one club and that's where they'll play all their golf, at that one club. We've got 800 members here at Baltray—that's all categories, of course—350 of them what you'd call full members. There are very few quiet days on this links when the weather is decent."

Paddy's mention of golfing societies reminds me that a battered old pickup truck loaded with "corporate sponsor" signs had preceded Harriet and me around the course that morning in preparation for some kind of outing—maybe a charity benefit—to be held later in the day. So we encountered these signs, all the same modest size—Coca Cola, Avanti, The Mall—as we moved from hole to hole. The egalitarian nature of the sign placement prompted a smile on the 15th tee, where we found a multinational corporation, Becton Dickinson, cheek by jowl with Monaghan's Poultry. But our favorite was the arrow-shaped directional marker as we left the 11th green. It pointed the way into the tumbling dunes and said: "McCabe's Garage." Doubtless it was in there somewhere, perhaps beside the 12th tee.

For a little over a hundred years the County Louth Golf Club was alone in this marvelous golfing country outside the village of Baltray. Now it has company.

When I learned of the Seapoint Golf Club, which abuts Baltray at a point on the second nine of both, I feared that it might suffer from an unflattering comparison. But though it is not a great course—after all, it possesses only a fraction of the superb duneland with which its neighbor is so generously endowed— it is certainly quite good. Put me down as a fan of this eighteen, which Des Smyth and Declan Brannigan designed and which opened in June of 1993.

When it is stretched to some 7,000 yards, against its par of 72, it must thoroughly test players of the first rank. (That, I suspect, is something that the club's developers, who benefitted from a substantial government grant and are building 60 houses on the periphery, would be most pleased to do.) The course can also be set up as short as 5,000 yards. The members play it at about 6,200.

There is little in the way of overall elevation change, not so much as 20 feet, I would guess, but we do not have the sense of playing over a dull stretch of flattish ground. A somewhat meadowy feel imbues both the holes and the turf on the first nine, which is at a considerable distance from the sea. However, a combination of water and boundaries keeps our attention firmly focused on the shot requirements. White stakes tight along the right on the 3rd and 4th lend a measure of menace to these two par fours. Water, in the form of streams or ponds, puts our score in jeopardy on the 1st, 2nd, 3rd, 4th, and 9th. On the 175-yard 9th, a lagoon, squarely between tee and green and running nearly the length of the hole, creates a very demanding shot indeed if the wind is up and is at us. But this peril pales before the second shot we are called upon to execute on the 380-yard 4th, where ponds both left and right of the green mandate that only our soundest stroke will find the harbor of the putting surface. I can't think of another hole like it.

Now if all this sounds rather more like American parkland than Irish seaside golf, perhaps it is. But these are nonetheless good and testing holes, and if we succeed in negotiating them acceptably, we will be in the proper frame of mind to tackle the holes that justify the club's name (and attendant promise). The second nine, so much nearer the sea, is routed over attractive linksland, beginning with the par-five 10th, which plays along a gently falling dune-lined valley and, at 475 yards, provides perhaps our best chance at a birdie. The next hole, also dune-framed and equally appealing, doglegs smoothly right—the doglegs are all nicely unforced—with the second shot on this 330-yarder played from very hummocky ground to an elevated two-tiered green. A cunning little swale immediately in front of the 390-yard 12th gives that very good straightaway hole just the spot of spunk it needs. The 13th, some 20 yards shorter and running in the opposite direction, is, unless you head for the back tees and thereby add 45 yards, of no sporting interest whatsoever: it is open, flat, and excruciatingly dull. Something,

I suspect, will be done about this, the only such regrettable hole in the entire round.

But redemption is immediately at hand, for the 370-yard 14th is a complete charmer, curving softly right as it rises to a big green backdropped by, of all things, four or five pine trees. They help to establish a secluded setting for a putting surface that is not at all far from the sea. It is a surprising and enchanting moment. For the first time, we truly sense the presence of the sea.

The 15th is a 140-yarder, with the tee set in a little glade and the green carved out of the base of a high right hand sandhill. Two bunkers lie concealed at the foot of the slope and the green falls off steeply at the left. Bunkering, I should note, tends to be light throughout. The greens, which range in size from moderate to large, have been designed with imagination, taste, and painstaking care—subtle borrows, restrained terracing, an attractive variety of shapes. Smyth and Brannigan must be very proud of them.

The 16th tee sits up in the dunes. This is a new experience for us here at Seapoint and a welcome one. When we reach this platform, we take in, for the first time, the sea as well as the course. It is an appealing vista, the two-shotter not far below us rippling away, parallel to the shore, a low range of sandhills separating it from the beach. It also turns out to be, this 16th tee at Seapoint, a supremely ironic situation—for unknown to us as we stand there on the heights, yet no more than six paces away on the other side of a screen of hillocky ground cloaked in long grasses that threaten to snag our backswing, lies the 14th tee at Baltray. Of all the special moments on the great County Louth Golf Club links, the 14th tee is the single most extraordinary—dramatically beautiful, the tee shot falling to a wildly rumpled fairway, much of the 12th and 13th holes also stretching away beneath us, to say nothing of the sea—and now here it is again, forcing comparison with its fledgling neighbor next door. And winning the comparison, despite the fact that the 16th shows Seapoint at its noblest and best. We have no choice but to smile and, having done so, to play the excellent hole on the newcomer.

The 17th is a strong knob-to-knob 165-yarder in the dunes. Played into a brisk left-to-right breeze—a circumstance that is not rare—the shot can all too readily finish down on the beach.

The last hole, a short par five of only 455 yards, is a bona fide beauty. From yet another tee high above the strand, we drive down to an angled fairway. A gambling second will eliminate some of the elegantly sinuous route that the fairway follows to the green, but failure to get home could result in a six instead of a four, for the rough in these low dunes is hostile. At Seapoint the architects have chosen to save the best till last. These final three holes constitute a rousing finish to a worthy course.

There is one additional grace note: the bright and comfortable clubhouse. So adroitly sited is this contemporary-style structure that though it is cradled in the dunes, every seat in the lounge and the dining room looks through a natural opening in the sandhills to the sea.

This area does not attract a large number of sightseers. Drogheda's motto, "God is our strength, merchandise our glory," may strike you as a funny—and desperate—attempt to reconcile the irreconcilable, but it does convey the split personality of this thriving trading center that sprawls over the hilly banks of the

Boyne. "Over 300 shops can cater for your every need," proclaims a chamber of commerce brochure, which then proceeds to spend its ink on St. Peter's Roman Catholic Church (late nineteenth century), St. Peter's Church of Ireland (mid-eighteenth century), St. Laurance Gate, Magdalene Tower (the remains of a fourteenth-century Dominican friary), St. Mary's Abbey (the remains of a thirteenth-century Augustinian friary), Millifont (the remains of a twelfth-century Cistercian monastery), and Monasterboice (the remains of two medieval parish churches and two richly carved High Crosses).

About a mile or so from this town of about 24,000 is the site of the Battle of the Boyne, where, in 1690, William of Orange defeated the deposed King of England, James II, in a battle that decided the fate of Ireland, to say nothing of the future of the English throne. History buffs incline to stare and speculate.

The Boyne Valley Hotel, just outside town in its own 16-acre park, is far from luxurious, but this restful eighteenth-century mansion has some very real virtues. It is quiet, the cooking is first-rate, the bar and the conservatory are convivial—and surprisingly stylish—gathering places, and the prices are reasonable. Guest rooms are decorated with modern furniture and incline to be small but not cramped; the beds are comfortable. An 18-hole pitch 'n' putt course is the proverbial icing on the cake: an amazing variety of 40- and 50-yard shots complete with ups and downs, cascading pools, ancient specimen trees, and carefully tended gardens. Most golfers find it irresistible.

One other accommodation I might mention could appeal to a foursome of men. We do not often get the chance to spend the night at an outstanding golf club. Such an opportunity awaits at County Louth. These rooms in the Baltry clubhouse are, for the most part, small and spartan. The bathroom is down the hall. But you sleep the sleep of the blessed, and when the cook knocks on your door the next morning to say that breakfast is ready, and when after wading through that trencherman's repast you head straight to the first tee of this superlative old links, well, then you know that you have stayed at the right place.

Chapter 8

A Newcomer Makes Its Mark

Not since the first chapter, when we toured the courses at Dromoland Castle and Adare Manor, have we played a round of inland golf. The diet has been relentlessly seaside. Now it is time to quit the coast, however briefly, and head for the midlands, to play at Mullingar, and at Glasson and to stay at Mornington House, the ancestral home of Warrick and Anne O'Hara, near Crookedwood.

There is a moment quite early on the drive to Mullingar, perhaps a dozen miles east of Drogheda on the N51, when we find ourselves in Slane. At the crossroads that mark the center of the village, four superb and identical Georgian gray stone houses, each occupying a corner, face each other diagonally. I think it is safe to say that there is nothing else like it in rural Ireland, nor, perhaps, in urban Ireland as well.

Except for its town hall and its courthouse, both eighteenth century, there is little of age in Mullingar, which, like

Drogheda, is both busy and hilly. The most prominent structure is the cathedral, not yet 60 years old. Its monumental gray stone twin towers dominate the surrounding countryside.

As it happens, the Mullingar golf course and the cathedral were built at the same time, in the 1930s, clearly a case of the town's two top priorities going forward hand in hand.

It was James Braid who laid out the course, in 1937. The five-time British Open champion's designs can be found just about anywhere you look in England and Scotland, but he did relatively little work in Ireland. Perhaps the fashion in which he tackled the Mullingar job indicates why.

The story is told that, after reconnoitering what was then a heath of gorse and scrub, the 67-year-old Scot called for a hatchet and 36 wooden pegs. Eyeing the terrain and moving briskly from point to point, he proceeded to lay out the holes as he pegged off 18 tees and 18 greens. That task completed, he collected his fee of £25, caught the train to Dublin, and promptly boarded the mailboat that would take him home to Scotland. It was all in a day's work. Forty years later Eddie Hackett made some revisions to the course, but it is basically Braid's golf holes that we play today. The Irish Professional Championship has been held here three times, with Fred Daly, the only Irishman ever to capture the British Open, winning in 1952, Norman Drews in 1959, and Christy O'Connor in 1965.

Mullingar is a pretty, rolling parkland course. Par is 72, and even from the championship tees the length is only 6,450 yards. The aspect here is one of openness, particularly on the first nine, and we seem to be playing over one vast and well-maintained lawn, where neighboring holes are uncomfortably close to each other. There is sometimes a lack of definition to individual holes, with the result that judging distances can be difficult. Ditches are to be avoided on our drives at the 8th and 16th, but the course presents no real water hazards. Nor is out of bounds a worry. Trees pose a problem on only a few occasions—fairways are quite broad—but there are a number of handsome old specimens, including some truly skyscraping firs that must be members of the sequoia family. Bunkers incline to be small and skillfully sited. The rough is short, but thick and wickedly tenacious.

If Mullingar is not a course of genuine distinction, it does possess two very important attributes: excellent turf and a handful of golf holes that are strong and fine. Coming immediately to mind are two one-shotters on the first nine, the 182-yard 2nd and the 173-yard 5th, kinsmen, both played from knob to knob across gentle valleys, each requiring a precisely struck 3- or 4-iron if we are to hit and hold greens that are neither particularly spacious nor yielding. In each case, the falloff at the green is steep and unforgiving. The 7th hole, 448 yards, is long and level and hard, the fairway curving almost imperceptibly right and the green, bunkered on two sides, rather too narrow for a hole this long and this testing. Also troublesome is the 10th, about 25 yards shorter but with three satanically sited small bunkers blind in the middle of the fairway just over a gentle rise perhaps 35 yards short of the green. The 17th is a wonderful penultimate hole: lofty tee shot down to the valley on a bite-off-all-you-dare left hand dogleg with low trees in the elbow, then a medium iron—the hole is 368 yards long—steeply uphill to a plateau green fiercely defended by three bunkers. To be sure, getting your figures at Mullingar calls for sound swinging and thinking, but still we could wish for more drama and memorability.

Adjacent to the golf club is Belvedere House, surely, in its prime, as beautiful a fishing villa as the world has ever seen. Unfortunately, this mid-eighteenth-century house is long past its prime and may never be restored to its original glory. However, derelict as it is and unfurnished, Belvedere House must be visited. Its setting, high on a promontory above Lough Ennell, is noble. Its extensive gardens, both formal and informal, are a joy. The splendid carved stucco ceilings in the gracious reception rooms are still miraculously intact. And one other thing: it possesses a nonpareil folly called the "Jealous Wall." Belvedere House was one of several mansions built in the eighteenth century by the Rochforts, then the richest and most powerful family in this part of County Westmeath. A hundred yards or so from the villa itself stands a great *false* front of another manor house, a mere stone facade with nothing behind it. Now somewhat deteriorated, it is nonetheless imposing. To what purpose was it built? To screen Belvedere House from nearby Tudenham Park, another Rochfort mansion, now in ruins, which belonged to one of Lord Belvedere's brothers, who had not been sympathetic to Belvedere when the lord's wife ran off with yet a third Rochfort brother! So, in order to effect a total estrangement from the master of Tudenham Park, Belvedere made it impossible, by means of this monumental sham, for him to catch even so much as a glimpse of Belvedere House from his manor.

For years Mullingar was consistently ranked among the top 25 or 30 courses in Ireland and generally regarded as one of the two or three best inland layouts. But the flood of new courses has washed it off the list, and the chance of its regaining its former eminence seems slim.

A newcomer that may soon find its way into that rarefied air is Glasson, which is located about an hour from Mullingar on the shores of Lough Ree, six or seven miles outside Athlone. Christy O'Connor, Jr., designed it. The course opened for play in 1993 on 175 gorse-splashed acres, and it is a beauty. The holes range from good to great and the setting is, at every turn, little short of enthralling.

The operative phrase is *at every turn.* Lough Ree is a large lake, some 16 or 17 miles long. One of its "arms" is Killinure Bay. Every one of the 18 holes at Glasson overlooks either the lake or the bay, in most cases from high above these bodies of water, which are parts of the Shannon River system. Golfers have a choice of arriving by either car or boat, but however they get there, they will know at once that they have reached as beautiful a spot as any golfer could conjure up. Keeping one's mind on the shots is an ongoing problem at—to give it its full name—Glasson Golf and Country Club. Why it isn't called simply the Glasson Golf Club I cannot say, for there is no sign of any other diversion.

This, be forewarned, is a hilly course, with an overall elevation change that must be very like 120 feet. The lush turf—until just a few years ago, this was pastureland and cropland—affords minimal run on the ball. And somehow I had the impression that those steeply uphill holes (4, 7, 9, 18) taketh away more than those steeply downhill holes (8, 10, 14) giveth. Par is 72, with the traditional mix of four long holes, four short holes, and ten par fours. From the ladies' tees, the course measures 5,580 yards (par here is 73). From the pro tees, the length is 7,120. The rest of us have two choices: 6,150 or 6,650. The difference is huge.

The first two holes—a par four and a par five, both medium length, over rolling ground where the stances can be tricky—give us a chance to get into the swing of things before the sterner challenges to come. The first one arrives at the 3rd.

This hole is a triumph of spectacle and simplicity: 190 yards over a swale from a moderately elevated tee to a plateau green backdropped by the shimmering vastness of Lough Ree, with wooded Hare Island in full view and the meadows of County Roscommon emerald on the distant shore. The green, neither large nor hospitable, is defended by bunkers pinching the entrance. The problem is twofold: choosing the right club (into a stiff breeze off the lake it can be a driver) and making the perfect swing. There is no finer hole at Glasson.

Which is not to say that there aren't four or five very much in its class, including the splendid 8th. This hole, a few yards under 400, doglegs sharply left in the tee shot landing area, then plunges to a green where a fancifully shaped pond skirts the left side and wraps itself around the back. At the right front is sand. Once again—and again from on high and starkly exposed to the wind—only our soundest swing will suffice. There is perhaps a little more golf in this hole than many of us can digest, but the flavor is nonetheless wonderful.

We finish the front nine with the third of the climbing two-shotters, where only the flag is visible and underclubbing must be rigorously avoided.

The first four holes on the second half are all good and varied and manageable, with the 10th, a shortish par five that drifts down and then up, a good birdie opportunity if we can keep out of the sand, and the lovely 11th a rising 160-yarder bunkered uncompromisingly across the front.

The finishing five show O'Connor, Jr., at his best, and now it is Killinure Bay that enchants and, at 14 and 15, makes us wary.

The 14th is one of the spectacular holes of the world. You can play it from 510 yards, 521 yards, or 566 yards. I urge you to take the bit in your teeth and climb to the top tee, a little platform of turf in the trees that is unnervingly high—not less than 110 feet, I should think—above the green. The panorama over Killinure Bay is surpassingly scenic. And the hole, once you have caught your breath, is rife with danger, as, plunging near vertically on the drive, it doglegs emphatically right (sand in the crook), then falls almost as steeply on the second (a lake eating into the fairway on the right here to catch a wayward wood), finally leveling out for the last 150 yards. The bay is close to the left side of the green; sand defends the front of the green and the right flank. At full stretch, this is a three-shotter worthy of the name. At any distance, it is unforgettable.

The 15th is a mere fraction of the 14th in length, but in its own short way it is also outstanding. Both tee and green jut into the bay. At 127 yards, where the men's forward markers are spotted, the forced carry is negligible. Not so at 170 yards, to say nothing of 185, especially into the prevailing left-to-right wind. Appropriately, the green is generous, though hitting it is no guarantee of par on this inventively contoured surface. Not incidentally, the greens at Glasson are excellent and varied, clearly designed to a very high standard by a man who thinks putting should call for artistry as well as sound mechanics.

The next couple of holes are demanding two-shotters, a pond on the right imperiling the drive on the 16th, where the approach must rise to a shelflike green. The 17th moves decidely right to left along a low-banked little cut of its own. A large cross bunker some 20 yards short of the green on this 425-yarder will be a little more than some of us can handle unless the wind is favoring. It probably represents the only gratuitously penal touch on the course and comes as a surprise.

The 360-yard 18th is a fitting climax—doglegging gently (to the left), climbing steeply. The narrow green—the flag is visible, but not the putting surface—is angled to the line of flight and all but ringed with bunkers. I cannot envision a day when this hole, finishing under the clubhouse windows, plays less than 400 yards.

The Glasson Golf and Country Club is a family business. Tom and Breda Reid had been farming their 275 acres—50 acres in turnips, 75 acres in cereals, 300 cattle, 1,500 pigs—for a number of years before they decided to make a big change. ("The children were not interested in farming and I felt I needed a new challenge," Tom says.) They managed to get a $600,000 grant from the European Regional Development Fund and to borrow nearly $2,500,000 from the banks to undertake this ambitious project. It was a gamble that is paying off. And it keeps the Reids—not just Tom and Breda, but their daughter Fidelma, the operations manager, and their son Frainc, who can often be found on a gang mower—very busy indeed. But not so busy that they don't have time to make their guests welcome.

The Reids have put everything they've got into this venture, including their home. Killinure House, an eighteenth-century Georgian manor, has been transformed into a clubhouse, and what an attractive one it is, complete with outstanding views over the bay. "My bedroom is now the bar," laughs Fidelma. "I don't know what to think about that."

From the moment Glasson opened, top Irish players such as Eamon D'Arcy, Philip Walton, and Des Smyth have been generous in their praise of Christy, Jr.'s course. One comment could perhaps be said to summarize all the encomiums. "I've played quite a lot of golf courses all over the world—this is magnificent, really championship stuff. . . . My God, the scenery is out of this world!" So said Christy, Sr. No getting away from it: Glasson is indeed a family—or two's—business.

Our base in the midlands, Mornington House, is yet another of the Hidden Ireland gems. And heaven knows it's hidden, tucked well away off the Mullingar/Castlepollard Road on some 50 rolling County Westmeath acres that include frontage on Lough Derravarragh.

Another Georgian manor house, Mornington dates to 1710. The additions have been totally sympathetic to the symmetry and elegance of the original structure. Warrick O'Hara is the fifth generation of his family to call Mornington House home. I might mention that he is not related to Brian and Lindy O'Hara, the owners of Coopershill House, in County Sligo.

Like Enniscoe House and Coopershill House, Mornington is a gracious family home still furnished with much of the original furniture and paintings. The reception rooms have open peat and log fires, and if there is even the faintest chill in the air, Warrick will have at least one of them burning. The emphasis here is on comfort, not museum sheen, and the hospitality is genuinely warm.

The four double bedrooms are bright, spacious, high-ceilinged and decorated with a number of antiques and family heirlooms. The same words might fairly be used to describe the attendant bathrooms.

On the first of our two visits—this is a house you will go out of your way to return to—we occupied a corner bedroom with heavy crown moldings and paneled shutters built into the window embrasures; wide pine floorboards painted black; a fetching Laura Ashley floral wallpaper and matching chintz curtains; a high, wide, and handsome brass bed complete with a tiny antique footstool for access; a white-painted wooden mantel over the fireplace, with dried flowers on the hearth ("Yes," said Anne O'Hara resignedly, "it does work, but the extra premium for fire insurance if we allowed guests to burn it is simply too high"); an airy white-painted Victorian adaptation of an eighteenth-century-style armoire; a small inlaid Hepplewhite desk with leather writing surface; and, in truth, much more in a room that is not at all cluttered. As for the view, it takes in an approach lane winding through the woods, a croquet lawn with its simple flower border, an immense 200-year-old oak casting its shade over a corner of the lawn, and, in the near distance, a steep green hillside.

Dinner by candlelight in the Victorian dining room, with its curious dark green porcelain stove in the fireplace, is a communal affair. All the guests eat at the same sturdy old oak table, having been introduced to each other over sherry by the fire in the drawing room. Let me confess at once that the company of strangers, night after night for, say, a ten-day stretch, would not be our choice, but for an evening or two it can be very stimulating, especially when accompanied by Anne O'Hara's outstanding cooking. The vegetables, fruits, and herbs invariably come from her walled garden, and the fish, fowl, or meat hardly hail from distant points. One evening's menu consisted of fried brie in a hazelnut dressing on a bed of raddichio; *carre d'agneau* with a Dijon mustard gravy; a meringue consisting of two chocolate layers framing a vanilla layer, the whole in a simple chocolate sauce; and three kinds of cheese, one a delicious goat's cheese. Warrick's wine list is not ambitious, but you should have no trouble finding a vintage that suits. Coffee, like the sherry before dinner, is taken by the fire in the drawing room.

I recall that our companions at dinner the first night we spent at Mornington House were two English women in their late 20s who had never been to Ireland before and whose profession was landscape architecture. They had created the gardens for several private homes in Wales, but knew that they must get some major commercial assignments—office buildings, industrial parks—if their partnership was to flourish. It turned out that several years earlier one of them had been employed as a dental hygienist in the Yorkshire Dales village of Thirsk, which the late James Herriott immortalized in *All Creatures Great and Small.*

"I worked just two doors away from his veterinary," she said, "and I knew him to say hello to. He did seem to be a kindly man. Herriott's not his real name, you know—just the name he wrote under."

Chapter 9

Round and About Dublin's Fair City

Draw a 10-mile-radius circle with its center at Dublin's O'Connell Street Bridge, and within its bounds you will find no fewer than 25 golf courses. The greatest and most famous of them is Portmarnock. Indeed, there are many who consider it the greatest course in Ireland and the worthiest of hosting a major international professional championship.

Portmarnock, which was founded in 1894, sits on a tiny peninsula in the Irish Sea, about eight miles from the center of the capital and six miles from the airport. In the early days golfers reached the club by crossing Portmarnock Inlet in a boat or, at low tide, by pony and trap. Today a paved road around the northern end of the inlet makes one's visit less venturesome, but you still have the distinct sense, once you've arrived, of being at sea.

It was the club's founders, W. C. Pickeman and George Ross,

together with its first professional, Scotsman Mungo Park, who laid out the eighteen, and though there have been minor revisions to it over the years by Harry Colt, Henry Cairnes, Eddie Hackett, and Fred Hawtree, the routing of the holes is little changed.

No other Irish club has hosted so many important competitions as Portmarnock. Both the British Amateur (1949, when London-based Irishman Max McCready rallied to down New York's Willie Turnesa on the 35th hole) and the Walker Cup (1991, the United States defeating Great Britain and Ireland, 14 to 10) have been contested here. But it is the numerous professional events that have earned the club world renown. The Irish Open Championship was inaugurated at Portmarnock in 1927, with George Duncan, 1920 British Open champion, winning. In the years since, it has been won here by Bobby Locke, Ben Crenshaw, Hubert Green, Seve Ballesteros, Bernhard Langer, Ian Woosnam, and Jose Maria Olazabal. And it was at Portmarnock in 1960 that Arnold Palmer competed for the first time in Europe, when he and Sam Snead teamed up to win the Canada (now World) Cup. Eddie Hackett served as the club's professional from 1939 to 1950 and was succeeded by Harry Bradshaw, a three-time Ryder Cupper who lost to Bobby Locke in a playoff for the 1949 British Open at Sandwich.

The professionals have an enormous regard for Portmarnock, which more than once they have named the best course on the European Tour. It is the essential fairness of the links that so appeals to them—blind shots are all but nonexistent, the generous and flattish fairways minimize capricious bounces, and the greens are relatively placid, so that the pure mechanics of the putting stroke hold sway.

There are no hills here; the overall elevation change could scarcely be 15 feet. The wind blows freely across every square inch of a links that is bounded on three sides by water; nowhere are you sheltered from it. And since the imaginative routing plan only once has two consecutive holes running in the same direction, the battle with the wind is a constantly shifting one. An occasional tree rears its wind-warped limbs, but nowhere near the line of play.

Portmarnock is one of the two or three toughest courses in all of Ireland (Waterville and Adare Manor are, in my judgment, the others). From the shortest men's tees, it measures over 6,600 yards. The ladies play it at 5,840 yards, the professionals at 7,130. Par is 72, but here there are only three long holes and three short holes, which leaves us with a dozen two-shotters of varying lengths. The bunkering is penal. There are about 120 of these often deep hazards, and they menace all but half a dozen of the swings we make. The rough is choking. Driving presents a number of forced carries over punishing country. There are no water hazards to speak of. In its uncomplicated severity, its straightforward presentation of targets and dangers, it reminds us of Muirfield and Oakmont.

Though both nines are sorely testing, we may find the second half harder and more memorable. From the tee of the 131-yard 12th, where the stringently bunkered green perches above us and beside the beach, the backdrop for the flag is nothing but sky. The 14th and 15th are perhaps Portmarnock's two most highly esteemed holes, the former a par four of 370 yards that doglegs very lightly left—a man-eating bunker here in the landing area must be given a wide berth—and then calls for a solid second to a long plateau green in the dunes defended across the face by two more equally devouring pits. Humps and hillocks surround the putting surface. Henry Cotton once took seven here to lose an Irish Open. The 15th is a stern beauty hard by the sea. It parallels the shore and requires only one swing, one that will advance the ball 180 yards. The pulpit tee is high in the dunes, affording marvelous views of the strand and the sea, with the quartzite rock of Ireland's Eye as well as the 400-foot-high porphyry rock of Lambay Island vying for our attention. We must ignore these distractions, for this narrow table of green with sheer little falloffs on both sides shrugs off all but the most precisely struck shot. And if the wind is strong off the water, right to left, then the shot calls for the courage to aim the ball out over the beach—itself out of bounds—and draw it back to the refuge of the green. No less a quartet than Palmer, Crenshaw, Faldo, and Norman have cited it as among the very greatest par threes in the world.

The 17th, which measures 420 yards, may lack both the beauty and the peril of the 15th, but what a strong straight-away par four it is, defended, seemingly every foot of the way, by 14 bunkers, to say nothing of a low ridge crossing just short of the green. On the 36-hole final day of the 1959 Dunlop Masters, the 17th was set up at 466 yards and proved to be the most difficult hole on the course. Twice did the redoubtable Christy O'Connor birdie it, the second time by feathering a 4-wood into the wind that finished eight feet from the hole and enabled him to edge Joe Carr by a stroke. Carr, whose father had been the steward at Portmarnock, was born in the clubhouse.

Speaking of the clubhouse, it is one of the most attractive in Ireland, a handsome and rambling white pebbledash structure with an orange slate roof. Inside, fine leather, old wood, and crackling fires strike a strong note of comfort, cheer, and hospitality. A far cry from the primitive shack that offered shelter in the early days, it makes an ideal place in which to lick our wounds—or to consider tackling the third nine. Fred Hawtree laid it out in 1971, and some consider it even more exacting than the original eighteen. At Portmarnock even the "relief nine" offers no relief.

Next door, in the summer of 1995, some months before this book was published, another golf course opened for play. Called the Links Portmarnock, it was built by Mark McCormack's International Management Group. Bernhard Langer, an IMG client, is the architect of record, but much of the work can be attributed to an American, Stan Eby. The course opened too late for me to play it, but I was able to tour it with the man responsible for bringing it to completion. His name is Peter Casbolt and he is the head greenkeeper. A Scot from Lockerbie whom I would guess to be about 50, he had held key posts at Turnberry for six years and at Connemara for four years. Said Peter modestly of his new charge, "I think we've got a special one here."

He invited me to join him in his Jeep and we roamed and bounced and rattled our way over just about all of what struck me as one of the outstanding seaside courses of Ireland, one that may soon be saluted as a great links.

Despite the beautifully natural look of the terrain, a lot of earth has been pushed around, with the result that the fairways have more movement—even those farthest from the sea—than those of its illustrious neighbor. The only time the ground does not undulate or ripple is when it tumbles, as indeed it does in the duneland over which the closing holes are routed. The overall elevation change seems not to exceed 20 feet, but there are still holes that provide ups and downs. The course can fairly be described as gently rolling.

There are a number of doglegs, almost all of them modest, though I recall a rather pronounced left-hand swing on the dune-framed 8th, where the shapely green is set just beyond a devilish little swale. "It's one of my favorites," said Peter with a grin.

He was particularly proud of the bunkering. There are 96 bunkers, all of them with revetted faces that would do justice to a bricklayer.

"They remind me of Muirfield," I said, paying them the highest tribute I know.

"And of Southernness," he answered, referring to the fine Mackenzie Ross course not an hour from his birthplace.

Some of the bunkers are as deep as eight, even nine feet. These tend to have nearly vertical faces. Perhaps a dozen of the 96 are cunningly concealed at greenside, either beyond a pit that we can see or just over a subtle rise.

The greens are varied and lovely, always interesting yet never extreme. Generally open to an appreciable degree across the front, they are also frequently raised a couple of feet above the fairway, on very low plateaus, as at the Old Course, with the result that chips and little pitches take on an added dimension. It is intended that this links will play firm and fast. Peter has used seaside grasses everywhere—no creeping bent. The greens, fairways, and tees (the tees are old-fashioned low rectangular platforms) are combinations of chewing fescues and fescue bent. Mantling the higher dunes, near the sea, is the natural marram grass. There are no water hazards and, from what I could observe, almost no opportunities to hit a ball out of bounds.

Peter was particularly eager to have me examine the last three holes. The 17th is a medium-to-long one-shotter through the dunes from a low knob to an only slightly higher knobby green that slopes just enough from left to right. The carry is over a forbidding wasteland of long rough grasses. Two elements combine to create the problem: that left-to-right tilt of the green, and the eight-foot deep bunker at the left front of the green, on precisely the line we must choose if we are to prevent our iron shot from slipping off the right side of the green into a deep hollow or another pit. An example of excellent strategic design.

The 16th and 18th are a pair of stout two-shotters, both from nicely elevated tees back in the sandhills, both doglegging right in cleverly bunkered landing areas, then proceeding over sometimes turbulent ground to target greens beautifully sited in the dunes. On the tee at 16 we take dead aim on an old graveyard beyond the green.

"I'm afraid," Peter said, "that into a stiff headwind the long forced carry here could make this hole the graveyard of a good score." His infectious grin made it clear that he relished the prospect.

I suggested that, given the IMG ownership, this course might well host an important professional tournament.

"I think we can count on Mr. McCormack seeing to that," he replied.

A scant three miles from the Dublin post office lies Royal Dublin Golf Club, in the Dollymount section of the capital. No other championship course is so close to the center of a major city. The temptation for its members to slip away from the office for a quick nine during lunch hour (hour and a half) must, on a fair day, be difficult to resist.

The club is located on Bull Island, in Dublin Bay. A narrow wooden bridge connects the property to the mainland. Founded in 1885 by John Lumsden, a Scot from Banffshire, and some of his friends, Royal Dublin is the oldest golf club in the Republic. It has never had women members, so although wives of members and women visitors play regularly, there are no women's competitions. The clubhouse—like Portmarnock's, white with an orange slate roof—does have a women's locker room.

When World War I broke out, the course was appropriated by the military for use as a rifle range and training center. Four years later it was handed back to the club rather the worse for wear, but a £10,000 compensation from the government allowed the club to bring in Harry Colt for what would turn out to be a complete revamping of the links. Though minor revisions were made years later by Sir Guy Campbell and then by Eddie Hackett, it is essentially the Colt layout that we play today. From the championship tees, it measures almost 6,900 yards. From the medal tees, it is 6,600, and members regularly play it at about 6,300. Par today is 71. Not too many years ago it was 73, but the 2nd and 18th, short par fives then, have been converted to long par fours. The two nines are decidely uneven in length. Going out—and this is a typical out-and-in course, the 9th green being the farthest point from the clubhouse on this narrow strip of land with the sea on two sides—par is 34 (one long hole, three short holes). Coming in, par is 37 (two long, one short), and the nine is a full 500 yards longer.

Aesthetically, Dollymount, as it is familiarly known, is among the least attractive of links courses. It is basically level—we cheer at the sight of a modest rise or dip, knowing that anything resembling a hill is out of the question. There is some undulation to the fairways, but mere hummocks and mounds must serve in the stead of bona fide dunes. There is an old and worn look to the land, and the views over the water are not always the prettiest, for this section of the harbor, occasionally marked by tall power generation chimneys, is rather industrialized.

Yet all that being said, Dollymount still has considerable appeal, for it is authentic links golf, simple and natural and keenly evocative of times long past. Whatever modernization has taken place is minimal—the addition of a bunker or two here and there to snare a tiger's tee shot, perhaps the building of a new tee.

This links demands accurate driving. The fairways are narrower than those on many seaside courses, the rough is formidable, and the breeze is only rarely a zephyr. On the outbound nine there are several good opportunities—1, 2, 5, 8—for a slicer to wind up out of bounds on the strand along Dublin Bay. The player inclined to hook must beware of Curley's Yard, a small and very old fortresslike stone enclosure between the 3rd and the 13th that now serves as a museum center for what is an officially designated animal preserve.

Which brings me to the hares of Dollymount, two or three packs of them, it seems, with about a dozen or so hares in each pack. They race willy-nilly over this old links, streaking across your bow out of nowhere as you contemplate the choice between a 4-iron and a 5, or suddenly hurtling down the rough on your right as you take your stance on a 75-yard pitch to one of the par fives. Possessed of surprisingly long legs that propel them across the course in great strides and at high speeds, these hares are cousins of the jackrabbit. Lahinch, you'll recall, has its goats; Dollymount, not to be outdone, has its hares.

There are several very good holes here, including the 3rd and the 7th, a couple of medium-length par fours, and the long par-five 11th, with an out-of-bounds drainage ditch along the right and an unusual fallaway green. But there are no great holes.

The course has been the venue for many championships, amateur and professional (Ballesteros won the Irish Open here in 1983 and 1985, Langer in 1984) and the setting on more than one occasion for high drama. In the 1966 Carrolls International, Christy O'Connor came to the 16th tee in the final round needing to birdie the remaining three holes in order to force a playoff. He won outright by two strokes. From the back tees, the par-four 16th measures all of 267 yards (shades of County Down). The green is rigorously bunkered. O'Connor drove it and rolled in an 18-foot putt. On the 17th, a straightforward 380-yarder, he made a straightforward birdie. This brought him to the celebrated home hole, then a par 5 of 478 yards, with its 90-degree right turn and its boundary ditch tight along the right daring you to shorten the distance to the green. The great man drove boldly over the corner, spanked a medium iron to the green, and dropped the putt for yet another eagle. Say what you will about the golf holes, this was still a thunderous finish. The crowd went wild, for not only was it an Irish victory, but this particular Irishman was the club's own professional. Christy O'Connor would hold this post for very like 30 years.

When I played Royal Dublin for the first time, more than 20 years ago, I caught up with another lone golfer on the 15th. A man who looked to be in his mid-30s, he invited me to join him for the last four holes. By what seemed to my wife and me to be an amazing coincidence, he turned out to be a Philadelphian. But he was obviously quite familiar with the course.

"I can see you've played here more than once," I said.

"I play here every day," he replied. "I'm a member. I've been living in Dublin for more than three years."

"You were transferred over here?" Harriet asked.

"No, I just decided to live here. I decided to come over because of the golf. It's good and you can play all year round, it doesn't cost much and it isn't crowded. Back home you either play at a crowded public course, which is cheap enough, or you join a country club and buy a bond and pay a big initiation fee. That was too much money for me. Then you've got the caddie fees and what you spend in the clubhouse. I couldn't see throwing away all that money, so I looked around—Scotland, England, even Wales—and finally I decided that Ireland was the best deal."

"How much are the dues?" I asked.

"Fifty-seven pounds. That's what the initiation fee was, too, fifty-seven pounds to get in, and the same for your annual dues."

We each hit half-wedges onto the 16th green that Christy O'Connor had driven, and as we walked up to putt I said, "It's great that you're able to get out so often. I mean, it's one thing that a club like Royal Dublin is such a bargain, but what's even better is being able to take advantage of that bargain the way you do."

"I'm a manufacturers' representative. So my time's my own. I generally arrange my calls so I can get a round in every day. Of course, there are days when I don't get out here till five o'clock."

This free spirit fascinated us. The very notion of simply picking up and going to Ireland to live because the golf was ideal—well, this was so preposterously at variance with such things as discipline and roots and the pursuit of Lawrence's bitch goddess that it was dizzying to contemplate. Dizzying and, if this is not redundant, terrifically heady. Think of it: a golf expatriate, an expatriate not because of taxes or career or love but for golf. I had to concede that it was not a noble rationale for self-exile. Nor was it ignoble.

Portmarnock and Royal Dublin are household names in the world of golf. Tens of thousands who have never played these two courses nonetheless know of them. Not so with a third

Dublin seaside course, where the golf is markedly better than at Dollymount and, arguably, very nearly the equal of Portmarnock. Yet the Island Golf Club, founded in 1890, is little known outside the Republic.

There are two principal reasons for this. The Island has never hosted important professional tournaments, which automatically confer a certain celebrity, and for close to a hundred years the plethora of blind shots prompted many accomplished amateurs to shy away from it. Well, the Island is still not a tournament venue, but thanks to extensive revisions in the 1980s by Eddie Hackett, working from a plan by Fred Hawtree—revisions that produced seven new holes blending beautifully with the best of the original eighteen—there are now no more than four blind shots in the entire round.

What sets this course apart from its Dublin counterparts is the land. Here is a links that instantly calls to mind County Down, Portrush, Portstewart, and Murvagh, a territory of grand and massive dunes that, in fact, the locals have always called "The Hills." So compelling was this terrain that its ten founding members were bent on playing golf here even though the only access was by boat from Malahide, on the far side of the estuary. This village's O'Brien family seemed to have a corner on the trans-estuary service. The brief trip could by choppy and hazardous, but there is no record of the O'Briens ever having lost a golfer to an angry sea.

I have played at the Island only once, in the spring of 1994. My companion was Frank Walshe, a member of the club's governing council. A 60-year-old engineer with Aer Lingus, he was a very strong 13-handicapper who in his prime had been a 4.

He owned a condominium in Clearwater, Florida, which he used for only two weeks a year and rented out most of the time. He was a member of the Donald Ross Society, had played several Ross courses in America, and had been to Pinehurst a number of times to play there with fellow members of the Society. A sturdily built man, he wore gray woolen knickers, two woolen sweaters, a traditional small-peaked woolen golf cap. He pulled a trolley on which rode a huge blue and white plastic trunk of a bag filled with graphite-shafted metal woods and newish steel-shafted irons. His driver was a low-priced imitation Big Bertha, and he pounded it.

He made no bones about the Island's interest in attracting the green fee business represented by touring golfers. "Everyone wants to play Portmarnock and Royal Dublin," he said. "No one seems to know we exist. I believe we must spread the word. I think we've got to make ourselves known to the golfers in your major East Coast cities, the ones that have large Irish populations, like Boston, New York, and Philadelphia. We want them to know that the Island offers very good links golf and the warmest of welcomes. We're eager to have visitors come here. And those few who have done so love this course and this club."

Why this strong interest in generating added revenue? I did not ask Frank. He said that the annual subscription had been climbing during the last decade and was now over £500. An increase in visitors could preclude further increases in dues, perhaps even make possible a reduction.

According to Ron Whitten and Geoffrey Cornish in their definitive *The Architects of Golf*, it was Alister Mackenzie who laid out an eighteen for the Island, and though no date is given, it would have to have been at some point between 1914 and 1934. But the club's official history makes no mention at all of the illustrious Yorkshireman, a curious omission indeed if he was responsible for the design.

The course measures 6,700 yards from the back tees, almost 6,400 yards from the regular tees, and nearly 5,700 from the ladies' markers. Par is 71, but the mix is scarcely what you would expect. There are just two long holes and three short holes—the other 13 are par fours. Like St. Andrews' Old Course (14 par fours) and nearby Elie (16 par fours!), the Island places the emphasis heavily on the two-shotter. The round begins with a strong and fine straightaway par four, a 400-yarder rising smoothly from a low tee through the dunes to an elevated green always in full sight and framed by sandhills. The fairway, generous enough, contracts subtly in the landing area, then broadens in its farther reaches. The round ends with an equally wonderful two-shotter, some 20 yards longer, that, paralleling the 1st but running in the opposite direction, starts from a tee high in the dunes, plays down and then gently up over the same rippling linksland to a green sited just as exquisitely as the opening one. And in between these two classic holes are 15 others—not 16, I regret to say—that range from delightful through exacting to splendid and great.

The weak link? Let us dispose of it quickly—though in fact it is not weak. Frank Walshe warned me of it before we teed off. "The tenth," he said, "is the one poor hole. It is a par five that just doesn't have much to recommend it." He was right: it is flat and featureless and unappealing, but, at 525 yards, it is not a pushover, and into a wind off the estuary it must be all but unreachable in three. "We've got to do something about it," he went on, "and we will."

That is the only hole they have to do something about. The others need no tinkering. They weave through dune valleys to cloistered greens, or plunge off giant sandhills into unruly terrain where a level lie or stance is a stroke of luck, or climb defiantly over a dune ridge to find the haven of a high shelf of green, or curve gracefully around a great shoulder of sandhill to disclose the green sited tantalizingly on a knob. We are consistently challenged, consistently invigorated, and consistently surprised by the routing of the holes, a routing wonderfully unpredictable and nonetheless sound for that. The views, it need scarcely be said, are captivating and include, as at Portmarnock, Lambay and Ireland's Eye.

Bunkering, I should point out, is quite light. The contours of the land itself, full of ripples, hummocks and hollows, dips and mounds, are all the defenses this course needs.

There are four consecutive holes on the second nine that deserve a close look. The fearsome 13th actually calls up the incomparable 16th at Cypress Point. From a tee high above the beach, it plays 218 yards across the corner of the Broadmeadow Estuary to a green perched equally high—and precariously—above the beach. Make your best and bravest swing and you will have hit a shot to look back on with pride, to say nothing of pleasure, for as long as you live. Come out of the shot just a split second too soon and the ball will disappear over the cliff and into the water. Bail out to the left and the ball will vanish on that side, to skate down a steep slope into heavy rough.

Tackling this mighty hole in anything like a stiff breeze is unimaginable—and yet it has to be done all the time.

The 14th is only 333 yards long. The tee is on the site of the former clubhouse, and the pilings of the old landing jetty, for years the only means of access to the links, can still be seen. This fairway is spoken of as the narrowest in Ireland. I think it must be the narrowest in the world, less than 15 paces wide. On the left are deep grass and a low dune ridge; on the right are deep grass, then a sharp falloff to wetlands. Once again, only our most courageous swing will do. The green is, of course, narrower than the fairway.

The 15th is magnificent, 510 yards from a high tee, the drive sailing down between tall dunes into an antic fairway that then proceeds to climb, drop, and finally level out. Two stout woods are needed to earn a view of the green. As for the 16th, just over 150 yards, it plays from a platform tee to what may well be the knobbiest little target in the world, one that does not incline to gather the ball.

The Island is a great course, compelling our respect for the testing quality of its holes, winning our admiration for its naturalness, endowing us from start to finish with the unique joy of seaside golf at its best. The world should be beating a path to its door.

Dublin has a number of parkland courses—Grange, the Hermitage, St. Margaret's, to name just three of the outstanding ones—but the only one I've played is Luttrelstown Castle, some eight miles west of downtown. It occupies 150 acres of a 560-acre estate, the centerpiece of which is the castle itself. Part of this graceful Gothic structure dates to the fifteenth century. Nicholas Bielenberg, who manages the entire property for its French owner, designed the golf course, which opened in 1994. It is his first such effort and he has done a creditable job, but it will be a few years till the course matures and the thousands of trees that have been planted fulfill their role in separating fairways and defining holes. At the moment the views from the clubhouse reveal rather more than we would choose to see. Par is 72. There are four sets of tees. From all the way back, the course measures more than 7,000 yards. For the ladies, it is just under 5,700 yards. Most of the time men will be playing it at about 6,350, which, because of the lush nature of the fairway grass, turns out to be a pretty long haul.

The clubhouse at Luttrelstown Castle Golf and Country Club is a charmer, with its countless gables and its long windows and what must surely be half the knotty pine in captivity. It struck me as a cross between a Swiss chalet and a Canadian hunting lodge. The facilities are tip-top and the food is outstanding. My wife and I had dinner there—salad of mixed leaves with bacon croutons, salmon *en croute,* chocolate terrine, Irish farmhouse cheeses—and came away suspecting that it just may have been the best meal we've ever had overlooking a golf course.

A word or two about the castle itself. In a sense, it is a hotel, but in a very restricted sense. It is rented only to groups—corporations, professional societies, incentive travel groups, etc.— who contract for the entire castle. There are 14 individually furnished double bedrooms, each with its own spacious and stylish bathroom. Over the years the castle has hosted Queen

Victoria, the King and Queen of Denmark, Prince Rainier and Princess Grace of Monaco, and many other notables. Recently modernized, and with its elegant eighteenth-century plaster-work, its frescoes, and its countless marble fireplaces all restored to their former glory, Luttrelstown is sublime.

In the eighteenth-century stable yard there are several self-catering apartments available. Each of these attractively furnished suites—sitting room, dining room, fully equipped kitchen, two double bedrooms, each with its own bath—can comfortably accommodate a foursome. And the castle staff will be pleased to make arrangements for you to play at the Portmarnock courses, Royal Dublin, and the Island.

Dublin, with a population of about 550,000, is small enough to be grasped easily. We generally know just where we are—in relation to our hotel and to the important sites—as we roam. The river Liffey flows through the city, but I'm afraid that, on the whole, the buildings that line its banks have neither architectural merit nor charm. Strolling along the Liffey is not to be equated with strolling along the Seine.

In addition to visiting the landmarks—Trinity College (home of the Book of Kells and an oasis of serenity at the foot of lively Grafton Street, itself now a shopping mall closed to automobile traffic), Dublin Castle, the cathedrals of Christ Church and of St. Patrick—you can also absorb a bit of Dublin's atmosphere simply by relaxing in her lovely city center parks. St. Stephen's Green, the largest and perhaps the best known, has, among its many amenities, a very pretty lake, sculpture fountains, and a scented "Garden of the Blind." Merrion Square, just a few blocks away, is lined on three sides by dignified Georgian mansions. Though many of them are now divided into offices, those of us on the outside don't find them a drawback. A short walk from here brings us to Fitzwilliam Square, the smallest and best-preserved of the city's Georgian squares. Yeats lived in a flat at No. 42 from 1928 to 1932.

There is one Dublin landmark that, for some people, puts all the others in the shade. That is the Abbey Theatre. For us, it really doesn't matter a great deal what's on the boards. We are simply pleased to share, if only for an evening, in the great tradition of a national theatre that got its impetus from the likes of Yeats and Synge and O'Casey, and from the lesser likes of Boucicault and Lady Gregory and Lennox Robinson, and that maintains a contemporary vitality by presenting the new plays of a Brian Friel.

These days the capital is chock-a-block with very good hotels. Among them are the Berkeley Court (in the residential Ballsbridge neighborhood, not far from the U.S. Embassy), the Westbury (a few steps off Grafton Street), the Conrad (opposite the National Concert Hall, in Earlsfort Terrace), and the Shelbourne, on St. Stephen's Green. The Shelbourne is the dowager of the group, the present building dating to 1865. And though it is old world, it is certainly not old hat. With its marble, its crystal, its oil paintings, and its *objets d'art,* there is an unmistakable air of period elegance. But it is an easy elegance and we quickly feel at home here, never more so then when enjoying high tea in the Lord Mayor's Lounge. I suspect that the Shelbourne is a finer and more comfortable establishment today than at any point in its long and colorful history (the Irish Constitution was drafted here in 1922), but I must confess to missing one of its former charms: No longer do young and smartly uniformed bellhops circulate through the public rooms paging guests—more precisely, *singing* out the guest's name—with voices fresh from a cathedral choir loft and with an engaging Gaelic lilt.

Chapter 10

Arnie
and Pat

When people have asked me about it since our brief stay there in 1994, I have blithely replied, "If you can't get to Versailles, then by all means go to the K-Club." Flippantly, I was attempting to convey this simple fact: The Kildare Hotel & Country Club is the single most luxurious golf-centered resort in my experience.

Approximately $45 million was spent to develop the K-Club, the principal elements of which are an 18-hole golf course and a 45-room hotel in the nineteenth-century chateau called Straffan House. There are also swimming, tennis, squash, and fitness facilities. This, then, is no vast pleasure dome. It would never be mistaken for Gleneagles, not to mention the Greenbrier or the Homestead. Still, it is very close to perfection.

No two guest rooms or suites are alike and all are palatial (cut crystal doorknobs are a reassuring touch), with fabrics, furniture, and furnishings fit for princes and princesses of the blood. There is a particular moment in the bath/dressing complex that I found quite arresting.

Having worked our way back past a pair of large built-in wardrobes with padded beige velvet doors and past a veined white marble tub on the right, with gold-washed fixtures, and, on the left, past a sunken stall shower at least double the size of an ordinary such unit and sporting more of the golden fixtures, we have now entered a generous area that is the setting for a double vanity, a toilet, a bidet, and a clever visual trick. Facing each other on a pair of opposite walls are large arched mirrors. The result of this juxtaposition is that when you look into either of them your image is repeated over and over and over in the glass, echoing away, as it were, to what is probably infinity, growing perceptibly smaller as it retreats into the distance. You have little choice but to laugh aloud at this legerdemain—and to count the number of laughs in the mirror. Ten was as far as my eyes would take me.

The cuisine at the K-Club is as kingly as the accommodations: spinach tagliatelle finished with a prawns cassolette lobster cream; terrine of foie gras accompanied by plum chutney; papillote of seafood with caviar butter sauce; hot praline soufflé served with prune and Armagnac ice cream; and so on and so forth. Yet the most extraordinary moment at dinner had nothing to do with the food. Having taken her seat, Harriet hesitated for only a moment before slipping her handbag down onto the carpet beside her chair in this romantically lit room. Almost before it had settled there, discreetly out of sight, a member of the dining room staff silently materialized with a tiny square bench, suggestive of m'lady's footstool, upholstered in a pale gray silk.

He unobtrusively placed it beside her chair, put the handbag upon it, bowed, and backed away. Dinner could now proceed.

The K-Club can take a little getting used to.

Arnold Palmer and Ed Seay get the credit for the superb golf course here. They also get the blame—justifiably or not—for the drainage problems that beset this eighteen over a period of three years. But this is all in the past, and it is possible now to evaluate the design without that uncomfortable sinking feeling.

This is not to suggest that water is no longer a problem. In fact, it is the central problem, imperiling the shot—sometimes more than one shot—on no fewer than 12 holes. The lovely Liffey, which drifts for a mile through this 330-acre estate, skirts the 7th, 8th, and 17th. A grand total of 14 other bodies of water, all man-made—ponds, lakes, lagoons, streams—take up where the Liffey leaves off. We are, in effect, playing in a vast water garden, which, you can be sure, also has its share of stately old trees, fancifully shaped sand bunkers, antagonistic mounding, clinging rough, and creatively contoured greens. Ernie Jones, head professional at the K-Club, said to me, "Palmer wants to challenge the golfer every foot of the way, from the opening drive to the final putt."

One million tons of earth were moved to build the course on what, I'm guessing, was once a rather unremarkable expanse of County Kildare woodlands and meadows. Some of that bulldozing involved the construction of tees. Every hole has four teeing grounds and five sets of markers. The ladies play from 5,350 yards, the professionals from 7,100 yards. Mere mortal men can choose a course that measures 6,160 or 6,500 or 6,800.

There is something here for everybody, and if you make the right selection, the round can be immensely enjoyable.

The very first shot announces the rigors of the examination awaiting. A large and fantastically shaped bunker looms threateningly from a swelling in the center of the fairway at about 160 yards. Along the left runs a boundary wall. Isn't "Mulligan" an Irish name? The narrow green on this 510-yarder is bunkered, but not too stringently, right and left.

The 2nd, 360 yards, doglegs smoothly left. A pond nudges the fairway on that side to swallow a pull (there is sand to snare a push). A second pond is hard by the left side of the green. Happily, there is only some low mounding on the right. Water and sand menace the 140-yard 3rd, as they do the 350-yard 4th, but here the sand is confined to a lone bunker at the left of the plateau green, while we must steer clear of water on the left with our drive and on the right with our approach.

Ernie Jones joined me for the first nine. He had won twice on

the European tour in his prime and then, in the mid-1980s, had captured both the British and Irish Senior PGA Championships. Captain of the British PGA in the early 1990s, he had come to Kiawah in 1991 as that organization's official representative at the Ryder Cup Match, played over Pete Dye's Ocean Course. "I was the one to make the toast to the President of the United States at the big dinner," he said, "though George Bush was not on hand. Dan Quayle was there to take his place."

Jones, a slim six-footer, continues to play beautifully, not simply making solid contact but lashing the ball as well. On the 6th he hit a high, softly drawing tee shot 260 yards. As we approached his ball, he said with a straight face, "I've been getting a little more distance out of that 5-wood lately." In fact, he had hit his driver.

I mentioned later that there was no question in my mind but that this is truly a championship course.

"There's good reason to say that," he agreed, "but I'm afraid you can't really call it a championship course until it has hosted a championship." In fact, it was subsequently chosen as the venue for the European Open from 1995 through 1998.

We get our first taste of the Liffey on the 7th, which, for men, can play just about anywhere from 530 to 610 yards. It is one of the most outstanding par fives I know and, for much of the way, one of the most unassuming. A double-dogleg with a nest of bunkers in the elbow as it swings right in the tee shot landing area, the hole now straightens out for the second shot, the Liffey paralleling the fairway along the left, concealed at first by trees along the bank—we actually hear its gentle flow before we see the broad stream—then coming into full view at about 120 yards from the green. Two noble trees along the right side of the fairway, a weeping beech and a conventional beech, force us to hesitate before giving the water too wide a berth. The green is on an island, but this is not an island green in the sense of the 17th at TPC Sawgrass. Called "Inish More" (the very name urges us to take enough club!), the island is actually many times larger than the putting surface. Still, there is no margin for error short or right, but there is space to spare left and long, though in both instances we shall find ourselves trapped in trees. It is an altogether wonderful hole—fair and fine and quite beautiful, with, to top it off, an enchanting little white cast-iron suspension bridge, more than 150 years old, providing access to the island just beyond the green.

Ernie Jones told me as we crossed the bridge that he had lived in the hotel for a couple of months before the course opened for play and that he often came down to this stretch of the Liffey to fly cast for trout in the evening. "The trout fishing has always been very good here, and you can see for yourself what a lovely spot it is. Now we've got salmon, too, and there are hotel guests who take advantage of the opportunity to try their skill—or their luck."

On the 330-yard 8th, called "Half Moon" because of its gentle dogleg shape, the Liffey runs along the left within a few paces of the fairway from tee to green. The merest suggestion of a pull is fatal. Rough-covered mounds punctuate the right side of the hole, and just beyond them lies a lake, but there is no excuse on such a short two-shotter to visit that hazard. At the 9th, which plays a good 400 yards as it climbs toward the clubhouse, voracious bunkering on the left eats into the fairway to endanger the drive, and there is even less respite on the second shot, for three large bunkers patrol the green, which slants away from front to back.

So much for the easier half, where most of the holes are routed over fairly level land. The second nine introduces a number of ups and downs to the equation while, if anything, providing even more water.

At the medium-length par-four 10th, the story is simple: trees right and water left on the drive, sand at the green. The up-hill 11th, 375 yards long and tree-framed, plays at least 400 yards and sports two defiant bunkers in the slope just short of the green. Only gently climbing is the 140-yard 12th, but the an-gled green is staunchly defended by sand and water. The par-five 13th, from a high tee that affords splendid views of the estate, sweeps downhill, and in the course of its double-dogleg, intim-idates with half a dozen bunkers on the left to trap the hooked drive, sand and water on the right just about where our second shot will come to rest, and sand across the face of the green. By this time it had belatedly occurred to me that there may be no such thing as a free swing on this entire golf course. Certainly there is none on the final four holes, where the Dali-esque water patterns all but stop us in our tracks on the spectacular downhill 15th and the rather level 16th, both calling for "death or glory" second shots. The Liffey reappears within two or three steps of the right edge of the green on the very short 17th, where a vast free-form expanse of sand awaits the weak or pulled iron. The last hole is no letdown. Another of those devilish double-doglegs that Palmer and Seay apparently couldn't get enough of, this 485-yard par five contains everything that has beleaguered us for the first 17 holes: sand, mounds, curves, trees, water (the green juts out into a lake). The big basher will have a go at the green on his second shot. The rest of us will prudently lay up, optimistic that we can safely traverse 110 yards of water en route to the flag. The hole is called "The Hooker's Graveyard," but that name may be entirely too restrictive.

Small wonder that Arnold Palmer had this to say about the second nine: "For excitement, I think they're the best consecutive holes I've ever seen. Not just on my courses, but anywhere." It is a bold and sweeping claim, but it cannot be dismissed out of hand. In any event, Arnold can be forgiven a touch of hyperbole, for this is not only thrilling stuff, it is terrific golf, though perhaps with a bit more in the way of Roman candles than the ordinary 16-handicapper can survive. One thing is undeniable: the gorgeous and extravagant Kildare Hotel and Country Club has a golf course that is in every respect worthy of it.

The K-Club is 40 minutes west of Dublin. Forty minutes south, at Brittas Bay, in County Wicklow, lies a new course that opened in 1993. It may well have cost less, including land acquisition costs, than Arnold Palmer's design fee for the K-Club; it is the first new bona fide links course built on the east coast of Ireland in the twentieth century; and it is, in a word of one syllable, great. Eighteen months after the full eighteen was opened for play, the European Club course (a bit grandiose, that name) was ranked sixth in all of Ireland. The five ahead of it on the 1995 list of the top 30 were Portmarnock, Royal Portrush, Royal County Down, Ballybunion Old, and Waterville. Among the 24 that followed the European Club were Mount Juliet, County Louth

(Baltray), the K-Club, County Sligo (Rosses Point), Killarney (Killeen Course), Lahinch, Royal Dublin, Portstewart, the Island, Tralee, Connemara, Donegal (Murvagh), and a dozen other outstanding courses.

The European Club is the realization of Pat Ruddy's dream. The longtime golf journalist and sometime golf architect acquired this stretch of linksland on his own, designed the course, built it and the clubhouse, and today is the sole proprietor of all he surveys (well, he and his wife, Bernardine, are the sole coproprietors). From the day they took title to the land to the day Pat baptized the links by driving the first ball, six years passed and six Ruddys—Pat and Bernardine, two sons, two daughters—committed their lives to this grand scheme. It was worth it.

What awaits at Brittas Bay is that ideal—and rare—combination of rugged sandhills, imaginatively routed yet perfectly natural golf holes, large and undulating greens, crisp seaside turf, penal but playable bunkers, and an ongoing requirement for sound thinking and sound shotmaking. Almost all of the 18 holes have splendid sea views.

There are no blind shots (I do not advance this as something to crow about, but simply as a statement of fact). Indeed, 14 holes actually provide full tee-to-green vistas. You know where you are going at Brittas Bay. Which is not to say that Mr. Ruddy hasn't been up to a few tricks. The fairways often seem to be no more than 30 yards wide, when they are actually much wider. The deception has been achieved by concealing portions of the fairway beyond hillocks, in valleys, and behind reeds. The clever use of what the British call "dead ground" (dips, the extent of which cannot accurately be judged) conceals a club length or more on some shots to the green. And the appearance of length is sometimes exaggerated by routing holes through long corridors of tall dunes, which has the effect of telescoping medium-length shots into challenges that look endless. Moreover, greens that on the whole are quite spacious appear at times to be a bit cramped, as the designer dearly loves to site them immediately in front of high sandhills, which dwarf the putting surface and distort what a photographer would refer to as "depth of field."

Oh, he has been sly, this burly, fun-loving, quick-witted Ruddy has, but once we are onto his tricks, what had at first looked like too potent a layout becomes more like an even match. And since the course is not long by modern standards— 5,400 for the ladies, 6,750 for the scratch player, and a choice between 5,900 and 6,450 for the rest of us—brawn will not be the chief requisite. Once again, as at the Island, it is the par four that rules the roost. The course has just two par fives and three par threes; the other 13 holes are two-shotters.

It is not easy to choose favorites from this banquet table. A medium-length par four rising very gently to an elevated green gets the game off to a promising start, followed by a 150-yarder from a pulpit tee to a heavily bunkered green. Now comes a beautiful short par five spilling downhill toward Arklow Bay over this heaving linksland. The landing area for the drive is generous, but stingy for the second shot, with the ground sloping decidedly from left to right and a brace of penal pot bunkers at the front of the green issuing a stern warning to those larcenous souls who would steal a stroke from par here. Two superb fours (the steep uphill drive to a spacious fairway on the 4th calls to mind the tee shot on the same hole at Lahinch) are followed by the two river holes. The stream is tight on the left of the green on the falling 173-yard 6th, and tight on the right every foot of the way on the 401-yard 7th, a secluded beauty carved through a marsh offering an abundance of flora and wildlife. The drive is hit over the twisting line of the river, and the safe route to the green expands and shrinks most unexpectedly. At the marvelous 395-yard 8th—another of those serpentine fairways, this one, on balance, bending right—we play along a dune-framed corridor and over a swale so deep that it might qualify as a chasm to a sand-free green in a dell of dunes.

The second nine brings us to the Irish Sea, with the beach much in play along the right on the 398-yard 12th and the 529-yard 13th. The par five is relatively flat. Four bunkers have been cut into a long low dune along the left for the last hundred yards, a not entirely happy alternative to that vast water hazard on the right. Says Ruddy with a relish, "Talk about being between the devil and the deep blue sea!"

We tuck back into the shelter of the dunes to play the superb knob-to-shelf 155-yard 14th, then drive out to sea on the next hole—open, windswept, exhilarating—the second shot along the clifftop as the hole curves smoothly left and we climb ever higher above the sea. When I played here in the spring of 1994, the surface of the green revealed the damaged inflicted by the salt spray from winter's wind-whipped seas exploding against the rocks more than 40 feet below.

A boundary fence protrudes into the fairway from the right on the pretty 16th, a 341-yarder with a tee at the cliff edge.

The 17th is a beautiful 380-yarder from a lofty tee—the back-drop for the hole is sea, sandhills, gorse, bracken, and moun-tains—where the drive falls endlessly into a deep valley. So soaring are the framing dunes and so elevated is the tee that the fairway, punctuated by four thorn bushes in splendid isolation, appears narrow. In fact, it is 80 yards wide. However, the rising shot to the cloistered green, defended by sand and high, rough-covered banks, offers no such freedom.

The final hole is controversial. The tee shot landing area is broad on this 385-yarder. Now comes a shock. The narrow pas-sage for our second shot through the dunes focuses our eye not on the green but, astoundingly, on a pond that fronts it and wraps around it on the left and part of the way across the back. Nothing has prepared us for this moment, not on this course, indeed, not on any links course with a claim to seriousness, to say nothing of greatness. We shake our head in wonder. What is this pond doing here?

"The ground was marshy, it was wetlands," Pat Ruddy told me. "I had a choice of draining it or making it into a real haz-ard. The American contribution to golf course design was wa-ter, and I will not turn my back on that. So view this, if you will, as my tribute to the great American golf course architects. I know it will not be everyone's cup of tea, but there is no deny-ing that it makes for a strong finish."

Indeed it does, however artificially strong it may seem. And if the jury is still out on the propriety of the pond (which, Ruddy says, he may later decide to do away with should in-formed protest persuade him of the error of his ways), there is no doubt as to the acceptance of the course. It is a welcome addition to the Irish pantheon, a joyful revelation that to be great a links need not be old. Might the European Club one day host the Irish Open, perhaps even the Ryder Cup? I would not bet against it.

Some 20 minutes north, just off the N11—and thus 20 minutes closer to the capital—Pat Ruddy was reunited with Tom Craddock at Druid's Glen, which opened in mid-summer of 1995. The team had a third member here, a man of means by the name of Hugo Flinn, whom Ruddy describes as "the main owner and inspiration for the place." He is also the man who built the golf course, a task he had carried out at St. Margaret's some six or seven years earlier when the three had created that worthy course.

Here, however, near the Wicklow village of Kilcoole, Mr. Flinn had loftier aspirations. "Can you," he said to Ruddy and Craddock, "lay out for me Ireland's best inland course?" They said they could.

Now you must understand that over the years Ireland had been blessed with very few inland courses of distinction. Once you had ticked off Killarney and Carlow (in the Republic) and Malone and Belvoir Park (both Belfast), there was little more to say. But then along came the K-Club, Mount Juliet, Adare Manor, and Glasson, and there were suddenly parkland, meadowland, and lakeland courses that could hold their heads up in any company. It is likely that not one of these outstanding new eighteens surpasses Druid's Glen.

It is a par 73 (five par fives) that the ladies play at a mere 5,300 yards, the men at 6,300, and the he-men at 6,850. The course wanders over not less than half of a 400-acre tract made up of the

Woodstock Estate and an adjoining farm. The well-wooded and well-watered site ranges from rolling to hilly, with an overall elevation change of some 115 feet. It is ideal golfing country, and routed over it is a series of golf holes that consistently delight and challenge us, in one fashion or another, from start to finish.

This basic fact, however, may tend to be obscured by the high jinks indulged in by the irrepressible Ruddy and the acquiescent Flinn. For instance, there is a graceful stone bridge over a narrow river on 13. It connects the ladies' tee with the fairway. The bed of the bridge is covered in an aromatic herb. The footsteps of the players crush the herb, releasing its exotic perfume and creating a marvelously heady atmosphere. Another instance is the curious "sugar loaf" mound that rears up behind the green on the 16th. It mimics precisely—and, in fact, is squarely on line with—a distant peak of the Wicklow Mountains. The joke may not be subtle, but it is funny. Then, at the island green 17th, you can cross to the putting surface by means of a stone weir. From the tee, those behind you awaiting their turn to play would swear that you are actually walking on water, for they cannot make out the flat stones just an inch or two below the surface that are supporting you. Says Hugo, "Now for those who don't trust the power of the druids, we do have a bridge around back."

Speaking of bridges, Hugo, now in his mid-70s, amassed his fortune through large-scale civil engineering projects in Africa. Knowing that, we should not be surprised to find a high and mighty suspension bridge spanning the ravine our drive must carry on the 9th. It is doubtless modeled on one or two of his favorite creations in Nigeria. In any event, we have to love the pair of them, Ruddy and Flinn, for not taking themselves or the game too seriously.

And once past the Disneyland aspect of Druid's Glen, we find ourselves treasuring these golf holes, starting with a 425-yard opener that sweeps down across a soft swale (sand on the right) and leans to starboard as it rises to a narrow green framed only by trees. We will write down 5 more often than 4.

Ruddy claims that he drew his inspiration for the par-three 2nd hole from the long second shot on the infamous Road Hole (17) at St. Andrews, and that the par-three 8th takes its cue from the 16th at Augusta National. Well, the analogies may limp, but the holes do not. They are superb. And to give him his due, there are a wall and a road to the right on his first one-shotter, and there is a lagoon to cross and a cruelly contoured green to negotiate on his second one-shotter.

The other two par threes may be even more memorable. At 150 yards, the 12th falls through the trees to a huge green defended at the front and along the right by that modest river. We are now in the druid's glen, and in the woods on the hillside to our right, as we troop down to the green, stand the remains of an authentic druid's altar, a small cluster of boulders dating back very like a thousand years. According to Pat Ruddy, if faced with a curling 3-footer, the player should turn to the altar and, arms upraised, invoke the pagan power: "Oh mighty druid, please let me hole this tiny teaser!"

The final one-shotter is the fearsome island 17th, where, the illusion of walking on water aside, we are called upon, from 180 yards (the championship tee is just over 200), to land the shot somehow on terra firma. The green is all but ringed with a broad belt of sand, thus enlarging the haven. But in any kind of an honest breeze, we will be relieved to touch down safely anywhere. I might add that from 203 yards the hole is simply a scandal.

I have bypassed the 13th and must now return to it. It is one of the great par fours you will ever play and one of the great golf course construction projects of our time. In this latter capacity it found Hugo Flinn entirely in his element. The hole is 450 yards long (470 from the tips). It is played from a nobly high tee down into a valley crossed, about 170 yards out, by a broad stream (that so-called "Irish river"), which then skirts the right side of the fairway to the point, perhaps 90 yards short of the green, where it is transformed into a full-fledged pond. The tee shot is exacting (it is all too easy to run out of mown grass on the left as the hole bends right) and the unconscionably long second shot over water is terrifying—there is no bailout right or left. For the record, the green is set among mature chestnuts and oaks. It is an awe-inspiring, beautiful, and heart-stopping creation, this 13th at Druid's Glen.

Which brings us to how it came into being: Ruddy and Craddock imagined it and Flinn constructed it. Hugo did this by literally shearing away a wall of granite 80 feet high and 100 yards long in order to make room for the tee and part of the fairway. And having moved this mountain, he now rerouted the rushing stream and excavated the pond. "Even the Japanese," boasts Ruddy, "would never have undertaken all this in order to build just one golf hole." The self-effacing Flinn makes no such claim, simply adding that the resulting stone has been used to erect bridges, line riverbanks, and build roads.

A word about the 18th hole. It is a short par five that begins with a forced carry over a lake and climbs steadily uphill from the landing area to a green guarded, on the left, by three little lakes cascading over weirs, one into the other, and on the right by a very narrow stream rushing down a rock-strewn trough. The tiger can indeed get up in two, but the margin for error on his aggressive second shot is minuscule. The hole is a fitting and dramatic climax to all that has gone before. And this time there can be no criticism of Ruddy's use of water to defend the home green.

It should be noted that the clubhouse is as fine as the course; and on the high ground, it is often in view as we work our way around the eighteen. Built about 1760 by a son of the Earl of Aldborough, it is a handsome Georgian country house of high ceilings, classical columns, long windows, and exquisite plaster decoration on walls, ceilings, and cornices. Hugo Flinn has spent about $3 million to restore it to what, one imagines, is even more than its original glory. He has also added a roof terrace that not only commands the course but encompasses the distant sea as well.

Pat Ruddy—is he not more deeply imbued with a love of the game than anyone else in Ireland?—said to me after I had finished the round, "I like most of the holes and love some of them. We have created a fun course with a good deal of beauty. We have built a lot of unreasonable shots into it on the basis that the charge was not to create commercial golf but good golf for good players. I think we may have honored our brief to come up with Ireland's best inland course. Certainly we have tried, we have been given the freedom, the grand site, and the money to do the job right. I hope we have succeeded so that I won't have to leave town!"

Quite nearby is the attractive Glenview House, a hotel that provides excellent food, engaging views of the Wicklow Mountains, and, from what we could observe, very comfortable accommodations. My wife and I have eaten at Glenview but not spent the night there.

Some 20 minutes south on the N11, closer to the European Club than to Druid's Glen, is Tinakilly House, just outside the village of Rathnew. A long rising driveway curves up to this substantial house, situated on high ground. Built in the 1870s, it strikes one as rather more Italianate than Victorian. The only four-star hotel in County Wicklow, it has 26 bedrooms and 3 suites and is highly regarded for its cuisine, its accommodations, and its rather opulent public spaces (the great reception hall is at least 30 feet high, and it is difficult to decide which is more imposing, the staircase or the fireplace). Our room was spacious and attractively decorated (a rich, multicolored paisley at the windows and on the bed struck exactly the right traditional note, and all the furniture and furnishings nicely echoed it). From the big windows we looked down over the gardens and the meadows to the sea, perhaps a mile away. It is a room in which to spend hours reading and relaxing. Tinakilly House, with Bill and Bee Power, the co-owners, seeing to it that all goes smoothly, is as rewarding as the golf at the European Club and Druid's Glen.

Chapter 11

From
Carlow
to Venice

On the map, the distance between Rathnew, where Tinakilly House is located, and Carlow, home of the Carlow Golf Club, appears to be less than 40 miles. But linking the two places are only tertiary roads through the Wicklow Mountains. You nearly have to feel your way. Check the signposts diligently at villages such as Aghavannagh and Hacketstown and Killerig, stick to a westerly heading, and don't hesitate to ask for directions, which, if the brogue does not defeat you, will keep you on the crooked and narrow. It may take somewhat more than an hour, but you will enjoy the remoteness and the beauty and the sense of times long past.

Just off the Dublin Road, on the north side of Carlow, lies the golf club. Viewed from the lane leading to it, the clubhouse is unprepossessing. From the golf course side, however, it is quite attractive. And inside it is spacious and smart, clearly the work of a professional interior designer.

In 1999 Carlow will celebrate its centenary. The club has been operating at this site since 1922, and the course we play today is largely attributable to the brilliant Tom Simpson, who was brought in in 1937 to revise it extensively, a year prior to his outstanding work at Baltray. Par is 70 (there are just two par fives), and from the back tees the course measures only 6,470 yards. Nevertheless, it has been deemed strong enough to host the 1977 Irish Amateur and, two years earlier, the Irish Professional Championship, which Christy O'Connor won. Christy, Jr., was the club's professional at the time of his father's victory.

The course is one of the most spacious anywhere, roaming over nearly 250 acres of fast-drying sandy soil that was once a deer park (in fact, its address is Deer Park, Carlow). Though its slopes—this course ranges from rolling to hilly—are studded with all manner of trees, many of them noble and venerable, and with white birch occasionally punctuating the dark green firs and pines, rarely do these trees restrict the shot. The fairways are extremely wide, the greens large and vigorously undulating, so even on a blustery day there is plenty of room to play, room to start a tee shot well right or well left, as needs be, and have it sail reassuringly back on line, room to fly a 4-iron out over a greenside bunker, confident that, if the swing be sound, the ball will float back to the safety of the putting surface.

And if it is a treat simply to be abroad on Carlow, with its splendid vistas (the views over the countryside from the pinnacle tees on 5 and on 8 prompt a sharp intake of breath, giving way to a smile of unfettered delight), we must not lose sight of the testing nature of the golf holes. Each of the four short holes is excellent, with two of them, the 6th and 13th, of that inviting hill-dale-hill species. Among the many fine two-shotters, four in particular stand out. The 8th, almost 430 yards, plays down between stands of trees, the endlessly falling tee shot launched from the highest point on the course. The long second shot from a downhill lie to a well-bunkered green is demanding. A rim of hills in the distance and the glint of water on the nearby 2nd hole (there are also ponds on 10 and 11) add to the appeal of this hole. At the 12th a deep, grassy plunge along the very left edge of the green makes this 370-yarder a little terror. And 14 and 16, 455 and 435 yards, respectively, are bold in concept—the high left-hand shoulder running the full length of the fairway on 14 gives this behemoth a rare individuality—and call for two excellent strokes. Speaking of individuality—this of a rather commercial nature and not uncommon on tees and tee markers of Irish courses—there was a large white sign on the 14th tee that is a model of simplicity and directness: "Joe O'Neill—Fresh Milk".

On a course that surrenders birdies grudgingly, the home hole may be our best chance to pick up a stroke. Again the lofty tee, and this time the hole swings gently left as it sweeps down the long hill toward the green on the level ground in front of the clubhouse. The card says 500 yards, and if the breeze is tailing even I can get within a run-up on the strength of two strong swings.

Less than 30 minutes south of Carlow on the N10 lies Kilkenny. It is often referred to in promotional copy as "the medieval city of Kilkenny." The term *city* may be stretching things a little, since the population is not even 20,000.

Kilkenny bestrides the river Nore on both low and high

ground. Hundreds of years ago the Irish Parliament met here. The most important sites are Kilkenny Castle, all gray stone towers and battlements on a hill above the Nore; the Cathedral of St. Canice, which the *Blue Guide to Ireland* calls "one of the finest unruined churches in Ireland"; and Kilkenny College, in whose grounds may be seen traces of the ancient town walls. Among the pleasures of simply walking—as opposed to visiting the certified monuments—are narrow winding lanes that climb and dip, occasional old cobbled passages, streets with a fair share of substantial Georgian structures, a house or two that go back to Elizabethan times, and the pretty river. Green's Bridge, dating to 1765, is a charming Palladian span with five arches. Also worth keeping in mind is the Kilkenny Design Workshops (ceramics, fabrics, and much more), with studios and showrooms in converted stables across the Parade from the Castle. Kilkenny is probably the best place to get some feeling for life in Ireland during the Middle Ages. You will not want to pass it by.

Just 20 minutes south, adjacent to the village of Thomastown, is Mount Juliet. It is frequently spoken of in the same breath with the K-Club. Each is magnificent. Each has as its centerpiece a distinctive golf course. The Mount Juliet eighteen, designed by Jack Nicklaus, opened for play on July 14, 1991. The K-Club followed on July 15. Many of the same people, including representatives of the media, were on hand for both debuts. It was, if I'm not mistaken, a case of killing two birds with one stone, or something.

Comparisons between the two resorts and the two golf courses were then—and continue to be—inevitable. One thing, however, is certain: both places are wonderful, and there is little point in attempting to slot one above the other. Though the two eighteens have a decidedly American look and feel to them—water and manicuring instantly suggest their heritage—the fact is that the privileged world that each inhabits is not to be found in the States. No Arnold Palmer course back home is attendant to a palace. No Nicklaus course back home comes with a 1,500-acre estate that is one of the finest of its kind anywhere. I believe that the American golf nomad will find both enormously attractive.

The quiet and pleasant village of Thomastown displays signs to Mount Juliet. Make it a point to head for the principal entrance to the estate, not toward the golf club, for once inside the handsome old wrought-iron gates, the driveway, if we may call it that, swings sinuously over rich and rolling meadowland for very like a mile, finally disclosing, with some distance still to go, the great manor house itself nobly sited on the high ground above the banks of the river Nore. Pheasants flutter up from the underbrush, and peacocks strut upon the lawn. It is magical stuff, this long approach, and it is just one of the ingredients in the mystique of Mount Juliet.

The estate, dating to the thirteenth century, is more than golf. And it is this "more" that makes a stay here, however short, so special. Mount Juliet is the home of the Ballylinch stud, breeding ground for past and present champion thoroughbreds. Also here, in the same tradition, is the Iris Kellett Equestrian Centre, which makes it possible for guests not only to indulge in dressage and arena jumping but to ride to the hounds with the local hunt. And since both the Nore and its

tributary, the Kings, flow through the estate, there are four
miles of river fishing, including a dozen named pools, for
salmon and trout. About it all is an atmosphere rather like what
must have obtained during long weekends of country-house
parties at Mount Juliet in the Edwardian Age. It should, however, be pointed out that there was then no golf course outside
the door for the pleasure of the guests. And certainly this Nicklaus eighteen is a thoroughly pleasurable experience for everyone. Ladies play it at just under 5,500 yards (par 73). Men have
a choice of the green tees (6,172 yards), the white (6,641), or
the blues (7,101). For them, par is 72.

It could fairly be claimed that the course is a reflection of the
great estate. There is a gentility about it, a decorous beauty, if
you will, as it moves with appealing naturalness over this lovely
meadowland. The fairways are broad, the greens are large (but
because of the bunkering and the contouring, they do not *play*
large), ancient oak and beech and lime trees lend a stateliness
and serenity to the scene, and even the water hazards strike us
as pretty first, then lethal. And so excellent is the turf, in both
texture and maintenance, that it has set a new standard for
greenkeeping in Ireland.

All of which is not to suggest that the holes themselves lack
bite. A number are quite testing. The 352-yard 2nd, where our
drive must carry a slit of a stream that then angles along the
right edge of the hole, lurking there to swallow even the slightest push, is an exacting short par four. The tee shot held a shade
too safely left finishes in mounds or behind trees. At the 350-
yard 4th a pond all but laps the right side of the green. The 5th,
a par five of 509 yards, drifts left, then right (clearly we live in

the age of the double-dogleg three-shotter), with five bunkers left and two right to snare the errant second shot. In the 1994 Irish Open, John Daly started the final round with six consecutive 3s (five under par). His eagle on this hole, which measured 534 yards, came as the result of a drive and a 9-iron. Alas, he tied for second, a stroke behind Bernhard Langer.

The 6th, which Daly parred in this stretch, is a 200-yarder (229 for the professionals). Because there is a patch of fairway short of the green, and because this is angled out to the left of the straight line from tee to green, the hole takes on the aspect of that perennial joke, the dogleg par 3. Nonetheless, it is one of the very best holes on the course.

There are several holes on the second half that are also outstanding, perhaps none so striking as the 518-yard 10th. At about a hundred yards from the green, the fairway splits. You have a choice of hitting your second shot left or right, because on the direct line to the green, standing implacably abreast, are three towering beech trees. They come as a considerable surprise.

Thirteen is a terrific two-shotter. Our drive disappears just over the crest on this 412-yarder. From a slightly downhill lie, Nicklaus requires that we unfurl what may well be a 4-iron to an elevated green jutting out into a small pond. It is a do-or-die shot on what might fairly be called a great hole. And the hole that follows, 177 yards from a pulpit tee across a valley to a two-tier green ringed by sand, is another beauty.

The Irish Open was held here in 1993, 1994, and 1995. Nick Faldo, firing a 7-under-par 65 in the final round, tied Jose Maria Olazabal for the title at 276 in 1993, then won the sudden-death playoff with a par on the 1st. It was Faldo's third consecutive victory in the tournament. "I find it relaxing here," he said. "Nobody dies of an ulcer in Ireland." Mention of Faldo reminds me that his mentor, David Leadbetter, has a golf school here, the only such facility offered by the guru in Ireland.

Faldo played well the following year at Mount Juliet, but his total of 280 left him five strokes off Langer's winning pace. This marked the German's third victory in the championship, his earlier wins having come in 1984 and 1987. In 1995 Scotland's Sam Torrance rolled in a 12-foot putt for an eagle 3 on the second playoff hole to eclipse Howard Clark and Stuart Cage after the three had tied with 11-under-par totals of 277 at the end of 72 holes.

It is Mount Juliet House, built by the Earl of Carrick more than 200 years ago, that serves as the hotel. There are 32 accommodations, including two "presidential" suites and seven smaller suites. The rooms, large and high-ceilinged, are individually decorated in a warm, traditional fashion that is luxurious but not ostentatious. Many have beautiful marble fireplaces and views over the river Nore to the meadows and the distant hills.

The public rooms are no less fine, and despite the undeniable elegance of them, they are not stiff. Dinner in the Lady Helen McCalmont Dining Room (the McCalmont family owned the estate from 1914 to 1986) is one of the high points of an Irish holiday. This is one of the most exquisite period rooms in the country. The carved plasterwork in the Adam style, white on Wedgwood blue walls and ceiling, is of a surpassing grace and delicacy, with classical figures in relief on medallions, and stylized vine tendrils lightly swagging the medallions. It is artifice raised to high art.

One might reasonably wonder whether the cooking could live up to the setting. It does, it does. Among the starters were panfried veal sausage on an onion confit with a gherkin and grain mustard dressing, and smoked chicken and melon salad with a passion fruit sauce. A cream of parsnip and turmeric soup was both novel and delicious. Entrées included pheasant and rabbit ("Duo of Game") set on a potato and celeric purée with a star anise jus, and broiled turbot in a light butter sauce, with a julienne of onion and wild mushroom. For dessert, Harriet chose the crème brulee with pear, and I had the chocolate bavarois on a trio of coulis. The wine list is extensive and the service flawless.

Katherine MacAnn, Mount Juliet's director of sales and marketing and for some years one of Ireland's outstanding women amateurs, told us that her thirtieth birthday occurred during the 1993 Irish Open. Unknown to her, several of the players had learned of this. "That night," she related, "at a big dinner with many of the well-known players, when it came time for dessert, the room suddenly went quiet. I looked up and there, coming across the room toward me, were Seve Ballesteros and Jose Maria Olazabal carrying a birthday cake with the candles all lighted and them leading everyone in singing 'Happy Birthday'! Can you imagine them doing that, for me?"

At Mount Juliet, yes. It is that kind of place.

Less than an hour south of Thomastown on the N9 is Waterford, an ancient port city on the river Suir that has preserved few buildings of any real interest and that is best known today as the home of Waterford crystal. Visitors may tour the factory, about a mile and a half out of town on the Cork Road, and observe certain stages in the manufacture of the pieces, particularly cutting and polishing. They may also take this opportunity to buy, and it is probably safe to say that nowhere else in the world is there such an extensive array of the Waterford line, everything in cut glass from a violin to the head of a driver (it's a paperweight). There is one feature of this facility that struck us as particularly nice: buy a gift, say, a cross, and have the recipient's initials engraved on it while you wait. Indeed, you will sit opposite the house engraver and watch him inscribe the letters on the glass. There is no charge for this service, but do not expect factory outlet prices at this factory outlet.

A few miles east of the city center is Waterford Castle Hotel, which, together with its golf course, occupies a 300-acre island in the estuary. A small ferry boat with a capacity of about six cars carries you from the mainland. Attached to an underwater cable, it seems to run perpetually. Certainly the wait is never more than six or seven minutes.

The castle dates to the fifteenth century, and with its ivy-clad gray stone walls and its battlements, its Elizabethan oak paneling and its massive stone fireplaces, it is all that it ought to be. For centuries it belonged to the powerful Fitzgerald clan, and Edward Fitzgerald, the translator of the *Rubaiyat of Omar Khayyam,* once lived here. Today, in its incarnation as a hotel, it manages to be both opulent and intimate at the same time. The guest rooms are big and comfortable and full of character, though perhaps not so luxurious as those at the K-Club and Mount Juliet.

The cooking is excellent, with an emphasis—not at all surprising—on seafood. The dishes incline to be uncomplicated: tartare of salmon with lime juice and dill, or panfried fillets of plaice on a grain mustard sauce, for appetizers; entrées such as poached turbot in a light cream sauce with cucumber and tomato, chicken breast filled with a herb mousse and served in a herb cream sauce.

We were able to spend only one night here and our schedule was such that I did not have the time to play the golf course, which Des Smyth and Declan Brannigan, who designed Seapoint, laid out in 1991. But I did manage to get an overview of it from several vantage points on the higher ground. From the back tees, it measures 6,850 yards against a par of 72. The ladies play it at 5,600 yards, and for them par is 74. Certainly the views over the estuary are lovely, with an occasional ocean-going vessel as a pleasant distraction, but the plantings, which are particularly important on what is a parkland course, were some years from maturity. I knew I would have to return to gain an accurate picture of what Smyth and Brannigan had accomplished here.

Just nine miles due south of the city of Waterford lies Tramore, a popular seaside resort that climbs a hill overlooking a bay framed by Brownstone Head and Great Newton Head, each with its prominent old stone tower. If by some chance you should seek a bit of relief from the high-rent districts (Mount Juliet and Waterford Castle), you might find that Rushmere House, which has six guest rooms, will do nicely for a night. It is a tall, white, semidetached B&B that looks out on the bay. Mrs. McGivenney is the proprietor and a friendly, obliging woman is she, for whom the faith appears to be very much alive. There is a holy water fount in the vestibule, a small Infant of Prague statue tucked under the staircase, and a porcelain crucifix in the upstairs hall. No rosary beads dangling from a clothes tree.

Tramore is not Biarritz. Style is not its stock in trade. There is a paved promenade—boardwalks as we know them are not common in Ireland—and it carries you along the beach and past the Loop-O-Plane, the ferris wheel, the souvenir shops, the ice cream parlor, and the amusement arcade (bumper cars and Bingo).

Mrs. McGivenney recommends the Pine Room for dinner. ("I'd better book for you—it's Ladies' Open Week at the golf club and there will surely be a crowd.") Virtually every table was taken when we walked in at eight o'clock. Men were in the minority. The room we ate in, capacity of perhaps 28, had walls painted a deep green, a white Victorian marble fireplace, wide pine floorboards, pine tables and chairs, and an open pine hutch with pretty china plates. The menu was short and simple, the food excellent—broiled sole in a lemon butter sauce for Harriet, duck à l'orange for me. Two nearby tables caught our attention. The closer one found half a dozen women (golfers?) in their 50s and 60s dividing up the check in a complex series of exchanges whose reverberations were doubtless felt in the great financial capitals of the world. And at a table for two against the wall was the Irish couple met so often in fiction: mother, perhaps 75, and son, about 50, plodding through their meal in unbroken silence.

The Tramore Golf Club celebrated its hundredth anniversary in 1994. It was the late Colonel H. C. Tippet, of Walton Heath (outstanding pair of courses at this suburban London club) who laid out the course here, in 1939. This site, on the Dungarvan coast road, about a half-mile from town, is the club's third. The first course was laid out in the sandhills, but heavy seas so often flooded it that it had to be abandoned. The club then moved to the land inside the local race course, but whenever the horses were running, the course had to be closed.

What Tramore now has is a pretty meadowland/parkland eighteen that measures 6,600 yards from the championship tees (both the Irish Professional Match Play Championship and the Irish Amateur Close Championship have been contested here), 5,600 yards from the ladies' markers, and 6,100 yards from the regular tees. Par is 72 for men, 74 for ladies.

The course is flattish and unadventurous. Stands of pine trees frame many of the holes, but the fairways are wide and offer very little in the way of bunkering. Gorse is a factor. Water and boundaries are not. There is no drama, no call for the heroic play. One hole, the 355-yard 4th, displays the kind of spirit that is too often lacking. Here our drive, a forced-carry over rough and broken ground to a somewhat constricted landing area—the hole doglegs right—is followed by a 6- or 7-iron over yet another patch of hostile territory to a modestly elevated green.

Turf quality is the hallmark of this course. The fairways are very good, almost seaside in their springiness and a delight to walk. And the greens are superlative—swift, true, silken.

Never in Ireland have I putted on finer surfaces. And if at the outset they seem to offer little in the way of imaginative contouring, they display considerably more character as we move into the round.

Following my game, I met the then acting manager, Johnny O'Connor, a small, intense, thin-faced man in his mid-40s, who proudly showed me around what is now the 25-year-old clubhouse. It has low, graceful, contemporary lines and offers five rooms for overnight guests (bath down the hall), a billiards room, and a squash court.

We drank a cup of tea in the main lounge, with its broad windows revealing much of the course and, in the distance, the outline of the Comeragh Mountains. When I asked Johnny O'Connor whether he played the game, he said he did, and with some regularity but not well today. Years ago—quite a few years ago, I gathered—he could be counted on for 83 or 84, but, he confided, "It was the beer. I would come out to the club, sit down at the bar, and never get to the first tee." The beer eroded his game and his life. Finally he joined AA and straightened himself out.

He told me that he shoots about 95 today and carries a 23 handicap. Four years earlier, in a pan-European handicap tournament, he won the Tramore club elimination stage of it with a net of 63. This advanced him to Killarney for the national competition, where again he won, emerging as one of the two Irish representatives who joined players from a number of other European nations in Venice for a two-day summit competition. There, on the Lido links, he captured the first day's event and finished fourth the second day. He was put up in the very villa once occupied by Ronald and Nancy Reagan. "Aye, there's a lovely photograph of the two of them on the wall there now, in commemoration of their official visit. And d'ye know, though my own visit was four years ago, there are those who still point me out as the man who won the golf trip to Venice."

Chapter 12

Cork Comes
of Age

The drive from Tramore to Cork via Dungarvan (if it's lunchtime and you want a sandwich, try the bar at Lawlor's Hotel there: dark wood, stained glass, modest prices, convivial atmosphere), then on the N25 through Youghal and Midleton (how there could be only one *d* in the middle of Midleton I cannot imagine), should take less than an hour and a half. Five or six miles short of the city, on the east side of it, you will see signs for the Cork Golf Club, Little Island. Sticking with the N25, however, for two or three more miles will bring you to Lotamore House, a handsome eighteenth-century manor well above the highway in its own small park and with very good views of the harbor. As you begin the steep, curving climb to the house, your instinct may be to believe that you are approaching a superior hotel, probably with a four-star rating. This is not the case. Lotamore House is a B&B. But it has 21 rooms, all with private bath, telephone, and television. It also offers a pleasant lounge and a cheerful dining room for breakfast (no other meal is served). But what particularly recommends it is the spaciousness of many of its guest rooms, spaciousness with an emphasis on simple comfort. At the suggestion of a Cork Golf Club member, we spent three nights here in Room #21 on our most recent visit to Ireland and did not regret it for a moment. Our accommodation was a corner room that measured $16 \times 10 \times 12$. It had two beds, a double and a single, each with a good mattress. Among the rest of the furnishings—and almost as important as the beds—was a pair of overstuffed wing chairs, one in tweed (there were nine more identical with it in the lounge) and one in mohair. Each presided over the view from one of the two generous front windows.

This panorama was scarcely idyllic. At the foot of the hill, and on the bank of the Lee River estuary, bulked a couple of squat oil storage tanks. Next to them was a lot that serves as a staging area for several hundred new cars brought here by ship from time to time. The storage tanks and the cars constituted the foreground. The broad waters of the estuary occupied the middle ground. On the far shore stood ancient Black Rock Castle, now a restaurant, and in the background were Passage, Monkstown, and the meadowlands to the south. Large cargo vessels that have entered the vast and complex harbor from the sea down at Crosshaven, or that have offloaded their shipments in Cork city itself, ply these waters regularly. Few painters are likely to be tempted to render this scene, but, perhaps perversely, we liked it. What it lacked in picture-postcard prettiness it more than made up for in sweep and vitality.

While Mrs. Hardy, the hospitable and crisply efficient proprietor of Lotamore Hotel, does not provide dinner, only a couple of minutes away is the Barn Restaurant, which prides itself on its authentic Irish cooking and which offers an extensive menu: nine or ten starters; perhaps a dozen main courses, including a good selection of seafood and one or two game dishes; an impressive dessert trolley; and several uncommon Irish cheeses. The decor may be a bit too colorful by some standards, and not every dish is likely to prompt applause, but there is a good chance that, on balance, your dinner here will be enjoyable. The Barn is very popular with the locals, and reservations are often necessary.

The Cork Golf Club is less than 15 minutes from Lotamore House. Though its course cannot be considered great, it has genuine distinction—indeed, it may be unique—and it has a way of inspiring both affection and admiration in all who play it.

The club was formed in 1888, quite near Lotamore House, as a matter of fact. The organizers were several of the leading citizens of Cork plus some officers of the then resident British Army and Navy. But this inland location proved unsuitable, as did a second one near Queenstown Junction, and it was in 1898 that the club moved to Little Island (actually a peninsula), to a strip of land with a large limestone quarry on the northern shore of the Lee estuary. Here David Brown, a native of Edinburgh who was the club's first professional, and Tom Dunn, an Englishman, laid out nine holes. Almost 30 years later, in 1927, Alister Mackenzie, then working his wonders at Lahinch, was invited to Little Island, where he extensively revised the existing holes and added a second nine. There is a lot of Mackenzie in the course that so delights us today, but it also bears the stamp of work done in 1975 by Frank Pennink.

Over the years the course has been the site of a number of important competitions for men and women, amateur and professional, including the 1932 Irish Open, the 1940 Irish Professional Championship, and the 1965 Carrolls International. But Little Island is today still best known as the home club of Jimmy Bruen, who won the Irish Close Amateur in 1937 and 1938, the Irish Open Amateur in 1938, and the British Amateur in 1946, defeating America's Robert Sweeny in the final. Bruen played in the 1938, 1949, and 1951 Walker Cup Matches. A pronounced "loop" at the top of his swing—the clubhead would fly so far past parallel that, as in the case of John Daly today, it would actually be pointing at the teeing ground—was the source of this big, powerful man's immense length, and also of his wildness. The opening hole at Little Island measures 368 yards. It rises very gently over the first 200 yards, then climbs to the green. On more than one occasion Bruen drove this green.

I was reminded of Jimmy Bruen—he served as both captain and president of Cork, and an oil portrait of him hangs in the clubhouse—when I returned to Little Island in 1995 after far too long an absence, and was fortunate to play a round with Niall Goulding, 24-year-old son of one of the club's outstanding players, Loyal Goulding. A couple of days prior to our game Niall had walloped his drive on the 1st to within six or seven paces of the green. He has scored 65 here from all the way back—6,725 yards, par 72—and had very recently returned from the United States, where he had competed with only minimal success in the South on a minitour for some months. A modest and very likable young man with an uncomplicated swing and the requisite husky forearms, he has all the shots, including a delicate touch around the greens, but, like the storied Bruen, he may not be straight enough off the tee.

The start at Little Island is tame and misleading. The 1st is quite manageable, if not at all the pushover suggested by the blasts of Jimmy Bruen and young Niall. And the short downhill par-five 2nd and very short 275-yard par-four 3rd yield plenty of birdies. So far, so easy, pretty parkland golf that cannot possibly contribute to the excellent reputation of this course.

And now we walk down a little slope behind the 3rd green and through a thicket and out onto a tee smack beside the shore of the broad estuary. Stretching away, parallel to the water on our right, is a great two-shotter, 425 yards from the shortest men's tee. The long forced-carry over very rough ground to a rippling fairway, with the mouth of the Lee lurking to devour a fade, is daunting. The rough on the left, punctuated by gorse, is scarcely a refuge. The second shot, a wood for most of us, climbs to a green that is neither large nor welcoming, and any work called for from its humpy surrounds will be hard work. The greens at Little Island have spirit to spare, a legacy from Mackenzie.

The 5th, a 510-yarder continuing in the same direction and again close beside the water, provides a bit of dipsy-doodling before doglegging right and climaxing at a green nosing into the estuary on a low, stone-banked promontory. The aggressive second shot is a gambling second shot, and the net of it all is another great hole.

The 6th completes what is a marvelous trilogy, and with it we enter the world of the quarry. We have already played parkland golf and waterside golf, and now we enter the land of limestone. The 6th is only 300 yards long. The drive, with our back to the water, is blind, a forced-carry over a forbidding wasteland of scrub to what turns out to be a wide fairway. The pitch is a short one, and well it might be, for the green is not *on* a knob, it *is* a knob. Framing it are the high gray rock walls, largely overgrown today, of the long-disused quarry. This swelling of a green, though not tiny like the fearsome 8th at Pine Valley, is unreceptive. If not truly crowned, it is certainly far from gathering. The shot, unless nipped with controlled authority, wants to edge away from the safety of the center and, at last, slip down the shaven bank—right, left, front, rear—into the short but tenacious rough. There are no bunkers, and we are unlikely ever to take 7 or 8 here. But how distressing to write down 5 when, as we stood there beside our drive only a few moments earlier, a 3 seemed within our grasp.

After very good drives into the breeze that left me with a hundred yards and Niall with little more than half that, we both failed to hold the green. My 9-iron wobbled in the wind and his artful knockdown half-wedge took a surprisingly big first hop. The 6th at Little Island is one of the most tantalizing holes I've ever played, and one of the best.

More of the quarry, bordering on the right, for the very good 170-yard 7th (platform tee) and the even better 8th, a 400-

yarder with an open aspect—the drive, lined on Tower Castle at Glanmire, slightly falling, the second shot rising to an elevated two-tiered green. The first nine comes to a close with yet another marvelous hole, a 185-yarder from one low knob to a second low knob, the green itself an almost fantastically convoluted surface. The hole, like the 4th and 5th, would be very much at home on the purest links course, so much is there of the seaside in its topography and its turf and its feel. Bunkering at the front and a steep falloff at the left demand a full-blooded stroke of very like perfection, especially in what is often a right-to-left wind.

The incoming nine begins with a strong par four of about 390 yards, where the narrow, bumptious fairway proves elusive. At the 11th, a 490-yarder curving right, we bid goodbye to the quarry—and we do so in style, for the green is perched on high ground at the very edge of the rock outcroppings. The daring second shot, or the indifferent third, that leans to the right is gone. Better to declare it lost and accept the penalty. On this hole in 1983 Seve Ballesteros, in an exhibition round, unleashed a monumental drive of 411 yards (powerful tailwind, rock-hard fairway). In commemoration, a Spanish chestnut tree was planted just opposite where the ball came to rest, 89 yards from the green. When I arrived at that point in two, it confirmed what I had long suspected: Seve is a club longer than I am.

The last seven holes are pure parkland, and though they do not measure up to the eight-hole stretch that began beside the water at the 4th tee, they are good and testing. The 16th and 17th are a pair of charmers, the latter a great driving hole from a spectacularly high tee to a fairway sloping right to left, where out of bounds awaits. The 16th, from a tee in a pretty glade, is a short two-shotter that plays out to a big fairway, then, turning sharply right, climbs steeply to a plateau green with a deep bunker under its right flank. Niall, gambling on cutting off some 75 yards with his drive and perhaps reaching the green, faded the shot more than he had intended, yet still, despite a restricted swing, managed a recovery from high rough and over intervening mature trees for a birdie.

When I marveled at the shot, he laughed and said, "That was my Trevino shot. That man can do things with a golf ball that no one else can. He's associated with a club in Florida where I was working in the shop last year for a while. We played together a few times. He'd just walk in and say, 'C'mon, get your clubs, let's go.' D' you know, I asked him once what he did to handle the pressure, for example, when he would be faced with a six-footer to win the PGA Championship. He said, 'I *change* something.' Then he explained that he would make some very minor adjustment, maybe lighten his grip or move the ball back a couple of inches in his stance or take the putter away from the ball a little lower, something that was just a bit different from the usual. This made him concentrate on the change and took his mind off the pressure."

So much for that basic precept of practice: do it the right way, the best way, a thousand times, so that in the clutch you will automatically do it the same way.

Loyal Goulding came out to meet us on the last hole, a rather flat and ordinary 410-yarder that curves slightly right. Here, as though in homage to the memory of Jimmy Bruen, Niall hit a

power cut some 275 yards into the middle of the adjacent 15th fairway, fired a 9-iron over the trees to within 12 feet, and knocked in the putt for a routine three. His father simply shook his head, slowly.

Loyal insisted that Harriet and I have lunch with him upstairs in the clubhouse lounge, with its grand views across the course to the water. We ate smoked salmon and brown bread, and if there is a better way to cap a round on a course you dearly love, I can't imagine what it could be.

A successful businessman in his late 60s, Loyal Goulding is retired. This enables him to play golf when and where he wants to and to visit America every year, almost always for the Masters. Thanks to his many friends here, he is able to tick off the shrines—Merion, Pine Valley, Baltusrol, Winged Foot, Pebble Beach, Cypress Point, Olympic, Bel-Air, and many more—that he has played over the years.

When Harriet asked him if his home overlooked the sea, he

said, "It does indeed. I could drop a boat in the water at the bottom of my garden and paddle my way to Boston."

For more than a hundred years, Cork, the third largest city in the Republic (population about 140,000), had only the one first-rate course. Now, following the opening of Fota Island in 1993, it has two, plus a third, Harbour Point, that is also a pleasure to play, though it would not stand up under the attack of the scratch golfer.

The Fota Island Golf Club, not 15 minutes from the Cork Golf Club (nor, for that matter, from Lotamore House), is next door to the Fota Island arboretum and gardens, which make for an enjoyable couple of hours' outing. The course is laid out on gently rolling parkland that offers views of Cork Harbor as well as of distant patchwork hills. Mature woodlands frame much of the tract, but the course itself is actually quite open, with none of the holes routed through avenues of trees.

Peter McEvoy, 1977 and 1978 British Amateur Champion as well as five-time Walker Cupper, teamed up with Christy O'Connor, Jr., who is getting a lot of work these days, to design the course. Obviously, they are both admirers of Augusta National, and the Mackenzie/Jones masterpiece is the inspiration here: very broad fairways, light rough, moderate bunkering, five or six water holes, large, imaginative, and sometimes improbably festive greens. The four sets of tees permit the course to be played at 6,900 yards, 6,440 yards, 6,200, and 5,500. Par is 72, with the very untraditional and very attractive allotment of five par fives, five par threes, and only eight two-shotters. This scheme produces a kind of built-in variety.

The game gets off to a very good and very stiff start with a

410-yarder where the drive is uphill and the long second, over the crest, is blind to a slightly raised green. Right off the bat we are likely to find ourselves playing the one shot we would prefer to postpone, a teasing little pitch or chip to a double-tiered green.

Following a level two-shotter of the same length comes the fetching 148-yard 3rd, almost totally surrounded by water but with a generous margin for error nonetheless. The hole pays witty obeisance to the district's senior course in its very name: "Little Island." Back-to-back par fives now call for big hitting and not much more—as almost everywhere at Fota, there is room here to swing away with impunity. A lone and deep pot bunker squarely in front of the elevated green at the 5th does give us something to think about on the pitch.

Beginning at the terrific 360-yard 6th—down from an elevated tee, then up to a plateau green patrolled across the front by a nest of bunkers in the slope—the course grows in interest and appeal. The slanting green on the 146-yard uphill 7th is sited just beyond a low stone wall. At the 8th, a rising dogleg left and the third par five on this nine, a stream bisects the fairway and there is a greenside lake on the left to warn off the player with thoughts of getting up in two on this 477-yarder. The closing hole on the first half runs steeply downhill to an extremely wide but shallow green, which is sand-free but triple-tiered.

So accustomed are we to being out in the open at Fota that the par-five 10th, plunging between a great grove of old hardwoods on the left and a high bank of gorse on the right, seems a virtual tunnel. The fairway turns sharply left beyond a stone wall at the bottom of the hill and proceeds to a relatively level green with water behind it. For me, it is an original hole: I can think of no other like it.

There are a couple of outstanding par fours coming in. The 14th, 414 yards long, is the #1 stroke hole. A majestic lime tree in the heart of the fairway some 275 yards from the tee is the guidepost. The faint of heart will play left of the tree on their second shot; this is the longer but safer route. The brave will aim to the right of it, confident of clearing a hidden lake that fronts the green. As for the 16th, there is neither choice nor danger, just a fine 400-yarder that edges mildly right between low mounding and sand, then rises gently to a vast and undulating green full of marvelous but manageable gradients.

The final hole, 477 yards and framed by trees in the early going, demands a straight drive, but there is plenty of room on the second shot as the fairway sweeps broadly downhill to a green uniquely cambered to fall away toward the lake at the back. The terracing in this green is perhaps the most extravagant I've ever encountered. It is essential to place your third shot on the same "table" as the cup. What with the downhill second encouraging an aggressive swing and with the water behind the green very much in play and with the fantastical contouring of the putting surface making three-putting commonplace and four-putting by no means out of the question, this 18th is, as Peter McEvoy says, "a hole where bold play can produce a 3 or a 7."

After my round I had lunch in the wonderful clubhouse—an old stone farmhouse has been enlarged and tastefully remodeled—with New York-born Kevin Mulcahy, the club's general manager and the son of the late Jack Mulcahy, founder of Waterville Golf Club. He told me that Fota Island would be the venue for the 1995 and 1996 Irish Close Amateur and for the 1995 Irish Club Professional Championship. I gathered that he, McEvoy, and O'Connor may well do a little tweaking and fiddling (something that's been going on at their model, Augusta National, for the 60 years of its existence) as they spot opportunities to improve an already very good course, one that boasts the best set of greens in Ireland. What we miss here is pressure on the swing, those truly demanding shots where failure can be costly, perhaps ruinous. As I write, the Fota Island course strikes me as a bit too benign. It needs, if you will, a little more Augusta. But make no mistake about it: this is a very welcome addition to the Cork golf scene and to Ireland's roster of first-rate inland courses.

Harbour Point, which, like the Cork Golf Club, has a Little Island address, enjoys similarly handsome harbor views, though despite the club's name, the holes never do get within a holler of the water. It can play as long as 6,700 yards and as short as 5,650. Par is 72 (four long holes, four short holes, ten two-shotters). The first seven holes are routed over mildly rolling terrain. The last eleven are, with the exception of a couple of par threes, hilly.

The course is lightly bunkered, there is little or nothing in the way of boundaries, there are no water hazards, and only the 6th, 455 yards, and the 7th, 445 yards, are likely to be unreachable in regulation. Harbour Point ought to be that rarest of golf experiences, a course we've never seen before where we can play to our handicap. I'm afraid it doesn't work out that way. The principal reason is the narrow fairways, which, from time to time, are preposterously pinched. For instance, on the eye-and-lung filling par-five 9th, with its tee on top of the world, the steeply downhill drive is blind to a fairway that is precisely 18 yards wide in the landing area. And though the rough is not high, it is healthy. There must be many days here, with the wind howling across these heights, when hitting a fairway becomes very nearly accidental. I might also add that the greens, frequently frisky, incline to be narrow at front.

Among the holes we remember best are the 190-yard 5th (across a dip to a well-bunkered green shaded by spreading old cedars); the 208-yard 12th (a long knob-to-knob challenge where only a perfectly struck wood or long iron can succeed); the 380-yard 13th (downhill, the vast estuary an entrancing backcloth, the hole playing much shorter than the measured distance); and the 390-yard 16th (steeply uphill, infinitely longer than the measured distance).

Harbour Point, which opened in 1991, has a smartly appointed clubhouse with good food and attractive views. It also has a 21-bay all-weather driving range, floodlit at night, that welcomes those who simply want to practice without playing the course. It is the driving range that must account for this facility's unusual name, Harbour Point Golf Complex.

If the city of Cork has few structures of compelling architectural interest and, on the whole, little in the way of even unpretentious charm—we seem ever conscious of warehouses and breweries and tanneries and dilapidated housing—you might well take pleasure in a short run down to Cobh or to Kinsale, both of which are no more than 30 minutes away.

Cobh (pronounced "Cove" and with a population of some 7,000) is the port of Cork and the principal shipping center in this vast and all but land-locked entity, stretching from the Atlantic Ocean all the way to Cork City, that goes under the name of Cork Harbour. Dominating the town from its hilltop site is St. Colman's Cathedral, begun in 1868 and built of granite in a Gothic style. It attracts tourists as much for its panoramic views as for its good architectural details.

Cobh was the gateway to the United States and Canada for some 2,000,000 Irish immigrants in the nineteenth and early twentieth centuries. It provided the last view of their homeland as they sailed away to create new lives in the new world. And here, at the old railroad station on the quay, has been established a Heritage Center. Contemporary audiovisual techniques have been employed to dramatize the horrific experience of voyaging, in steerage, from Ireland to America in the small sailing vessels—the notorious "coffin ships"—that were barely seaworthy. And though this is, of course, an Irish story, it could just as easily be an account of the poor who dared to cross the Atlantic from any of the nations of continental Europe. It is a skillful dramatization of the way it must have been for many of our ancestors, and it is difficult not to be moved by it.

I should also mention that Cobh was the last port of call for both the *Lusitania* and the *Titanic*. The tragic sinking of these two liners is also graphically depicted here.

Well, there is none of the poignancy of Cobh in Kinsale, a colorful and bustling fishing village on the estuary of the river Bandon. Call it what you will—restoration, gentrification, modernization, commercialization—but this picturesque little port is booming. Behind gaily painted masonry fronts are all manner of shops (trinkets and wearables the most prevalent offerings), to say nothing of cottages, picture galleries, pubs, and restaurants. There are those who point to Kinsale as the cuisine capital of Ireland, which, on the face of it, sounds excessive but may just be the case. We have not eaten there in recent years, but an examination of menus as we strolled through the town in 1995 convinced us that the cooking is ambitious (and so is the pricing).

Kinsale is a holiday town and it has holiday golf, a nine-hole course at Belgooly that measures 2,850 yards against a par of 35. The mix of holes is a plus—two par fives, three par threes, four par fours.

My guess is that the course is straitjacketed into no more than 35 acres. What I'm certain of is that the view—regardless of the hole or the shot, it is essentially the one view of the estuary, narrowing through a gap in the hills covered with a patchwork quilt of meadows—is enchanting. The clubhouse rests atop a high hill, and the holes run up and down it. We are either driving down, in which case the second shot will be a half-wedge, or driving up from the riverbank, in which case the second shot will be anything from a 5-iron to a 3-wood. Bunkering is light. The greens are reliable putting surfaces and, on occasion, unaccountably large. The 350-yard 6th hole, for instance, boasts a tripled-tiered green that is 190 feet long. Putting here can be adventurous.

Speaking of adventure, within six or eight months of the publication of this book, a new course on the Old Head of Kinsale is scheduled to open. Since it will be widely reported, I

want to mention it here, though when I was in the neighborhood in the spring of 1995 the course still lacked shape, to say
nothing of definition.

It is called the Old Head Golf Links, and its site may be
without parallel in the world of golf. The course is being laid
out on the headlands of a rock-ribbed peninsula jutting into
the Atlantic. No fewer than 10 of its 18 holes will hug the
clifftops, sometimes as much as 200 feet above the roiling seas.
One is instantly reminded of Pebble Beach and Cypress Point,
but the effect here will be starker and more theatrical.

Paddy Merrigan, a Cork-based golf course architect whose
best-known design is Slieve Russell, in County Cavan (I've not
yet played it), is responsible for the layout. Consulting with
him are Liam Higgins, longtime head professional at Waterville, and that greatest hero of Irish amateur golf, Joe Carr. The
start of the project was considerably delayed by the protests of
environmentalists, who decried in vain the transformation of
the once natural and lush and wild beauty of the Old Head into
a man-made playground. Nevertheless, assuming that the golf
holes themselves turn out to be good (not always a safe as-
sumption), count on the Old Head Golf Links to become a
magnet for Irish golf. And certainly the Cork area, once noted
for the beloved course at Little Island, will become a golf destination in its own right, with Fota Island and Harbour Point
and now the Old Head to take their places alongside what was
for so many years "the one and only."

Which brings me, at long last and however circuitously, to
the one and only Ballymaloe House. Less than a half hour east
of Little Island and Fota Island, it is not simply another of

those excellent country-house hotels; it is the wellspring of the truly outstanding cooking, once virtually nonexistent in Ireland, that we can now count upon enjoying in many parts of the land.

Ballymaloe House is owned by Ivan and Myrtle Allen, now in their early 70s, and operated by them and their extended family. The text on the cover of their menu, which Myrtle Allen penned, is informative: "Ever since we placed our first advertisement in the Cork *Examiner* in May 1964, headlined 'Dine in a Country House,' it has been our endeavor to emulate the food in the best country houses in Ireland. To this end we have always gone down to our own garden and glass houses, into our local butcher's shop and to the pier at Ballycotton to collect our produce. We write a new menu each afternoon when we see what we have got. . . . We are constantly bringing in new ideas from our school and from our guest lecturers, but our main repertoire is still based on our traditional foods and our old recipes."

From the initial ad, the Allens have been packing them in, first the diners, then the overnight guests. Now there are Ballymaloe cookbooks and a Ballymaloe cooking school, and one of their daughters-in-law, Darina Allen, has even run a cooking series on television. The influence of all this has been far-reaching and pervasive. Other country-house hotel owners, willingly more often than not, were soon at pains to raise the standards of their own table. We are all indebted to the Allens.

There was a full house that Thursday evening in Mid-April a year ago when Harriet and I found our way there. From Midleton, which is on the N25, you take the Shanagarry road via Cloyne, across the meadows and croplands. The early nine-teenth-century gray stone manor house, partially mantled in lavender wisteria, is the centerpiece of a 400-acre farm. An ex-uberant fanlight shaped like a peacock's tail surmounts the front door.

There is no bar at Ballymaloe House. Cocktails are drunk and menus perused in the spacious drawing room (a fire going here most evenings), and dinner is served in several small or medium-sized rooms. These dining rooms display an interest-ing collection of modern Irish paintings, including canvases by Jack B. Yeats, brother of the poet.

Harriet had a cucumber timbale with coriander dressing, followed by potted crab, and, for her main course, baked sea trout with spinach butter sauce. I chose the French peasant soup (a hint of bacon in this ambrosial confection), salmon *en papillote* with spring herbs, roast lamb with rosemary and garlic mint sauce and Swiss chard. Half a dozen cheeses, several of Irish farmhouse pedigree, were offered, then a nice selection of desserts that, thankfully, were marvels of restraint. Coffee with petits fours brought the meal to a close. I should mention that the wine cellar, which Ivan Allen presides over, lives up to the cooking.

So relaxed is the atmosphere that at no time do you feel you are worshipping in a temple of gastronomy. But when the meal is over, you find yourself concluding that it was one of the four or five most enjoyable dinners in your memory.

Myrtle Allen was pleased to show us a couple of the 30 guest rooms, which can be found in the main house, in the annex across the cobbled courtyard and in the sixteenth-century gatehouse. Those we saw were spacious, comfortable, studded with antiques and heirlooms, and offering pretty pastoral views. There is a heated outdoor swimming pool at Ballymaloe House (any outdoor swimming pool in Ireland that is not heated is of doubtful utility), a tennis court, and, of all things, a seven-hole pitch 'n' putt course. The Allens have thought of everything.

Chapter 13

One of the Great Ones
and a Handful
of Others

Scattered between Cork and Waterville, which is some 75 miles and more than two hours due east of Cork on the celebrated Ring of Kerry, lie a handful of uncelebrated golf courses. With the exception of Parknasilla, there is little reason to seek any of them out. But since they pop up on a good road map and so might pique your curiosity, and since I once played at five of these clubs a good dozen years ago, I will tell you what I thought then and what I know now, in case you should ever be tempted.

The Skibbereen Golf Club, closest of the five to Cork and closer yet to Kinsale, had a dull course, the nine holes laid out on a broad and mildly sloping meadow. There were no notable holes, but a couple of them, the 195-yard 5th and the 415-yard 7th, were tough. The greens were small and flat and without interest. Bunkering was minimal. Evergreens, sparingly planted, were used to separate the holes. Alternative tees provided a little variety for the golfer who decided to go around a second time. There were neither sea nor river views to brighten this exercise, but there was a notice on the clubhouse bulletin board that caught my eye. It advised that here, at the club, on November 17, 1983, a debate would be held on the topic "Has Society Become Too Liberal?" I daresay a golf club is as good a forum as any in which to examine that provocative question. (Who knows? Perhaps the matter of women's prerogatives on the 1st tee Saturday before noon was even aired.) Recently, Skibbereen added a second nine. A number of holes run along the side of a hill and, I have it on good authority, the new greens are anything but flat.

The nine-hole course at Bantry, northwest of Skibbereen on the N71, had one bunker, at the left front of the 1st green; eight holes running up and down a grand hill in front of the clubhouse (the 6th was totally concealed behind the clubhouse, for reasons that escaped me); and smashing views over Bantry Bay. The course measured 3,218 yards against a par of 35, and on balance it was an enjoyable place to swat the ball against a backcloth of heavenly scenery.

Only moments away is Bantry House. This magnificent early eighteenth-century house functions in two ways: as one of the Hidden Ireland group, it offers nine accommodations for overnight guests; and as one of the finest stately mansions in Ireland, it opens its public rooms to visitors. In one capacity or another, it should not be missed. We have not stayed there, but we have paid our admission fee and explored the house and gardens. The house is furnished with an impressive collection of furniture and works of art brought together by the 2nd Earl of

Bantry as a result of his continental travels throughout the first half of the nineteenth century. He also designed the grounds and, inspired by the gardens of Europe, laid out a formal Italian garden and a "staircase to the sky" rising up the steep terraces commanding the bay. The current owner, Egerton Shellswell White, is a trombonist with the Cork School of Music Symphony Orchestra as well as with a local brass band, so there is always music at Bantry House, whether live or recorded. Concerts are held in the library, which houses a piano made by Bltuthner of Leipzig. We noticed a little sign on it, hand-lettered in red: "If you are an experienced pianist and would like to play, please tell us at the desk. A selection of music is on the rack. Thank you. Piano is tuned to concert pitch (440)."

On the west side of Bantry Bay is the Glengarriff Golf Club. Despite the fact that its nine was a full thousand yards shorter than the course at Bantry, there was a clear kinship, for both were hilly, both partook of the splendid sea views, and both laid claim to only one bunker. Sand is apparently at a premium when the course is not squarely beside the sea.

There was potential danger on the opening shot at Glengarriff. The 1st tee was hard by the N71; the markers, by actual measurement, were 18 feet from the principal thoroughfare—the *only* thoroughfare—across this part of the southern coast of Ireland. The teeing ground was a tiny platform on a low rise beside the road. A vigorous off-balance swing coupled with a sudden gust of wind could, in literal truth, have been the death of me, had I tumbled off the minuscule perch down into the path of an oncoming vehicle.

And so, however warily, I began the game at Glengarriff,

which was an unbroken series of exhausting ups and exhilarating downs punctuated by numerous blind and semiblind shots and by captivating water-and-mountain vistas. My most vivid memory is of the exotic 5th, which packed a lot into 285 yards. The green was hidden somewhere around to the right beyond a small grove of trees. For the first 200 yards the hole was a toboggan slide. Very near the bottom, just off the left edge of the fairway, lurked the hidden trickle of a burn. The hole now made a 90-degree right turn and, for the last 50 yards, leaped neatly uphill. Down, water, right, trees, up—all of it in the space of 285 yards. After I'd putted out, it struck me that the green was probably driveable if only I had known where to aim.

The 3rd, a 270-yard par four, may also have been driveable, but its real claim to fame was that the tee overlooked the estate of Maureen O'Hara, who enjoyed stays of varying length here several times a year. Shortly before I played Glengarriff, she had come back with Ed Koch, then mayor of New York, in tow.

In the village was the Bluepool House Hotel, where we stopped for sandwiches and a drink. We were the only customers (shades of Mrs. Peacock's!). Our host was the proprietor himself, Paddy Downing—friendly and funny, late 40s, balding, grossly overweight, obliging to a fault. When we asked for cheese and tomato sandwiches, he said they were fresh out of tomatoes and summoned a 12-year-old daughter to run down to the green grocers. We refused to permit this—I had to all but blockade the door—and changed our order to ham and cheese.

We chatted with him about Maureen O'Hara ("a couple of stone heavier than in her salad days but still a beauty when she's all dolled up"); about the tourist business ("not too good this past summer when the weather got so warm that the holiday crowd were looking for a beach and Glengarriff hasn't got one"); about the economy ("Ah, the young marrieds had been buying houses and fitting them out, but with the recession they're not able to make the payments"); and about the extraordinary beauty of this part of Ireland ("I'm afraid we pretty much take it for granted").

When Harriet asked Paddy where we might find the best buys on Waterford crystal—remember, this was 1983—he volunteered to open his shop across the road to see whether he might have what we were after. And though he didn't have the particular pattern in stock, he did find it in the catalog and offered it at a 25 percent discount. We signed up for ten water goblets at $16 each and were delighted. I made a lighthearted to-do about having stopped at the Bluepool House Hotel to get a sandwich and winding up spending $160 on Waterford goblets in a store that wasn't even open!

It is the N71, needless to say, that links Glengarriff with Kenmare. For beauty and spectacle, this 30-minute drive may be unsurpassed in Ireland. Up, up, up we climb through subtropical foliage and gardens, emerging from this heavy vegetation into moorlike terrain dominated by great outcroppings of rock and by expanses of rusty bracken. As you reach the summit of a Caha Mountain peak, you look back to bid goodbye to the panorama of Bantry Bay. In moments you are sailing through the first of the three short rock-piercing tunnels that carry the road through this high traverse ridge. Then, with the tunnels in your wake, begins the long, swinging glide toward the floor of the Sheen Valley, with the lower reaches of the mountainsides a quilt of sectioned meadows, the upper reaches encased in rock and bracken, and yet, somehow, none of it forbidding for all of its steepness and remoteness.

In 1983 there was only a pretty nine-hole course in Kenmare, laid out beside the broad estuary of the Kenmare River. Like the Old Course at St. Andrews, it started and finished right in town, no more than a couple of hundred yards up the street from a cozy pub called the Purple Heather (a redundancy in the name and a log fire in the hearth), where we had our usual simple lunch.

The course measured just 2,410 yards and had no hills. Only one of the half-dozen par fours could claim any real length, in this case 400 yards. There were about 20 bunkers, but most were quite small and appeared to be afterthoughts. As golf, it was negligible, but as a walk with the mile-wide estuary, backed by the mountains, in full view at all times it was an undiluted pleasure. Today, the course of the Kenmare Golf Club has 18 holes. Eddie Hackett laid out the second nine on a compact and hilly piece of land. The holes here are very much an up-and-down affair and the walking itself is strenuous. Certainly the two nines present a vivid contrast.

Next door to the golf club is the renowned Park Hotel, a five-star establishment with 40 bedrooms and 9 suites. We've never stayed there, but a good look at its public rooms (old pieces and paintings and carpets, all of unmistakable quality) strongly suggested why the hotel is so well regarded. Its cooking is among the best in Ireland.

Some 15 miles south of Kenmare and on the same bank of the

estuary lies Parknasilla, a tiny and charming resort where the bathing is good in its sheltered waters as well as from the open strand just beyond the village. A Great Southern Hotel is the principal—perhaps the only—public accommodation here. The original nine-hole course, which had captivating sea vistas in abundance, lots of awkward stances and lies, and very little in the way of serious golf holes, has recently been replaced by a nine that Dr. Arthur Spring designed. I have not seen it, but the architect, a man I like and trust and about whom more will be said in the next chapter, believes that it is an improvement over its predecessor and that I would enjoy playing it. I'm sure he's right on both counts, and that now there is not only great natural beauty at Parknasilla but some testing golf in the bargain.

Well, the N70, which brought us down from Kenmare to Parknasilla on a leg of the Ring of Kerry, can now carry us in about 30 minutes over to Waterville, at the tip of the rugged and remote Inveragh Peninsula.

Here, in the sandhills above Ballinskelligs Bay, lies a great links, one that richly deserves its ranking among the half-dozen best courses in Ireland. This is big golf—par 72 and 7,200 yards from the championship tees, 6,550 from the regular markers, a course to hold its own under the barrage of the finest players in the world. (I hasten to add that for the ladies it measures an agreeable 5,270 yards.)

Golf has been played at Waterville since the 1870s, when the men who came to work in the giant transatlantic cable stations nearby found natural holes just waiting in the dunes. But its full potential was not realized until John A. Mulcahy, a New York businessman and Winged Foot member with an abiding love for his native Ireland and for the game, arrived in the early 1970s. He hired Eddie Hackett to take what was a near derelict nine and, together with an additional tract of linksland, layout the eighteen that we play today. The visionary and knowledge-able Mulcahy contributed much to the design himself, with the result that the attribution often reads "Eddie Hackett/John A. Mulcahy." Nor did the founder ever stop tinkering with what the two of them had wrought.

I met Jack Mulcahy in 1980, on my second visit to Water-ville. I was playing that afternoon with the club's professional, Liam Higgins, one of Ireland's finest golfers—and probably its longest hitter—during the 1970s and 1980s. Mulcahy joined us as we approached the green on the very long par-four 2nd, a 469-yarder from Liam's markers, a 425-yarder from mine. He was then 74. He struck me as quite fit but also as a man who may have been husbanding his energy, walking at a deliberate pace, talking with restraint, gesturing not at all. He explained that he had recently changed this hole, moving the green down near the water's edge and thus lengthening the hole by a good 65 yards. This necessitated another change, he continued, shortening the 3rd so that it, too, became a long par four in-stead of what it had been, a very manageable par five of 490 yards. His alterations were clearly not aimed at making the course easier, which is one reason why it has earned the respect of those professionals who have found their way here. The 2nd was one of the two holes (the other was the 14th) selected from Waterville by Christy O'Connor for his all-Ireland greatest 18. No other course contributed more than one.

Over the years a chorus of champions has hymned the links' praises. Raymond Floyd said that Waterville "is one of the most beautiful places that I have ever seen," and that here he had enjoyed "some of the finest links holes I have ever played." Tom Watson was once prompted to suggest that, as a group, the par threes at Waterville may be the best in the world. It was Sam Snead who dubbed this links "the magnificent monster," and he agreed with the witty name bestowed on the first hole, a straightforward two-shotter of 430 yards: "Last Easy."

Before Jack Mulcahy left us at the 7th, a strong medium-length one-shotter with a dune backdropping the green and a pair of tiny ponds (Eddie Hackett's "water bunkers") fronting it, he said to me, nodding toward Liam, "Make sure he tells you about the 16th."

The last two holes on the first half are stern par fours, both over 400 yards, the 8th doglegging left on the long second shot to a green secluded in the dunes, the 9th swinging right as it rises over starkly exposed ground to a tightly bunkered green (there are a dozen pits on this hole, most of them small and gathering) on a low plateau.

And now we are ready—or if we are not ready, I'm afraid it's too late—to foray into the tall and shaggy sandhills that make up the second nine. The 10th, a merciless par four of 450 yards from the white tees (475 from the blues) with its green in a dell of dunes, is followed by the great 11th. Called "Tranquility," it meanders for every one of its 495 yards along a dune-framed corridor, the undulating fairway appearing to inhale and exhale as the sandhills alternately bite into it or draw back. The tee is elevated and there is a teasing dip just short of the green. Gary Player has said that it may be the most beautiful and satisfying par five of all. Who, having played the hole, would gainsay it?

The 12th is also celebrated. Wholly enveloped in the sandhills, this 154-yarder (200 for Liam) plays over a vast and deep hollow to a generous elevated green. It is called "The Mass Hole," and the hollow is truly sacred ground: Here during Cromwell's Penal Days, more than 300 years ago, the local population would hear Mass in hiding. Engaging in such "popish practices" was punishable by death.

The 13th, a par five with concealed burns right and left in the high rough to catch the wayward second shot, plays from a high tee back in the dunes out into the open, but the 14th, a bear of a two-shotter at 410 yards (456 from the blues), promptly returns to the sandhill country. And the 15th, a medium-length par four threading through low dunes, has an especially nice rhythm, gently uphill on the drive, gently downhill on the approach to another of those wonderfully natural secluded green sites.

I had not forgotten Jack Mulcahy's admonition, and as Liam and I walked onto the tee of the 350-yard 16th I said to him, "What about this hole? What happened here?" The green is nowhere to be seen. From a platform tee high above the beach, the hole doglegs left around a wilderness of scrub and sandhills.

"Oh," he replied with what I suspect was a practiced nonchalance, "a few years back I holed it."

I was bowled over.

"I went for it," he explained, "knocked my drive right over

that jungle out there, on the direct line to the green. It's probably about 335 yards going that way. Now this wasn't the first time I'd tried the shot, nor even the first time I'd hit the green. Just the first time I'd holed it." He hesitated, then laughed. "There has not been a second time."

The scorecard today commemorates that miraculous shot, for the hole, once called "Round the Bend," is now called "Liam's Ace."

The brisk breeze was into us, as much right to left as against. Reaching the green was not a physical possibility that day. "I have no chance," he said, then all but came out of his shoes as he nailed a low searing draw that followed the curving fairway and finished some 75 yards short of the putting surface. It was certainly the shot of a man who, given favorable circumstances, just might do the unthinkable again.

The 17th, called "Mulcahy's Peak," is one of the game's most theatrical moments. It measures 153 yards from the whites, 196 yards from the blues. Playing it is a four-part undertaking. First is the near-vertical ascent to the tee, a flattened summit of the tallest dune on the links. Second, we catch our breath. Next we attempt to assimilate the grandeur of the world that is Waterville, the links rumpled and woolly, the bay blurring into the sea, Lough Currane, and, in the far distance, the mountain range known as Macgillycuddy's Reeks. Finally, we have no choice but to hit the golf ball. The green, looking smaller than it actually is, beckons from atop a low dune. Between us and it lies a valley of densest vegetation. A broad sandpit blockades the front of the green.

I have neglected to mention the wind. Of all the storied sea-side courses, Waterville seems to me the windiest, and the 17th is the most wind-ravaged hole at Waterville.

After all that has preceded it, the 18th could have been anti-climactic. It is not. A tee high above the water and a broad fair-way combine to encourage an aggressive drive, a necessity on this formidable 550-yarder, where the beach parallels the fair-way on the right, low dunes and high rough skirt it on the left, and the green is guarded by five bunkers. It is a fitting close to a remarkable course.

I would do well to give the late Henry Cotton, three-time British Open champion, the last word. After playing here in 1987, he said, "Waterville has to be one of the greatest golf courses ever built. If it were located in Britain, it would un-doubtedly be a venue for the British Open Championship. I have never seen a more consistent succession of really strong and beautiful golf holes than I have seen here."

The touring golfer has two very attractive—and disparate—choices when it comes to accommodations here. The former Waterville Lake Hotel, which Jack Mulcahy built in the 1970s, was acquired five or six years ago by Club Med. The result of that chain's extensive and costly renovation is a stylish three-story facility with 80 double bedrooms (many of which over-look Lough Currane), a large indoor heated swimming pool, and an up-to-the-minute fitness center.

Waterville House itself, once Jack Mulcahy's home and to-day the property of the New York consortium that owns the club and course, is now a luxuriously appointed guest house. This late eighteenth-century dwelling, in its own 40-acre es-

tate on the shores of Ballinskelligs Bay, has 10 accommodations, some with fireplaces. It also has immediate access to what
many consider Ireland's best salmon fishing: virtually outside
the door is Butler's Pool, a favorite fishing haunt for years of
none other than Charlie Chaplin. There is no record of the great
little clown's ever striking a golf ball.

In 1974, the first time I played golf in Ireland, my wife and
I were driving through County Kerry some 35 miles north of
Waterville one afternoon when we noticed a sign that said
"Dooks Golf Club." I had not heard of it. A short distance farther along the road was a man on a bicycle. I pulled up beside
him and said that I was surprised to see that there was a golf
course in the neighborhood.

He nodded with a rueful little smile and said, "Dooks, ah,
'tis a poor thing."

I gave the course no more thought. Seventeen years later,
chiefly because we were spending a few days at nearby Caragh
Lodge, I decided to play Dooks, which is located in Glenbeigh,
on the Ring of Kerry (N70).

In certain aspects it was still "a poor thing." The holes themselves, particularly on the first nine, were often ill-defined. The
tees were worn and bumpy. The fairways were too wide and
there may not have been as many as a dozen bunkers on the entire course. The rough was light and the gorse never gets in the
way. A narrow drainage ditch crosses the 16th and 17th but
scarcely gives pause on either. To top it all off, from the tiger
tees the course measures only 6,010 yards, against a par of 70.
It is not easy to take Dooks seriously.

But despite its shortcomings, this is not a negligible golf

course, and surely Eddie Hackett, who in 1978 drew up a plan for revisions and improvements for the then 89-year-old links, must get some of the credit. The fairways, a seaside fescue, heave and tumble. The greens, often sited on little plateaus and sometimes artfully angled to the fairway, incline to be small. They also tend to be firm, so hitting and holding them, especially in a wind worthy of the name, is a tough assignment, and you must have some feeling for the bump-and-run seaside game. This is authentic links golf, and the magnificent views of Dingle Bay—5, 9, and 11 actually get quite close to the water—only reaffirm that fact.

There are some delightful holes. The 394-yard 6th doglegs sharply left to a hidden fairway, then heads nicely uphill. At the 531-yard 11th, which plays along the sea, the hole turns right just about where we would like to place our second shot, and a steep bank squarely in front of the green renders our third shot blind. The small green on the 150-yard uphill 13th is grotesquely wrinkled and, as such, quite a shock. But then so is the embankment in front of the home green, earthworks that suggest nothing so much as World War I trench warfare and a foolhardy lieutenant shouting, "Over the top, boys!"

As mentioned, we were staying at Caragh Lodge, an Edwardian country house just a mile off the Ring of Kerry Road. Though not luxurious, it is in every respect comfortable and charming. And it is set in magnificent award-winning gardens —palm trees, rhododendron, azaleas, magnolias, camelias, and countless rare subtropical shrubs—that sweep down to the lake shore. Here you can swim, sail in the lodge's boat, or fish for salmon and trout.

Nothing more convincingly demonstrates the hospitality you can expect from the proprietor—Mary Gaunt not only owns and runs Caragh Lodge, she is also the chef—than our reception on a gray and chilly morning in April a couple of years ago. Immediately following a transatlantic night flight from JFK, we drove from Shannon down to Caragh Lodge, a 2-hour-and-20 minute run. We arrived at 9:30, weary. Our room had not yet been vacated. Mrs. Gaunt promptly showed us to one of the seven garden rooms so that we could get some rest. We awoke three hours later and moved into the room that she had reserved for us in the main house.

And what a lovely accommodation it was, #3, large, attractively decorated in antiques and a colorful red chintz, the double bed with its pretty canopy "au polonaise," a tufted sofa in a pale green moiré facing the fireplace with its unusual green, gold, and brown floral tiles. And the view over serene Caragh Lake, seven miles long, fringed with woods, and backdropped by the towering Macgillycuddy's Reeks, was nothing short of mesmerizing. It is the identical view that is enjoyed downstairs from the lounges and the dining room.

Mary Gaunt is a very good cook. The dishes are generally simple—Irish stew is one of her favorites—and the menu is not extensive (four entrées to choose from, three appetizers, three deserts), but the ingredients, in most cases obtained locally, are fresh and of high quality, and the preparation is careful. There is a considerable reliance on seafood, and we remember with pleasure poached bass with Hollandaise sauce and sole stuffed with salmon.

One evening while we were eating, a large and lively party of local people came in. They turned out to be members of Dooks, and we struck up a conversation. One of the group, Joe O'Dwyer, headmaster of a boys' school in nearby Killorglin, had been captain of the club during its hundredth anniversary year, 1989. This is a signal honor, and he was proud of it. I told him how much I liked the course, particularly the plateau greens.

"Ah," he said, "I did the ninth green."

"That's one of the ones I'm talking about," I said. "Plateau and set on an angle to the shot."

"Yes, yes indeed it is," he warmed to the subject. "And if you three-putted, you can blame me for it. It was almost five years ago now, in preparation for the Centenary [pronounced in Ireland "cen*teen*ary," with the accent on the second syllable], when a number of us took the responsibility for returfing the greens, each man to handle one green. I picked the ninth. A good friend of mine volunteered for the eighth. Now with nine being just a one-shotter, the eighth green happens to be fairly close by. Well, he thought nothing of hauling new turf all the way out to the eighth green to pile it up there for the creation of a grand new putting surface. And night after night—we worked mostly in the evenings—when he had gone, I would slip over to the eighth and help myself to some of that marvelous sod of his and lay it down on the ninth. So we got two very good greens in a row, eight and nine"—he was laughing now at the memory of it—"thanks to him. I don't think he ever knew."

Chapter 14

A Dead Crow
and a Red
Jacket

Its name is the Killarney Golf and Fishing Club, and there are always a good half-dozen skiffs and dinghies awaiting those who would cast a line on Lough Leane. But I've never known anyone so inclined. No, golf is the lure, 36 holes on the shores of the largest and perhaps loveliest of the Lakes of Killarney. Lough Leane, with its 30 islands (most of them, in truth, islets), sparkles against a mountainous backdrop that changes in hue from the deep forest green of heavily wooded slopes near the water's edge through the soft rust-brown of bracken to the subtlest of purple in the barren higher reaches. Never is this well-nigh incomparable scene more bewitching than when, on a sunny day, the light, white clouds dreamily wreath the highest peaks. It is arguably the most beautiful setting in the world of inland golf, though those who favor Banff or Capilano or Crans sur Sierre for that honor can scarcely be ignored.

The two eighteens are routed over similarly pretty parkland.
From 1939 until 1971 there was just one course here. It was in
large part the work of Sir Guy Campbell, but with important
contributions by Lord Castlerosse, owner of the land (also a
hugely successful London newspaper gossip columnist), and his
good friend the late Henry Longhurst. A little more than 30
years later Fred Hawtree was called in to lay out 18 additional
holes. Old and new holes were then intermingled to produce, if
you will, two new courses: O'Mahony's Point and Killeen.

It is difficult to choose one over the other. I gather that at
least some of the members prefer O'Mahony's Point, which is a
couple of hundred yards shorter and somewhat less exciting as
well. Both are par 72.

O'Mahony's Point, just under 6,400 yards from the white
tees, opens amiably with a 350-yarder that finds both fairway
and green expansive. But the next two holes, a 430-yarder doglegging right and rising modestly, and a 440-yarder leaning
left and falling modestly, are tough and terrific. Fortunately for
most of us, they are also atypical, and the holes that follow on
the outbound nine, including a couple of short holes where we
hit over swales, are not beyond our reach. But the immense and
boldly contoured greens that characterize this eighteen require
a very sure stroke.

The second half, beginning with a clever medium-length
par four that turns sharply right and has a low holly tree smack
in the middle of the fairway a hundred yards from the green, is
more stringent. The 453-yard two-shot 11th reminds us of the
two early tartars, except that this one is complicated by a triple-
tiered green on a little plateau.

Of the remaining holes, three are outstanding. The 13th, a par five of only 470 yards, is my particular favorite on this course. The downhill drive is blind. Unless the wind is into us, we should have no difficulty on our second shot carrying the stream that crosses the fairway at the bottom of the hill. But the third shot, probably a pitching wedge, climbs almost vertically to a small knob of a green with slick falloffs all around and three bunkers lurking partway down these wicked slopes. However short, this shot is unnerving.

The 16th is another excellent short par five. This one rolls nicely downhill to a green sited just short of the lake. Again, a stream must be carried on the second shot, and there are also narrow burns on both sides of the fairway that menace the aggressive wood. The vista of lake and mountain is transfixingly beautiful. Small wonder that the hole is called "Heaven's Reflex."

The shore is on our right the entire length of the 380-yard 17th, which brings us to perhaps the most photographed hole in Irish golf, a par three of nearly 180 yards with an inlet of the lake tight along the entire right side of the hole. It is actually neither so dramatic nor so dangerous a shot as you may have been led to believe, but the green, generous enough in a glade of rhododendron and pines at the water's edge, is memorably sited, and the hole itself is a perfect reflection of the abundant charms of O'Mahony's Point.

The Killeen Course was extensively revised in the 1980s by Eddie Hackett and the beloved Dr. Billy O'Sullivan (Dr. Billy, a club member, won the Irish Open Amateur here in 1949). It was toughened even further in 1990 in preparation for the Irish Open, which was played over it in 1991 and 1992. Killeen measures 7,027 yards from the championship tees, 6,250 from the whites, and almost 5,400 from the ladies' markers. The easy opening hole, 335 yards, doglegs sharply to the right around an inlet of Lough Leane, with the green set quite close to the shore. The next three holes continue in the same direction, the strong 180-yard 3rd calling for a solid long iron across a little corner of the lake, often into the breeze.

My wife and I had a very curious and rather chilling experience on the 4th more than 20 years ago, when we first visited Killarney. The green on this medium-length par four, with the shore tight on the right all the way, is invisible from the tee. I would not have been confident of the correct line had it not been for what looked like a marker in the fairway perhaps 150 yards out. As we walked toward it, it became clear that what we had assumed to be a flag or at least some sort of fabric stuck on a pole actually had bulk to it and was black. The pole was nothing but a skinny tree limb. At roughly five paces from this marker we stopped, momentarily reluctant to move closer.

fairway marker on the 4th hole

"It's a bird!" Harriet breathed.

"It looks like a crow," I said, "a dead crow."

Now we edged closer. The crow was neatly impaled on the limb, head dangling, beady eyes still open.

"Not exactly your run-of-the-mill fairway marker," I said, trying without success to pass it off lightly. Harriet was shaken. The crow-as-marker was violent, gratuitous, and starkly at odds with this otherwise idyllic setting. I remember that she quickly urged me on to my ball, some 60 yards beyond, and that she did not look back.

The 5th demonstrates the simplest way to toughen a course—simply move the tee forward 15 yards on a par five and call it a par four. That's what happened here, and the result is a 470 yard two-shotter that, for most of us, is still a three-shotter. On its final hole, you may recall, Royal Portrush pulled the same trick.

The 6th intimidates. It is only 160 yards from the white markers (203 from the blues), but the raised green, clearly crowned, is encircled by a narrow moat—and that is carrying the royal metaphor too far! There are many more 5s than 2s reported here.

Water in the form of a barely visible burn, an all too prominent lake, or tiny ponds no bigger than a self-respecting bunker (Eddie Hackett?) imperils the tee shot on three of the next four holes, and by now we realize that Killeen is a stern test of driving. The fairways are surprisingly narrow, and the rough, deceptively low, is nonetheless choking.

The 13th is superb, almost certainly the single best hole of the 36. Measuring 430 yards from the regular tees, it calls for a very good drive to one of those stingy fairways, followed by a full-blooded second over a rough dip (the fairway has momentarily disappeared) containing a stream. The elevated green sits on the far—very far—slope. Nothing less than a perfect blending of power and precision will do on a hole whose straightforward excellence is immediately apparent.

Seventeen and 18 add up to a grand finish, the former sporting a high plateau green not unlike that terror right beside it, the 13th on O'Mahony's Point. In the 1992 Irish Open, Nick Faldo, the defending champion, looked to have run out of holes when he arrived here late Sunday afternoon two strokes behind the leader, South Africa's Wayne Westner, with two holes to play. But Westner, determined to be up on the steeply climbing second shot, knocked his short iron over the green and bogeyed the hole. Now Faldo was only one off the pace.

The 18th at Killeen measures 430 yards from the regular markers, 450 from all the way back. The tee is high—that entrancing panorama of lake and mountain, to be sure—and water short and left of the green imperils the underhit or pulled second. Westner played the hole solidly for a four. After a strong drive, Faldo fired a brilliant 8-iron to 10 feet, rolled the putt home to force a tie, and won on the fourth hole of sudden death as Westner again failed to put his second shot (to say nothing of his third) on that inhospitable knob of a 17th green.

As the round unfolds on either of the two 18s here, your instinct is to suspect that the golf cannot possibly measure up to the rare natural splendor of the setting. And, in truth, it just may not. But it is very good nonetheless, and replete with first-class holes that owe little to the beauty of this place. The

Killeen course, it might be noted, has been chosen for the 1996 Curtis Cup Match.

It is likely that more visitor rounds are played at the Killarney Golf and Fishing Club than at any other club in Ireland. Tee times have become increasingly difficult to arrange, and traveling golfers have not always been able to schedule as much golf as they would like here. But relief has very recently arrived, and though neither of the two new facilities can take the place of O'Mahony's Point and Killeen, you will certainly want to be aware of them.

Michael Moriarty, the proprietor of the famous shop at the Gap of Dunloe (tweeds, linens, sheepskin rugs, blackthorn walking sticks, shillelaghs, Waterford crystal, and much more) has built a nine-hole course nearby which he calls the Dunloe Golf Course. Adjacent to it is a driving range with 30 indoor/outdoor bays, a large 18-hole putting green, and an area for pitching, chipping, and bunker practice. The course, only 2,500 yards long from the tips, is a par 34 (one long hole—a dogleg right 517-yarder no less—and three short ones) laid out on what looked to me to be less than 40 acres. It's a charmer, with ongoing interest and variety and more challenges than you might have thought possible, some attractive elevation changes (two of the one-shotters move nicely uphill), and a routing plan that is not at all predictable. The bunkering is thoughtful and inventive, and the turf is good. Great care and imagination were brought to bear on this essentially modest undertaking, which also affords delightful views of Lough Leane and of the mountains, including Carrantuohill itself, the highest peak (3,414 feet) in Ireland.

This little course may turn out to be useful to the American golfer in a very special way: for a quick nine late on his day of arrival in Ireland (after landing at Shannon, driving to Killarney, napping for several hours, and awaking at four o'clock that afternoon with an unquenchable thirst not for a Jameson's or a Bushmills or a Bailey's but for nine holes of golf), or for a quick nine on the day of departure, just before jumping in the car to make the drive back to Shannon.

The other new course, which opened in 1995, is rather more ambitious. Its name is Beaufort and, five miles from Killarney, it is routed over very gently rolling pastureland on the Churchtown Estate. The clubhouse was fashioned out of a large old gray stone barn and, like a somewhat similar clubhouse at Fota Island, has warmth and style. The manor house itself, all of 75 yards away, continues to be just that and has not been incorporated into the golf facility.

I played the course just once, shortly before its official opening, with Dr. Arthur Spring, its designer. Very tall (close to 6 feet 3 inches) and very slim, Dr. Spring, whom I put at about 50, has been one of Ireland's fine amateurs for a good 30 years. On a chilly overcast morning, with a light breeze that occasionally brought a light rain, the willowy Dr. Spring, wearing a bulky kapok-lined jacket that brushed his thighs and using borrowed golf clubs, fired, in humble demonstration of how his holes should be played, shot after shot after shot (210-yard 3-iron, 195-yard 4-iron, 165-yard 6-iron) to the heart of his greens. Each shot, struck so effortlessly, was hit high and with a suggestion of a draw.

Arthur Spring is a Tralee native who received his M.D. at

Cork University in 1969, practiced medicine as a G.P. in Tralee for the next 20 years, observed closely the building of Tralee and the new course at Ballybunion, and, when the opportunity to lay out a 9-hole course in the dunes on the Dingle Peninsula for the Castlegregory Golf Club presented itself, grabbed the main chance and gave up healing the sick. Since then he has designed six or seven courses, some 18 holes, others nine. He is a modern-day Alister Mackenzie.

And if at Beaufort he has not produced a Crystal Downs, a Pasatiempo, a Royal Melbourne, or, to come much closer to home, a Lahinch, he has done a thoroughly creditable piece of work that will become even better as it matures. Par is 71. The course measures just over 6,600 yards from the blue tees, 6,160 from the whites, and 5,300 from the ladies' markers. Bunkering is moderate and there is very little water, but the fairways, which average between 30 and 35 yards in width, are corseted by thick, clinging meadow grass. You will always be able to make your swing here, but you will not always be able to make your shot.

The round begins tamely, a 490-yarder with a surprising buttonhook dogleg right at the very end. The two greenside bunkers at the left are hidden just beyond a low rise. Dr. Spring, a modest man who seems genuinely to value the opinions of others, asked me whether I thought that another bunker on the same side, this one 15 or 20 yards short of the green in full view, should be added. I liked the idea and said so. I look forward to returning soon to see whether he actually did it.

On the first nine I particularly enjoyed the falling 170-yard 2nd, where what is actually a large green runs diagonally across the line of the shot and thus plays smaller; the 5th, a dogleg right

330-yarder with a short but exacting approach to a nicely bunkered elevated green; and the pretty 173-yard 8th, where the shot is hit out of a stand of old oak trees to a very broad green in the open that is beautifully defined by mounding and bunkers.

The entire course—open in feel and aspect, with black and white cattle grazing just beyond the boundaries—is pure meadowland. A few trees have been planted, but nothing is to interfere with the simple bucolic vistas, many of which culminate in the distance with the ever-present mountains of Macgillycuddy's Reeks. The overall elevation change is little more than 20 feet, but we have no sense of playing over boringly flat ground. The land must be much as the architect found it—much, but not entirely.

On the second nine, particularly on holes 11, 12, and 16, Arthur Spring did move dirt. And this half of the course, on the east side of the handsome tree-embowered lane that leads to the clubhouse, is, as a result, considerably stronger, more adventurous, more compelling. Every hole has undeniable merit, to some extent because the greens, somewhat larger, are more creatively contoured. The 400-yard 16th, for instance, boasts a triple-tiered green that is 55 yards deep but only 15 or 16 yards wide. Among the outstanding holes on this half are the par-five 12th, the last half of it played up a narrow mound-framed corridor (the second shot is demanding, unusual on a par five to a closely bunkered green); the starkly romantic 165-yard 13th, memorable for what remains of fourteenth-century Castle Core off to the left of the green (a tall, graceful fragment of a wall); and the 360-yard 15th, where the drive must carry a corner of a man-made lake to a fairway swinging right, the double-terrace green requiring that our iron finish on the same level as the cup if par is to be likely.

Admittedly, there is nothing here of the contrived danger—and attendant pressure on the swing—that we encounter on many new courses. It is safe to say that no hole could be labeled a "card-wrecker." Restraint has been the hallmark of Spring's design. But only good shots will produce a good score at Beaufort, with the result that there is plenty of very satisfying golf to be had in a setting where pains have been taken to retain its simple charms.

Killarney's immense tourist magnetism stems not from the town itself, which is generally crowded and long on commerce but short on artistic, aesthetic, or antique appeal. Certainly the pubs are worth a visit or two. I recall an evening some years ago walking along the main street aimlessly after dinner. We heard singing coming from down a little lane (there are four or five attractive cobbled alleys in the heart of town). It was emanating from a pub called the Laurels, and we decided to join the fun. The customers in this large and simple tavern were mostly young people, predominantly Americans of college age, though where they might have been studying we could not guess. The singing—professional or amateur, solo or group, or the entire gathering—was enthusiastic and nonstop, and the atmosphere ranged from convivial to uproarious. It was a typically engaging moment in Killarney after dark.

Most of the sight-seeing here is in the environs, and there are a number of worthwhile attractions, like Aghadoe Heights, which affords even more striking panoramas of this lake-and-mountain scenery than do the two golf courses; Ross Castle, on Lough Leane, extensively restored in recent years so that its interior, in seventeenth-century style, can now be fully appreciated; Muckross House, an Elizabethan-style manor with fifty acres of gardens, including an extensive rock garden cultivated on natural limestone (The Burren!); and the Gap of Dunloe, a mountain defile of imposing proportions.

But perhaps nothing is quite so rewarding as simply to drive on the least traveled roads you can find. One afternoon we headed away from the town toward Kilgobnet and then, turning left shortly beyond that village, toward Glencar. It was a somewhat overcast day, with more gray clouds than blue sky. The road belonged to us. This is hilly country, alternately rocky and wooded, an occasional stream, an occasional lake, an occasional white stone cottage. It is not farmland. Sheep manage to keep alive on the slopes, but cattle are uncommon. There is a remoteness, a primitiveness, and, in the end, a tranquility to it all that makes you—at least for stretches of ten or twelve minutes—almost forget who you are and where you come from and what you must soon be getting back to.

We drove at no more than 20 mph. To go much faster on these twisting, dipping, climbing, narrow byways would be unwise. One moment on the road between Kilgobnet and Glencar is still vivid in our memories. More than halfway up the mountain on the far side of the valley, a little boy in a red jacket was skipping home across meadows and over stone fences. I stopped the car and we watched him making his bounding way toward the only cottage in sight, the scarlet of his jacket brilliant, his pace unflagging. We sensed that we could never survive the simplicity—even, to be truthful, the barrenness—of this existence, but its pull at that moment was strong.

Other than Dublin itself, Killarney is the most visited place in Ireland, so there are accommodations, as the promotional literature is always quick to point out, for every taste and every pocketbook. Over the years we have stayed at four or five hotels, including the Three Lakes, a high-rise in the center of town that offers not so much as a glimpse of the three lakes that give it its name; Killeen House, a hospitable 15-room inn where the guest rooms incline to be small and the cooking top-notch; the ivy-clad Great Southern; and the Hotel Europe.

The Great Southern is a Killarney tradition going back more than 140 years. This downtown four-star hotel, set in 36 acres of gardens and within an easy walk of everything, offers not only old world comfort but a new leisure center featuring an indoor swimming pool, sauna and steam room, jacuzzi and gymnasium. The cuisine in the Malton Room, which leans toward the continent for inspiration, is regarded by some as the finest in the Killarney area.

The other leading contender for this honor may well be the Hotel Europe. We are not likely to forget the marvelous *carre d'agneau provencale* we had there on our last visit to Killarney, less than a year ago. The Europe is a five-star hotel on Lough Leane, its beautiful gardens running down to the shore. Roughly four out of five of the hotel's 200 accommodations overlook the lake, most of them from their private balconies or terraces. The Europe is what might be called a full-facilities hotel, in this case referring to its indoor swimming pool and indoor tennis (the latter a rarity in Ireland), its sauna and solarium, its stables. Though attractively decorated, it would not be considered particularly smart or sophisticated. The emphasis here is on comfort and service, and both are supplied in full measure in a pleasantly relaxed atmosphere. For golfers the Europe is ideal: next door is the Killarney Golf and Fishing Club. And, for those prepared to reach a bit further for their golfing pleasures, it is about 20 miles to Tralee, and 40 miles to Ballybunion, where our circumambulations will come to a close.

Chapter 15

The End
of the
Game

 Harty was the name and hearty was the man, to say nothing of large-spirited, helpful, informative, and—a native propensity, some would say—voluble.

Harriet and I had ducked into this cozy, dimly lit pub on the main street of Tralee for a bar snack at about 2 P.M., and now that we had finished our sandwiches and beer, one of the staff, who turned out to be the proprietor, Tom Harty, delivered the check and began to clear off the table. I asked whether he could tell us how to get to the golf club.

"Ah," he said, "I could indeed. So you're going out to Barrow. I'll get you a map." In moments he was back with a crude sketch and, as it happened, rather more. He carefully explained the route we must follow, with a few "look out for's" and "beware's" that he trusted would keep us on the path.

"It's a grand course," he said, "not seven years old yet but surely one of the best in Ireland. Here, let me give you a pre-

view of what it is you'll be seein' this afternoon." And with that
he pulled from his white apron pocket a thick deck of three-by-
five color snapshots of the links at Barrow. And along with the
pictures—he seemed to have photographed every hole from
every angle—went a running commentary: "Not easy to tell
from this, but that's a steep slope you're playing down from a
high tee"; "You must keep the drive left here for fear that the
prevailing wind will toss it over the cliff if you've any slice at
all on the ball"; and "That's Kerry Head, there, in the background—glorious view, isn't it, but don't let it distract you.
Ah, what a treat you're in for!"

By the time we reached the 5th green it was clear that Tom
Harty now had a full head of steam up, and I could see the afternoon slipping away right here, with the real possibility that
I might not get the full round in. "Do you think I'll need a
starting time?" I interjected.

"Ah, well, now, it is a Monday, so—but then, on the other
hand, it's such a fine day—I'm sure I can't say for certain. There
could be a crowd."

This, in late 1990, marked our first visit to the Tralee Golf
Club. For the biggest part of 80 years the club had played its
golf on a "downtown" nine-hole course at Mount Hawk. In the
early 1980s Arnold Palmer and Ed Seay were commissioned to
lay out 18 holes beside Tralee Bay at Barrow. The course, which
was the design team's first in Europe, opened in 1984. Under
no circumstances is it to be missed.

This is a combination links-and-headlands course, much of
it running along the clifftops high above the sea. Mount Brandon, Ireland's second highest peak, is the backdrop for the first

nine, and Kerry Head, a long, embracing promontory on the far side of the water, is in full view almost the entire round. For sheer visual exaltation, Barrow is in the same class as County Down, Portrush, Portstewart, Rosses Point, and Rosapenna.

Par is 71, and from the tiger tees the length is almost 7,000 yards. Men ordinarily play the course at a bit under 6,500 yards, ladies at about 5,250. Bunkering is minimal—there are not 25 sand hazards to be found.

The first nine—open, exposed, windswept, yet with little in the way of undulation on what must once have been pasture-land—has moments that call to mind the Monterey Peninsula's two most celebrated courses. A couple of dogleg holes in par-ticular—the par-five 2nd and the par-four 8th—with their greens perched precariously atop the cliffs, remind us of the 6th and the 8th at Pebble Beach. And the 3rd—155 yards from the whites, 193 from the blues—has just a hint of Cypress Point's peerless 16th about it, sidling dangerously close, on our right, to the cliff edge and a plunge to the rocks and the oft-angry sea far below. The safe aim is left, on the stone Tudor gun turret just down the little slope behind the green. It has guarded the entrance to Barrow Harbour for centuries.

The second nine is in marked contrast. Now we sortie into mountainous sandhills cloaked in the long rough grasses. This area is called the Warren, and there are those who contend that it was never meant to have golf holes carved through it. It con-tains abrupt and startling changes in elevation, and the greens are sometimes sited on all but inaccessible plateaus. Again and again our drives must traverse violently broken ground as we seek the rumpled and constricted fairways. Shots to the green are often imperiled by treacherous falloffs that end in what can fairly be called abysses.

We enter this wild and primitive dunescape at the 11th, a double-dogleg 560-yarder called "Palmer's Peak" that ascends heartlessly to a triple-tiered green (the greens, nothing if not spirited, come in all shapes, sizes, and convolutions). The 12th, an about-face, is forever etched in memory. The blind drive on this 440-yarder is steeply downhill, a low stone wall close on the left, fierce bracken and the great dunes on the right. The second shot is just as steeply uphill, the fairway choked to near extinction, chasms short and left and right if our long and brutally demanding play from a downhill lie should fail to scale the heights on which the tabletop green is set. No sand, no water, no boundary—and, mercifully, no other two-shotter in the world even remotely akin to it.

The holes that follow scarcely constitute a letup. There is more cavernous crossing on the 155-yard 13th. The 14th offers the delightful prospect of a lofty tee, a sloping fairway, and a right-hand shoulder of dune at the green. On the sharp dogleg left par-four 15th, the play is from yet another elevated tee, this time down to what is essentially an island of fairway in the sandhills, with the hidden raised green sited just beyond more sandhills. From the 16th tee, cloistered in the dunes, we enjoy magnificent views of the bay and the infamous rocks—Mucklough, Oilean na Bearnach, the Flag—on which several trading vessels came to grief over the years. The shot, just under 170 yards, is to a green barely clinging to the cliff's edge. The hole is called "Shipwreck," and the slightest push will prove calamitous. As for 17, it is well-nigh indescribable—a frantically topsy-turvy fairway that is extremely difficult to hit from the high tee and that turns right just beyond another of the colossal sandhills in order to reveal the green, now almost vertically above us, on a lofty summit. This hole could not be said to fall naturally on the land. But then, it is likely that no hole could be said to fall naturally on this particular scrap of land.

The 18th returns to the open ground over which the first ten holes are routed and, down then up for a distance of 443 yards, is straightforwardly demanding. I never thought I would see the day when such a hole was a breather.

As for those seven holes in the Warren, they are not merely adventurous, they are audacious. They have managed to outrage many a traditionalist. Still, there are great holes here. This is the swashbuckling Palmer and the creative Seay at their take-no-prisoners best, and if, by some chance, the second nine at the K-Club is not, as Arnold has claimed it is, "For excitement . . . the best consecutive holes I've ever seen," then maybe he ought to be reminded of the seven holes that he and Ed Seay devised at Barrow in the Warren. Which reminds me: you do encounter rabbits—actually hares, of the Royal Dublin stripe—in that mountainous maze from time to time.

After the round, we joined the affable Michael O'Brien, a former captain of the club, up in the glass-walled lounge of the sparkling new clubhouse. It is all there from this expansive room—the fine sweep of the Dingle Peninsula, Kerry Head, Ballyheigue, Banna, and Carrahane. Pointing toward the distant 1st green, Michael said, "And did you know that the beach below it—it's called the Long Strand—is where some of the big scenes in *Ryan's Daughter* were filmed? 'Tis a marvelous spot."

In truth, it is *all* a marvelous spot. No wonder Tom Harty keeps that deck of photos so close at hand.

Out on the very tip of the Dingle Peninsula is the most westerly course in Europe, Ceann Sibeal. Take the low road, along the southern coast, where early on you find yourself gazing across Dingle Bay in an effort to pick out Dooks. This is farming and grazing land, much of it gently rolling, silent, almost devoid of people. You pass through tiny Inch (appropriately named!) and Annascaul and Lispole—you are now on the N86—and head on out to Dingle Town, a thriving fishing port and tourist mecca. The pastel-colored houses on the steep streets leading up from the harbor lend a note of gaiety to the scene. So do the numerous pubs—probably the highest pub-to-people ratio in the country is here—many of which provide traditional Irish music. Dingle is also a noted center for pottery and weaving and for the speaking of Gaelic (English sometimes seems like a second language). Among several very good restaurants, perhaps the best known is Doyle's Seafood Bar. The name itself gives a good picture of the place.

Beyond Dingle Town the countryside becomes hillier as the road carries on toward Slea Head, another location that David Lean used in filming *Ryan's Daughter*. Close beside this narrow, twisting, lofty byway are the unique stone cells, shaped like beehives, that monks built for meditation many centuries ago. You may want to park the car here for a moment and get out. The cliffs are sheer and high, the sea churning on the rocks and boiling up onto the strand.

Just a few miles farther along lies the hamlet of Ballyferriter and, at nearby Sybil Head, the golf course named for this promontory, Ceann Sibeal. It could reasonably be claimed that we have reached "the back of beyond."

The clubhouse, which opened in 1993 and is quite spiffy and comfortable, offers views over the course to the hills and the ocean. The course does not look particularly pleasing—no dunes, wide open, very little in the way of elevation changes, all of it at a considerable distance from the sea. Fortunately, it turns out to be better than it looks. Eddie Hackett laid out the first nine in the 1970s. Christy O'Connor, Jr., added the second nine in 1990. You get the impression that Mr. Hackett was operating on a shoestring, and the result is a bit too minimalist for most tastes.

Par is 72. The course can play as long as 6,650 yards, but it is usually set up at about 6,200 yards for the men, 5,600 for the ladies. The turf is quite good, on both fairways and greens, and the grass is a seaside fescue. A narrow stream snakes its way across a number of holes and actually menaces the shot seven or eight times.

There are a couple of good par fours on the first half, including the 370-yard 1st, where our approach must carry the stream, and the 425-yard 9th, routed over nicely undulating ground to a slightly elevated plateau green beneath the clubhouse windows. Unfortunately, there are three consecutive holes—6, 7, 8—that are flat and distressingly dull. A host of bunkers are strung out along the straightaway 520-yard 6th in what looks like a desperate effort to impart interest and character. They do not help much. Extensive revisions to these three holes would have a salutary effect on the nine—indeed, on the entire course—and I suspect that this may not be long in coming.

The second nine, which has no such poor patch, begins with a terrific 185-yarder, the green modestly raised, elongated, shapely, and, for the most part, concealed beyond some mounding. The 11th and 13th are a couple of good dogleg par fives, both given spunk by the presence of the stream. On the 13th, which sweeps boldly right, the water endangers both the drive and the pitch. And at the delightful 16th, 371 yards, which moves slightly downhill and doglegs right, that stream is back again to complicate our approach.

There is no water on the 500-yard home hole, and none is required. This is a beauty, with a stout forced-carry over rough ground from the tee, serious bunkering right and left along the way, the broad and ambitiously contoured green perched beyond tumbling and rising ground. This green is just one of a number of festive putting surfaces on the second nine.

Ceann Sibeal is no world beater, but it does have merit, and its setting, with stunning views of the Blasket Islands to the south and Mount Brandon to the north, is outstanding. Then, too, the drive that brings us down the Dingle Peninsula is consistently rewarding, and the alternate route back, which I earnestly recommend, contains one of the sublime moments in Irish motoring. Come out of Dingle Town and go north toward Kilcummin. Extraordinarily hilly, this narrow, lightly traveled road, with its twists and elbows, its long dips into lonely glens and its abrupt climbs back out of them, seems almost whimsical, aimless. You are heading toward Connor Pass now. The ascent is dramatic, even tense, with the valley on the right slowly slipping away beneath you as the car labors to reach the pass. And then, quite suddenly, you are there. The road has crested and you have broken through the mountains. You have not scaled the peaks; this is a pass, a cut through them, though you had to climb a long way to reach it. And now you are poised, as though on a high dive, gazing directly down on a pale green valley some two thousand feet below and stretching away toward the north as far as the eye can see. There is nothing in sight but the eternal land—no cottages, no cattle, no sheep, and perhaps, if you are lucky, not even another car. It is overpowering—simple and noble and beautiful.

The descent is even more precipitous than the climb. You keep a firm foot on the brake all the way down, and much of the way you remain in low gear. Finally you bottom out on the valley floor and aim northeast, through Kilcummin and Stradbally, on to Tralee and, some 20 miles due north, to Ballybunion, the last stop on this pilgrimage, where the river Shannon enters the Atlantic Ocean. We have traveled well over a thousand miles since our opening shot at Lahinch and have played some 50 courses along the way. And now it is time to savor the final two, the Old Course at Ballybunion and the new, now called the Cashen Course.

The club was formed in 1893, and for more than 30 years there were just nine holes. In 1927 the course was extended to eighteen. Tom Simpson was brought in nine years later to recommend changes, a few of which were promptly implemented, others being carried out over the years that followed. Among Simpson's basic views were two that are clearly exemplified at

Ballybunion: a course should look as natural as possible, and no two greens should be alike. Simpson contributed importantly to the eighteen we play today, but the routing of the holes owes much more to the ideas and efforts of various club committee members, a greenkeeper or two, probably a club professional. Records are at best sketchy, and even the club's official history, which reviews the speculation that Old Tom Morris and James Braid may at one time or another have been consulted, is unable to make a definitive attribution.

Because the club hosted several national championships— men's and women's, amateur and professional—beginning in 1932, the Irish themselves knew full well what an outstanding links this was, but the world was almost totally unaware of even its existence until, in 1968, Herbert Warren Wind visited it and subsequently reported his impressions in a piece dealing with half a dozen of the best Irish courses (the other five were Portmarnock, Royal County Down, Royal Portrush, Lahinch, and Rosses Point) that was published in 1971 in the *New Yorker*. America's preeminent golf writer asserted that "Ballybunion revealed itself to be nothing less than the finest seaside course I have ever seen." The lack of equivocation from a man noted for his considered judgments was stunning. Suddenly Ballybunion was, at the very least, on the map. Then, in 1981, Tom Watson, who had already won three British Opens and would win two more and who could thus be said to have some knowledge of links golf, made his own discovery of Ballybunion. He subsequently wrote the introduction to the hole-by-hole guide that some golfers like to have in their pocket before teeing off.

Watson opens by saying, "After playing Ballybunion for the

first time, a man would think that the game of golf originated here." He closes by saying, "Ballybunion is a course on which many golf architects should live and play before they build golf courses. I consider it a true test of golf." And in between he speaks of "the wild look of the place . . . some of the finest and most demanding shots into the green of any course I've played in the world . . . a magnificent challenge."

The sequence is clear: first Wind, then Watson, and now the world. Everyone wants to play the Old Course at Ballybunion. Most days, from April through October, everyone seems to be doing just that—and it would be difficult to find any among them not thrilled by it.

I still find myself checking the scorecard from when I first played here more than 20 years ago, wondering whether the enthusiasm of my original judgments should not be tempered by time and a broader perspective. Well, I have not backed down despite several return visits over the years. That first card, with all its cramped scratchings, shows no adjective beside eight holes. Of the other ten, nine are marked "Great" and one, the matchless 11th, "Greatest!" This on a course which, from the regular tees, measures 6,200 yards (6,590 yards from the blues, 6,000 from the "society green markers," 5,320 from the ladies' tees).

Standing on the elevated 1st tee and scanning the vast sweep of gray-green linksland, treeless and uncompromising, we are instantly struck—as at County Down, Carne, Cruden Bay, and only a very few others—by the formidable nature of the landscape: the huge, billowing, grass-covered sandhills that disclose only an occasional patch of playable turf. Not only are these dunes markedly higher and bolder than those of any other links, but they tend to run transversely across the course from the sea. Instead of paralleling the shoreline, they run at right angles to it. The net effect of this unusual topography is a broad variety of dogleg holes sculpted through the sharply contoured land as well as straightaway holes where the sandhills patrol the access to the green in stern sentinel fashion. The outlook here is unyielding. The round, we have no doubt, will be eventful.

The 1st, 366 yards and pleasantly downhill, confronts the slicer with a 300-year-old graveyard (a generous assortment of Celtic crosses) and the rest of us with a couple of bunkers in the left center of the fairway about 200 yards out. The 2nd hole, perhaps because it comes so early in the round, is an overlooked gem of 400 yards that plays 450 yards. The long second shot must be fired through a gap in a pair of facing dunes to a green high above us on a modest escarpment. The demand on the swing is implacable.

The 3rd is a falling 200-yarder to a large green with a boundary tight on the left, and the next two holes, a pair of straightaway 490-yarders, are birdie opportunities routed over rather featureless interior ground. Still, there is some good bunkering along the way, and, however plain, they cannot be taken for granted.

At the 6th, 345 yards, we turn left to reenter the great dune country—never again to leave it—and the shot to the disquietingly narrow green would be a tester if it were only 20 yards long instead of 120. Abutting the green and high above the strand is the great 7th, a 400-yarder that closely skirts the cliff's edge every foot of the way. A bunker at the left of the green seems a veritable haven when contrasted with the plunge to the beach on the right.

Turning our back now to the ocean and from a tee high above it, on the short par-three 8th we play inland and almost straight downhill between two dunes to a deep but narrow green defended by a necklace of bunkers and little grassy hollows. Watson wrote, "In a wind it's one of the most demanding shots I've ever faced."

My instinct is to say exactly the same about the second shot on the wonderful but backbreaking 430-yard 9th, where, following a downhill drive, most of us will be relying on a 4-wood to reach the green well above us, a green that is set into the shoulder of a rise and is defended by a hollow some 20 yards short of it, by a mound and another hollow on the right, and by a slippery falloff on the left.

The incoming half begins with a 340-yarder that edges left along a dune-framed valley. If it is not a great hole, it is certainly a perfect one. Both words could fairly be used to describe the 11th, which is surely among the four or five greatest seaside two-shotters in the world, cast in the same heroic mold as the 8th at Pebble Beach, the 14th at Dornoch, the 4th at Seminole, and the 17th at St. Andrews.

The 11th here at Ballybunion measures 400 yards from the white markers, 450 yards from the blues. The tee is 60 or 70 feet above the broad golden beach on our right, the fairway skirts the cliff's edge, and the massive grass-cloaked dunes stand guard down the left side of the hole. At first we are reminded of the 7th, but the landing area for the drive here strikes us as less generous, perhaps because of the height of the dunes that erase any bailout area on the left. The green is concealed behind fronting dunes. The fairway is actually broken into three different "pieces," if you will: the landing area for the drive; then, about a hundred yards farther on and on a lower level, a shelf; and finally, still lower, a narrow path of cut grass threading its way between the fronting sandhills till, on the far side of them, the green is revealed, an undulating carpet with a falloff right and a bit of breathing room left. All of this, it need scarcely be pointed out, with the ocean cliffs tight on the right all the way. Such a combination of majesty and ferocity, of originality together with the integrity of the truly natural, is rare indeed. And so probing an examination is it that on a typically breezy day, regardless of how you choose to maneuver, you cannot guarantee a bogey.

With no diminution of excellence and with only a shade less pressure on the swing, the seven remaining holes continue to challenge and delight. You will be quite surprised, starting at the 12th, to play five consecutive holes without a par four in the bunch—and what extraordinary, even brilliant, holes they are. The two par fives, 13 and 16, dogleg left, the 13th softly, the 16th emphatically. Each is 480 yards long. On 13 a dune-top tee leads down to a valley where the pitch—or the aggressive second—is played over a hidden stream short of an angled green isolated by mounds, bunkers, and falloffs. The 16th, from a seaside tee, plays up a narrow channel through the dunes, rising relentlessly over the last 200 yards. I remember battling this hole against the wind, needing three solid woods to get home, and, having gotten there in regulation (!), three-putting.

I also remember standing on that 16th tee and gaining a fresh insight into the cliff-erosion problem that has beleagured the club for many years. I was paired with a member, Kevin Fitzgerald, a Tralee grocer who played most of his golf at Barrow. He turned to me as we gazed down on the shore and said, "A law was passed recently that forbids the hauling of sand from the beach. The local farmers have been doing that for years in order to provide bedding for their horses and cattle. They'll take anything that's free. Well, they'll not take this sand anymore. You see, that's what has permitted the tide to rush right in, even beyond the rocks, to the sandhills and undermine the golf course. That's why we are always having to shore up the holes along the sea with rocks and wood planking and metal caging pressed into the cliffside. Golfers think that playing the game here is a battle. And indeed it is. But so is just keeping the links in place."

To return to the trio of superlative one-shotters, each takes its character from the imperious dunes, the shots in all three instances over intimidating rough country from which rescue is most unlikely. On both 12 (180 yards) and 14 (135 yards), the plateau greens are above us. On 15 there is a gently falling nature to the shot—and, at 210 yards, well there might be. This hole, aiming out to sea, our target a broad double-tiered green in the dunes, is one of the most glorious one-shotters in golf and reminds us of nothing so much as the even longer 6th at Turnberry's Ailsa.

The 17th, doglegging decisively left from a pinnacle tee in the dunes, heads straight out to sea at first, the path of the drive framed right and left by massive sandhills, the invitation to draw the ball around the giant left-hand dune a tempting one indeed. Succeed and you are left with only a short iron to a green, which is, believe it or not, beside the sea and at sea level.

The home hole, 365 yards, has long been controversial. It begins on a modest platform of a tee only four or five feet above the beach, and the drive plays over a corner of the 17th green and up a narrowish fairway flanked on both sides by the ubiquitous sandhills. A vast bunker devours the fairway some 240 yards out. This is no ordinary sand hazard. Its name, Sahara, lacks originality, but its composition does not. Neither does its provenance. The bunker actually contains a curious mixture of sand, shells, ashes, stones, and bones. According to archeologists, it was used as a midden, or dump, by ancient tribes, beginning perhaps as far back as the fifth century. It is to be avoided at all costs. The second shot, which crosses the Sahara, is blind, the green lying high above us at the top of an extremely steep hill and in a dell-like setting there. At the left front is a hidden bunker.

I mentioned controversy. The reason for it is that blind uphill approach. On a course where the target, either fairway or green, is consistently in sight, the notion of the final—and often decisive—stroke being blind is anathema to many purists. As this book went to press it looked very much as though something might be done about it. Tom Watson was retained by the club in 1995 to advance a few ideas—nothing at all major, you understand—that might somehow enhance this nonpareil links. One of them—you be the judge of whether it is major or minor—would be to lower slightly a part of the face of the Sahara so that the player who had positioned his tee shot in precisely the right spot (also a Watson judgment, I should imagine) would find himself looking up the hill not at the sky but at the flagstick. He would still, of course, be unable to see the putting surface, but the flag would beckon.

I think it an unwarranted alteration, but then, if you've come this far with me, you know I have a fondness for blind shots. To me, they are very much a part of genuinely natural golf whenever the terrain is hilly.

The change on 18 aside (though it is earth-moving, it is scarcely earth-shaking), I want to go on record here as declaring the Old Course at Ballybunion to be the best seaside course I've ever played. There are two reasons for this conclusion. First, it seems to me to have more great holes than can legitimately be claimed by any of the other renowned links—and it has no poor holes. Second, for pure golfing pleasure—a combination, for me, of honest challenge, natural beauty, exhilaration, originality, and variety—I find it without equal.

There is a splendid new clubhouse at Ballybunion these

days, and it represents a rather different outlook from that expressed in the club's Minute Book a hundred years ago: "Club can manage without cottage or pavilion till it sees how it gets on as regards members." The new structure opened in 1993, and it is very nearly as awe-inspiring as the Old Course itself: a roofline full of massive and unexpected stone "outcroppings," all manner of planes and angles and slopes and overhangs, vast windows giving on the sea, a terrace or two, and a spectacular glass-ceilinged atrium at the heart of it all. It is determinedly unlike any other clubhouse in Ireland, and it is entirely the right place to relax and regroup and ready yourself for the rigors of the round on the second eighteen, itself somewhat unconventional.

The Cashen Course, which opened in 1984, has thus far failed to elicit anything like the admiration and affection prompted by the Old Course. Put bluntly, golfers—the overwhelming majority of golfers, members no less than visitors—have vehemently disliked it from the day it opened, insisting that it is contrived, insensitive, even outrageous. They have shied away from playing it. Still, with the passing of time and the implementation of certain changes, there is growing, if grudging, acceptance of what I feel is a masterpiece. A flawed masterpiece, if you will, but a masterpiece nonetheless.

Robert Trent Jones was 74 years old when he agreed to design this eighteen, immediately south of the clubhouse in the same kind of monumental sandhills through which the Old Course is routed. His enthusiasm was that of a man half his age. "I was given a once-in-a-lifetime opportunity," he said, "and a terrifying challenge. . . . The property I had to work with is perhaps the finest piece of linksland in the world ... natural sites for greens, bunkers and passage through the dunes were everywhere offering a spectacular combination of long and short holes that demand power, precision, and imagination. This God-given land, with its tumbling, undulating, free-flowing rhythm of line is beauty beyond description. ... The boldness and variation of this terrain meant that the construction of a golf course would be no easy matter, but somehow it has been achieved."

In his twilight years Trent Jones appears to have set out here to leave his mark not just on Ballybunion, not even on seaside golf in general, but on the very fabric of golf architecture—and it just may be that he has succeeded.

To be sure, there were excesses. Four or five greens were satanically contoured (one thinks instinctively of the 10th, so scandalously hummocky that the model for it must have been a crumpled piece of paper), and several fairways (those of both par fives on the second nine) were much too pinched by the encroaching sandhills. A number of these so-called problems have been solved over the past six or seven years.

Changes in elevation, up and down, were occasionally too precipitous, and a few forced carries were judged to be too severe. It was decided to abandon the original 12th hole. No longer would a player be asked to climb to the top of one sandhill in order to hit to the crest of an opposing—and even higher—sandhill. So exacting was the shot on this 223-yarder that the hole was designated a par four, not a par three. The falloff on the right—the *abyss* on the right—called up the "War Hollow" on the 14th at Portrush. For pure effrontery, this stupefyingly original hole eclipsed even the 12th at Tralee. Nor shall we see its like again.

But if a certain toning down has taken place, this is still stirring stuff, with far more than its quota of remarkable golf holes—and no hole less than good in a highly unusual assortment that contains five par fives and five par threes. It is difficult for me to name favorites, but surely among them would have to be the 3rd, a 145-yarder sequestered in the sandhills, the green itself extravagantly contoured; the 5th, 373 yards, steeply uphill out of the dunes to a green on the heights perched within three or four paces of a long, sheer drop to the beach on the left; the 13th, a dogleg left 375-yarder, gently up, then less gently down, the perfect plateau green bunkered across the front and isolated on the far side of a very deep swale; and the 17th, writhing 476 yards through the dunes to finish on a baldly exposed rumpled knob of a green above the sea.

The Cashen Course is actually short—against a par of 72, it is less than 6,300 yards from the blues, about 6,000 from the whites, and a mere 4,700 from the ladies' markers. Power is no prerequisite. What is required is a willingness—as on the first nine at Portstewart and the second nine at Tralee—to accept brilliant and daring and innovative golf holes which may, in the bargain, have a wart or two. The Cashen Course takes a little getting used to. My friend Liam Higgins, the professional at Waterville, whose brother Ted held the same post for years at Ballybunion, said to me, "When I first played the new course, I shot 68 and 69 to win a tournament going away. I vowed never to play it again because I was convinced it was the worst course I'd ever seen and I hated it. Then I did play it again, and I did a complete flip-flop. I now believe it must be the single greatest course in the world and that it puts the Old in the shade!"

I think Liam goes too far, but I believe he is heading in the right direction. And one thing I am convinced of: the Cashen Course is not only a worthy companion to the Old, it is a great course in its own right. Together the two of them may well constitute the best 36 holes of golf in one place anywhere.

Ballybunion certainly attracts adherents. Some, like Watson and Wind, proclaim their devotion in words. Others make their statements more dramatically. On New Year's Eve, 1987, an avid American golfer by the name of Martin McDermott was buried in the cemetery beside the first hole on the Old Course here. "It was the one wish he had," said his wife, Vicki, who had the body of her 43-year-old husband flown 6,000 miles from their home in Los Angeles in order to respect his last request. Martin McDermott had played Ballybunion twice, in 1984 and 1986. Father Michael Galvin, the local parish priest, officiated at the interment. Sean Walsh, longtime secretary of the club, said, "I really was not all that surprised; it is the kind of thing the Americans might do. They hold this course in very high esteem and come back year after year to play it. This man came back for good."

Chapter 16

Updating Courses and
Hotels, 1997—2006

Since 1996, when this book was published, the Irish have not been content to rest on their laurels. Many new courses have been built, and some of the outstanding older courses have been revised. In the pages that follow you will find commentary on 20 courses that were not dealt with originally and some half-dozen courses that have benefitted from substantive alterations. Also added here are 34 places to stay, ranging from modest B&Bs such as Highfield House, near County Louth Golf Club, at Baltray, to the opulent Four Seasons Hotel Dublin.

For this chapter, it seems to make sense to follow the same "routing plan" that is used in the rest of the text, which is to say that the game will begin at Lahinch and head north as we move clockwise around the Irish land mass, the last leg of the trip carrying us up from Waterville to Doonbeg.

The big news from Lahinch comes courtesy of the gifted

Martin Hawtree, the third generation of Hawtree golf course architects. A links that has been dearly loved by the world for decades is now inarguably one of Ireland's half-dozen greatest courses. Grandeur and exhilaration and shotmaking delight mark every step of the round. Among the many Hawtree changes are the elimination of the old 3rd, a prosaic one-shotter near the parking lot; the creation of a new and altogether splendid par-three 8th; the transformation of the par-four 12th into a lustrous par five along the water. In truth, every hole without exception has profited from Hawtree's artistry, with the result that Lahinch, markedly more testing than at any time in its long history, is a masterpiece.

On the outskirts of town is irresistible Moy House, the centerpiece of a property with woodlands, gardens, a charming little river, and pasture land for cattle and horses that slopes down to Liscannor Bay. Some of the nine guest rooms have fireplaces, many have sea views, all are spacious and richly appointed. Plus the cooking is exceptional. In the heart of Lahinch are three moderately priced hotels—the Aberdeen Arms, the Atlantic, and the Shamrock Inn—which are professionally run and provide reliably good cooking.

Nearly two hours northeast of Lahinch, the Connemara Golf Club, at Ballyconneeley, now offers a third nine, designed by the late Tom Craddock. It measures only 3,145 yards from all the way back, but it is full of fun and surprises. Just about anything goes: big and antic greens, occasional long forced carries off the tee; water (to be crossed on both drive and approach on the par-four 2nd); sharply uphill climbs on the 4th, 6th, and

8th; and holes routed unpredictably to every point of the compass.

Forty-five minutes due east of Ballyconneeley is Cashel House, at the head of Cashel Bay. Woodlands and gardens provide solitude. This 30-room hotel is immensely inviting, with its antiques, old pictures, and turf-and-log fires. Its international reputation stems in part from the extensive seafood choices on the menu—lobster, crab, mussels, clams, oysters, scallops, sole, salmon, monkfish, turbot, and trout are all likely to be offered on a given day. Within a mile of Clifden, the unofficial capital of Connemara, is the 27-room Rock Glen Hotel, which purveys warm hospitality and good food in equal measure. Though inclined to be small, the bedrooms are nonetheless comfortable.

A third nine is opening at County Mayo's Carne Golf Links, Belmullet, in 2008. Count on it to be a humdinger. The architect is Denver's Jin Engh, whose courses include Sanctuary and Redlands Mesa, in Colorado, and The Club at Black Rock, in Idaho. Himself a member at Carne, Engh has routed a series of dazzling holes through this turbulent duneland. Among the most memorable moments is the dogleg 5th, a 540-yard valley hole that climbs out of the towering sand hills to finish at an elevated green above the ocean.

Belmullet now boasts a brand spanking new hotel, the Broadhaven Bay. Thoroughly comfortable, it has 90 guest rooms (most with grand water views), a spa, and excellent cuisine. Some 40 minutes east, in Ballycastle, is the Stella Maris Hotel. It is owned and operated by Frances Kelly, a Ballycastle native, and her Yank husband, Terence McSweeney. This is a stylish inn with 12 accommodations, open fires, an inviting bar, imaginative cooking, and a sunny 100-foot long conservatory within steps of Bunatrahir Bay.

At the western end of County Sligo is the Enniscrone links, which came into its own just a few years ago when Donald Steel summoned forth six new holes from an adjacent tract of glorious duneland. No fewer than four of these six are great—the double dogleg 500-yard 2nd, for instance, squirms along the floor of a dune-framed valley to a low plateau green brilliantly backdropped by the Atlantic Ocean—with the result that Enniscrone is now one of the top dozen courses in Ireland.

Three quarters of an hour east of Enniscrone, and still in County Sligo, is Strandhill Golf Club, with its sparkling sea-and-hill vistas and its diversity of first-rate golf holes. The two sternest par fours are the downhill 1st, 455 yards and curving left, and the uphill 18th, 442 yards and curving right.

Perhaps 30 minutes from Strandhill and off the Dublin Road is Cromleach Lodge Country House and Restaurant. There are ten guest rooms in the long, low, contemporary structure that looks down from the heights onto island-dotted Lough Arrow. Moira Tighe's gourmet tasting menu ("intense flavors—light portions") somehow manages to outshine even this extraordinary view.

Pat Ruddy was chosen in 2000 by Donegal Golf Club to upgrade the links at Murvagh. In addition to introducing some strategically sited bunkers—the lone pit just short of the green on the 520-yard opener is a stroke of genius—he built seven new greens, reshaped four fairways, and rerouted burns on the 12th and 14th to enhance the playing value of these two par fives.

At Rosapenna, with its 45 holes of seaside golf, Ruddy is again front and center. He recently lengthened the first nine of the Old Tom Morris links and added a superlative second nine to serve as its companion: rippling fairways, spacious greens on plateaus or in dells, huge gashes in the faces of sand hills to produce what are today called "blowout bunkers." And then, next door, he created Sandy Hills, a bona fide masterpiece. Rigorously challenging, it seems designed for the truly accomplished player and it is jam-packed with holes ranging from very good to great. The duneland topography—at times rolling, at times hilly, and ranging from rumpled to heaving—is perfect for the construction of arresting golf holes. And Ruddy has made the most of it.

Thanks to extensive revisions five years ago by the county's favorite son, Portsalon can now play as long as 7,100 yards. Ruddy built eight new holes, improved almost all of the other ten, and reduced but did not entirely eliminate the captivating quirkiness. The gorgeous sea-and-mountain panoramas make playing this authentic links an invigorating experience.

In the village of Portsalon is an antiques-filled guest house called Croaghross. Three of the five bedrooms—all five have bathrooms ensuite—enjoy stirring views over Ballymastocker Strand. And Kay Deane's cooking is superior.

A rather plain village with only about 600 inhabitants, Ballyliffin still offers a nice choice of accommodations, though the cooking is pretty much confined to the staples (chicken, pork, surf and turf). The spruce and comfortable Ballyliffin Hotel provides 36 rooms, many with views looking toward the sea.

The Strand has 20 rooms, individually decorated and inclined to be small, some with generous views to Pollan Strand and Malin Head. The 13-room Trasna House's accommodations are simply appointed and of modest size. Its pub frequently offers traditional Irish music. Rossaor House is a hospitable B&B with four rooms, each with private bath, that are attractively furnished but short on space; the full Irish breakfast includes smoked salmon and scrambled eggs.

We cross the border now into Northern Ireland and drive east along the coast road to Portrush. Royal Portrush Golf Club, with its fabled Dunluce Course, also takes pride in a second outstanding eighteen, the Valley Links; it too, was laid out by England's Harry Colt. Here towering sand hills embrace the acreage. The restlessness of this sublime linksland, the constricting dunes that give rise to narrow fairways, and the small, deftly sited greens (on plateaus, in dells) all demand accurate shotmaking.

Not five minutes from Royal Portrush is Bushmills Inn, a re-creation of an ancient coaching inn and mill house. Beam ceilings, old fireplaces, countless nooks and crannies are all to be found in the public spaces. Some of the more generous guest rooms have whitewashed stone walls, dark paneling, and four-poster beds. The cooking is topnotch, a skillful blend of "new Irish" cuisine and fresh County Antrim produce.

Often cited as the best inland layout in Northern Ireland is Malone, a few miles south of Belfast. It's a rolling beauty, with a wealth of oaks, sycamore, and pines, not to mention the river Lagan bordering it on the east and 27-acre Ballydrain Lake lending tension to the 13th, 14th, and 15th holes. At Ardglass, a 35-

minute drive north of Royal County Down, six holes are
linksland and the other twelve incline to be meadowy. Among
the handful of distinctive holes are three splendid one-shotters
(the 2nd, 10th, and 12th). The course is routed over ground high
above the water, with the result that the views—across the Irish
Sea to the Isle of Man, down over Coney Island Bay, south to the
Mountains of Mourne—are intoxicating. Some 15 miles north of
Ardglass, in the village of Portaferry and beside Strangford
Lough, is the Portaferry Hotel. Guest rooms as well as public
spaces are cheerful and cozy; the menu emphasizes fish.

Also in County Down but nearly an hour's drive north of
Ardglass is the Kirkistown Castle course, true links golf—a
turf base of sandy loam makes it quick to dry—with revetted
pot bunkers, a number of greens perched on the high ground
that takes the full brunt of the wind, and an impressive assortment of sturdy two-shotters.

Some 20 minutes south of County Louth Golf Club, at Baltray,
is the Laytown & Bettystown course, dating back almost a hundred years. Pulpit tees, plateau greens with sharp little falloffs,
and dunes cloaked in long marram grass combine to make the
game on this links an enjoyably sporty one. Ten minutes north
of Baltray, in Termonfeckin, is Highfield House, a farmhouse
B&B with three guest rooms, each of them spacious and with a
private bathroom. Next door is the Triple House Restaurant,
where the cooking is hearty.

Less than an hour south of Termonfeckin, in Maynooth, is Carton House Golf Club, with two eighteens. The first course was

designed by Mark O'Meara, who made minimal alterations to the existing landscape, which is a very attractive combination of mature woodlands, moderate elevation changes, and the pretty river Rye. There is an idyllic quality to the game here. The second course, laid out by Colin Montgomerie and lacking both water and trees, is a so-called inland links, replete with 140 bunkers, many of them deep, and with green complexes full of giddy contours and frustrating hollows. It was the venue for the Irish Open in 2005 and 2006.

Roughly ten minutes away is the K Club. The second eighteen here is called the Smurfit Course, in honor of the resort's founder, businessman Michael Smurfit. Also laid out by Arnold Palmer and Ed Seay, the Smurfit may not be so visually engaging as the Palmer Course, site of the 2006 Ryder Cup, but it, too, is studded with strong golf holes. Elevation changes are more pronounced here than on the original eighteen, the contouring of the immense and swift greens is bolder and more intricate, and bunkers are deeper and often steep-faced. This test is on no account to be missed.

A short distance north of Dublin and about 15 minutes from The Island Golf Club is Roganstown Golf & Country Club, with its 7,000-yard parkland course designed by Christy O'Connor, Jr.—gently rolling first-rate turf, water on 12 holes. The clubhouse/hotel has 52 spiffy and comfortable guest rooms, and the cooking is excellent.

Two of the most important Dublin courses, Royal Dublin and Portmarnock, have been improved by Martin Hawtree. At Royal Dublin he has employed deft bunkering and mounding to lend considerable character to the green complexes. At Portmarnock, Ireland's leading venue for major competitions over the years, Hawtree's efforts included moving the first green to the left in order to produce a more demanding approach shot, installing bunkers at the right side of the tee shot landing area on the 5th, creating a new—and richly contoured—green on the great 160-yard 12th, building an entirely new green complex at the 577-yard 16th, and fashioning a new green surround for the 472-yard 17th, the course's toughest two-shotter.

Three worthy places to stay should be noted. Almost next door to Portmarnock Golf Club is the stylish four-star Portmarnock Hotel, the central part of which was formerly the manor house on the Jameson Whiskey family estate. Not 15 minutes away, at the harbor in the picturesque fishing village of Howth, is the King Sitric, which bills itself as a "fish restaurant and accommodation." The eight guest rooms, all but two of them small, have sea views, and the cuisine is superlative. In the upscale Ballsbridge section of the capital is the Four Seasons Hotel Dublin, where the 259 accommodations are opulent: crystal, marble, polished chintzes, inlays, one-of-a-kind carpets.

South of the city in County Wicklow and immediately adjacent to Pat Ruddy's Druids Glen course is his Druids Heath eighteen, which opened in 2003. To characterize the Heath in three words, it is *thrilling, scenic, unyielding*. A brutally long par 71 at 7,450 yards from the championship tees, it boasts forceful elevation changes (the only level hole is a long par three over water from tee to green); sand (109 pits, a number of them deep); four water holes; two natural rock quarry holes; gorse, trees, and throttling rough; greens that are often very large, complex, and baffling; a fresh breeze off the mile-distant Irish Sea; and at least six great holes. The other 12 range from good to excellent.

The Druids Glen Marriott Hotel has 148 accommodations, all of them smart and comfortable. There are three dining options: Flynn's Steakhouse (char-grilled Irish beef the specialty), Druids Restaurant (Irish lamb stew on the dinner menu), and the Thirteenth Bar, with its zesty pub food served throughout the day. Fifteen minutes away, in Ashford, is the family-run Chester Beatty Inn—12 guest rooms (with pristine bathrooms), a bar with fireplace, and cooking that is simple and satisfying.

The Old Head Golf Links, on a 220-acre promontory some 20 minutes from Kinsale, in County Cork, and jutting about two miles into the Atlantic Ocean, opened in 1997. Six individuals played important roles in the design and construction of Old Head: the late Joe Carr, Ron Kirby (American golf architect), Paddy Merrigan (Cork-based golf architect), Liam Higgins (erstwhile head professional at Waterville), the late Eddie Hackett, and Haulie O'Shea, course constructor.

This is not a links course—no dunes, no rippling or tumbling sand-based terrain. Like Pebble Beach, Old Head is a headlands course, often clinging to the clifftops, which soar 200 to 300 feet above the sea. Nine holes skirt the ocean on the heights. Of these cliffhangers, no fewer than four are great, among them the precarious 415-yard 4th, where the broad fairway doglegs sharply left around a rocky inlet, then climbs to a green all but teetering on the brink some 215 feet above the water. Small wonder that this hole is called "The Razor's Edge."

No course you've ever played will prepare you for the extravaganza that is Old Head, unsurpassed as a triumph of seaside grandeur. More important, the holes here are not only compelling but, again and again, rigorously and fairly challenging.

Kinsale is awash with attractive accommodations. Old Bank House, opposite the sailboat-filled harbor, is an inviting B&B with 17 guest rooms, an antiques-studded sitting room with a fireplace, and a cozy breakfast room where Ciaran Fitzgerald, the proprietor, serves up hot porridge, sausage, black pudding, and scrambled eggs with salmon. Just across the street is Perryville House, another high-end B&B, this one with 22 rooms ranging from snug to spacious, many with harbor views. Or stay at the Trident, which, at the water's edge, looks as though it's about to set sail. The hotel's Wharf Tavern has tasty bar food and its Savannah Waterfront Restaurant specializes in fish dishes. Ballinacura House is the Kinsale area's most luxurious lodging, a country house hotel with 13 handsome guestrooms, a bar, dining room, sitting room, drawing room, and study.

In 2002 the Waterville Golf Links board of governors commissioned Tom Fazio to effect certain revisions. Though inexperienced on links courses, Fazio came up with changes that were both appropriate and insightful, so much so that the great course is now markedly greater. He created two entirely new holes, the downhill 6th, 194 yards through the sand hills, a burn threatening on the right; and the 424-yard 7th, which bends smoothly right as it rises, perfectly framed by dunes left and, as on the 6th, a burn on the right. He also radically altered five others, including the 16th, a medium-length two-shotter with an uphill approach shot to a green whose right edge is now mere steps from a steep falloff to the beach. As for the oceanside 18th, 594 yards from the tips, it is almost as breathtaking as the 18th at Pebble Beach and, thanks to Fazio's skillful bunkering and his aggressively contoured green, it is notably harder.

In the heart of the village of Waterville and overlooking the sea is the Butler Arms Hotel. Among the 42 accommodations are 12 luxurious junior suites, some with fireplaces. The beam-ceiling restaurant offers ocean views, an extensive menu, and well-prepared food.

Killarney's Lackabane Course, laid out by Donald Steel and Tom MacKenzie, opened in 2000. Unlike Mahony's Point and Killeen, Lackabane provides no view of Lough Leane and almost no suggestion of the mountains. Still, this is a lively layout. On seven holes, water menaces the shot, and on nine holes out-of-bounds is a clear possibility.

Not 15 miles east of Killarney, on gemlike Caragh Lake, is stately Hotel Ard Na Sidhe ("Hill of the Fairies"), a graceful beige-gray stone structure more than a hundred years old and with 20 guest rooms. The superior cooking takes its cue from local ingredients such as salmon, trout, and Kerry lamb. The terraces offer stunning views of the lake far below.

In the town of Tralee is the 58-room Meadowlands Hotel, set in exquisitely landscaped gardens. The suites have a king-size bed, a steam shower and jacuzzi, and a separate sitting room with fireplace. The bar is noted for its food and, on many nights, live music featuring Irish folk songs. Somewhat closer to Tralee Golf Club is Brook Manor Lodge, a B&B that is one of the two four-star luxury guest houses in the Tralee area. The large, sunny bedrooms are individually appointed, and the communal living room has a peat fire to take the chill off. Have dinner a short drive down the road in Fenit at the West End Restaurant, a bright and boisterous seafood spot where the cooking is merely marvelous.

Thirty minutes east of Ballybunion, on the south bank of the river Shannon, is 200-year-old Glin Castle. With its eye-opening collection of Irish furniture and paintings, it is one of the Republic's most important Heritage Houses. Of the 15 accommodations, all of them roomy and decorated with antiques, some have a four-poster bed, some have a fireplace, and some have both. Cocktails in the library, with its secret door in the bookcase, is almost as much of a treat as dinner in the formal dining room. For lodgings all but next door to the Ballybunion Golf Club, try the Marine Hotel. The 13 guest rooms look over the ruins of Fitzmaurice Castle to the Shannon, and the restaurant specializes in fresh seafood.

Directly across the road from Adare Manor is the 66-room Dunraven Arms Hotel, dating to 1792 and full of antiques. The fitness facility has a 55-foot indoor swimming pool. The cooking is quite good in the moderately priced In Between Restaurant as well as in the upscale Maigue Restaurant. Fifteen minutes south of Adare, in Ballingarry, is The Mustard Seed at

Echo Lodge, which characterizes itself as a restaurant with rooms. The cooking is of the highest standard, and the rooms are luxurious.

Twenty minutes northeast of Adare lies the Limerick Golf & Country Club, its par-72 layout measuring 6,900 yards from the tips. The distant views over meadows and pastures are fetching, the greens are provocatively contoured, water comes into play on ten holes, and doglegs abound.

In 2000 the course at Dromoland Castle was sweepingly revised by Joe Carr and Ron Kirby; Kirby had worked with Jack Nicklaus, Gary Player, and Robert Trent Jones. By and large, Carr and Kirby stuck with the original routing plan. But they lengthened the course to 6,845 yards and completely reconfigured the green complexes. Water imperils the shot on eight holes—we must take on the marshes, the tiny river Rine, and formidable Lough Dromoland.

Roughly halfway along the coast between Lahinch and Ballybunion awaits another majestic links, Doonbeg, laid out by Greg Norman seven years ago. Here, in the midst of grass-cloaked dunes soaring as high as 80 feet above the crescent beach, he has routed a parade of holes that are never less than good and that are often great (in fact, no fewer than seven indisputably great holes). Fairways meander through tranquil dune-framed valleys. Greens perch two-thirds of the way up the flanks of sand hills or beckon from the seclusion of dells or reside with supreme naturalness mere steps above the beach. Bunkers can be pitilessly deep. Though this is an uncompromising examination, especially in a heavy wind, the game here can still be a joyous occasion. One of Ireland's ten best, Doonbeg is a course for the ages.

At the golf club itself is a cornucopia of five-star accommodations. These suites—living room, kitchen, and as many as four bedrooms, each with bath—are sumptuously appointed. Owned by members, most of whom are Americans, they are rented to visiting golfers on a limited basis. The cooking in the clubhouse is superb.

Just beyond the practice range is Links Lodge, a B&B with ten bright and welcoming guest rooms, each with private bath. In Doonbeg village is another winning B&B, An Tintean ("our hearth"), which has seven very pleasant guest rooms, each with bath ensuite. Also in the village is Morrissey's Seafood Bar & Grill, where locals and travelers mingle amiably and the cooking is good.

Well, we've come full circle with this newsy chapter, and I'm optimistic that this paperback edition of *Emerald Fairways and Foam-Flecked Seas* now contains essentially all the information about where to play and where to stay in Ireland that you will need to put together what may turn out to be the golf trip of your dreams.

Golf Courses in Ireland

ADARE MANOR GOLF CLUB
Adare, Co. Limerick
Tel: 353-61-396204

**ADARE MANOR HOTEL &
GOLF RESORT**
Adare, Co. Limerick
Tel: 353-61-396566
www.adaremanor.ie

ARDGLASS GOLF CLUB
Castle Place, Ardglass
Co. Down BT30 7TP
Northern Ireland
Tel: 44-28-4484-1022
www.ardglassgolfclub.com

BALLYBUNION GOLF CLUB
Sandhill Road, Ballybunion
Co. Kerry
Tel: 353-68-27146
www.ballybuniongolfclub.ie

BALLYCASTLE GOLF CLUB
Cushendall Road, Ballycastle
Co. Antrim BT54 6PQ
Northern Ireland

Tel: 44-28-2076-2506
www.ballycastlegolfclub.com

BALLYLIFFIN GOLF CLUB
Ballyliffin, Co. Donegal
Tel: 353-74-937-6119
www.ballyliffingolfclub.com

BANTRY BAY GOLF CLUB
Bantry, Co. Cork
Tel: 353-27-50579
www.bantrygolf.com

BEAUFORT GOLF COURSE
Churchtown, Beaufort, Co. Kerry
Tel: 353-64-44440
www.beaufortgolfclub.com

BUNDORAN GOLF CLUB
Bundoran, Co. Donegal
Tel: 353-71-984-1302
http://www.bundorangolfclub.com
/contactpage.htm

CARLOW GOLF CLUB
Deerpark, Carlow, Co. Carlow
Tel: 353-59-913-1695
www.carlowgolfclub.com

CARNE GOLF COURSE
Belmullet, Co. Mayo
Tel: 353-97-82292
www.carnegolflinks.com

CARTON HOUSE GOLF CLUB
Carton, Maynooth, Co. Kildare
Tel: 353-1-505-2000
www.carton.ie

CASTLEROCK GOLF CLUB
65 Circular Road, Castlerock,
Co. Londonderry BT51 4TJ
Northern Ireland
Tel: 44-28-7084-8314
www.castlerockgc.co.uk

CEANN SIBEAL GOLF CLUB
Ballyferriter, Co. Kerry
Tel: 353-66-915-6255
www.dinglelinks.com

CONNEMARA GOLF CLUB
Ballyconneeley, Co. Galway
Tel: 353-95-23502
www.connemaragolflinks.com

CORK GOLF CLUB
Little Island, Cork, Co. Cork
Tel: 353-21-435-3451
www.corkgolfclub.ie

COUNTY LOUTH GOLF CLUB
Baltray, Co. Louth
Tel: 353-41-988-1530
www.countylouthgolfclub.com

COUNTY SLIGO GOLF CLUB
Rosses Point, Co. Sligo
Tel: 353-71-917-7134
www.countysligogolfclub.ie

DONEGAL GOLF CLUB
Murvagh, Ballintra, Co. Donegal
Tel: 353-74-973-4054
www.donegalgolfclub.ie

DOOKS GOLF CLUB
Dooks, Killorglin, Co. Kerry
Tel: 353-66-976-8205
www.dooks.com`

DOONBEG GOLF CLUB
Doonbeg, Co. Clare
Tel: 353-65-905-5246
www.doonbeggolfclub.com

DROMOLAND CASTLE HOTEL
& COUNTRY ESTATE
Newmarket-on-Fergus, Co. Clare
Tel: 353-61-368144
www.dromoland.ie

DRUIDS GLEN GOLF CLUB
Newtownmountkennedy
Co. Wicklow
Tel: 353-1-287-3600
www.druidsglen.ie

DUNLOE GOLF COURSE
Gap of Dunloe, Killarney, Co. Kerry
Tel: 353-64-44578
www.dunloegc.com

ENNISCRONE GOLF CLUB
Enniscrone, Co. Sligo
Tel: 353-96-36297
www.enniscronegolf.com

THE EUROPEAN CLUB
Brittas Bay, Co. Wicklow
Tel: 353-404-47415
www.theeuropeanclub.com

FARRANGALWAY GOLF CLUB
Kinsale, Co. Cork
Tel: 353-21-477-4722
www.kinsalegolf.com

FOTA ISLAND GOLF CLUB
Fota Island, Carrigtwohill
Co. Cork
Tel: 353-21-883700
www.fotaisland.ie

GALWAY BAY GOLF &
COUNTRY CLUB
Renville, Oranmore, Co. Galway
Tel: 353-91-790500
www.lawrencetown.com/galgolf.htm

GLASSON GOLF HOTEL &
COUNTRY CLUB
Glasson, Athlone, Co. Westmeath
Tel: 353-90-648-5120
www.glassongolf.ie

GLENGARRIFF GOLF CLUB
Glengarriff, Co. Cork
Tel: 353-27-63150

HARBOUR POINT GOLF COMPLEX
Little Island, Cork, Co. Cork
Tel: 353-21-358-3094
www.harbourpointgolfclub.com

THE ISLAND GOLF CLUB
Corballis, Donabate, Co. Dublin
Tel: 353-1-843-6205
www.theislandgolfclub.com

KENMARE GOLF CLUB
Kenmare, Co. Kerry
Tel: 353-64-41291
www.kenmaregolfclub.com

KILDARE HOTEL &
COUNTRY CLUB
Straffan, Co. Kildare
Tel: 353-1601-7200
www.kclub.ie

KILLARNEY GOLF &
FISHING CLUB
Killarney, Co. Kerry
Tel: 353-64-31034
www.killarney-golf.com

KINSALE GOLF CLUB
Kinsale, Co. Cork
Tel: 353-21-477-4722
www.kinsalegolf.com

KIRKISTOWN CASTLE
GOLF CLUB
142 Main Road, Cloughey,
Co. Down BT22 1JA
Northern Ireland

KIRKISTOWN CASTLE *(cont.)*
Tel: 44-28-4277-1004
www.linksgolfkirkistown.com

LAHINCH GOLF CLUB
Lahinch, Co. Clare
Tel: 353-65-708-1003
www.lahinchgolf.com

LAYTOWN & BETTYSTOWN
GOLF CLUB
Bettystown, Co. Meath
Tel: 353-41-982-7170
www.landb.ie

LIMERICK COUNTY GOLF
AND COUNTRY CLUB
Ballyneety, Co. Limerick
Tel: 353-61-351881
www.limerickcounty.com

MALONE GOLF CLUB
Upper Malone Road, Dunmurry,
Co. Belfast BT17 9LB
Northern Ireland
Tel: 44-28-9061-4917
www.malonegolfclub.co.uk

MOUNT JULIET
Thomastown, Co. Kilkenny
Tel: 353-56-77-73000
www.mountjuliet.com

MULLINGAR GOLF CLUB
Belvedere, Mullingar, Co. Westmeath
Tel: 353-44-48366
www.mullingargolfclub.com

NARIN & PORTNOO
GOLF CLUB
Portnoo, Co. Donegal
Tel: 353-75-45107
www.narinportnoogolfclub.ie

OLD HEAD GOLF LINKS
Old Head of Kinsale, Co. Cork
Tel: 353-21-477-8444
www.oldheadgolflinks.com

PARKNASILLA GOLF CLUB
Parknasilla, Co. Kerry
Tel: 353-64-45233
www.sneem.net/parknasilla

PGA NATIONAL GOLF CLUB
Johnstown, Co. Kildare
Tel: 353-45-906901
www.palmerstownhouse.com

PORTMARNOCK GOLF CLUB
Portmarnock, Co. Dublin
Tel: 353-1-846-2968
www.portmarnockgolfclub.ie

PORTMARNOCK HOTEL AND
GOLF LINKS
Strand Road, Portmarnock
Co. Dublin
Tel: 353-1-846-0611
www.portmarnock.com

PORTSALON GOLF CLUB
Portsalon, Co. Donegal
Tel: 353-74-915-9459
www.golfeurope.com/clubs/portsalon/

PORTSTEWART GOLF CLUB
117 Strand Road, Portstewart
Co. Londonderry BT55 7PG
Northern Ireland
Tel: 44-28-7083-2015
www.portstewart.co.uk

ROGANSTOWN GOLF &
COUNTRY CLUB
Swords, Co. Dublin
Tel: 353-1-843-3118
www.roganstown.com

ROSAPENNA HOTEL &
GOLF LINKS
Downings, Co. Donegal
Tel: 353-74-915-5301
www.rosapenna.ie

ROYAL COUNTY DOWN
GOLF CLUB
Newcastle, Co. Down BT33 0AN
Northern Ireland
Tel: 44-28-4372-3314
www.royalcountydown.org

ROYAL DUBLIN GOLF CLUB
Dollymount, Dublin 3
Tel: 353-1-833-6504
www.theroyaldublingolfclub.com

ROYAL PORTRUSH GOLF CLUB
Dunluce Road, Portrush
Co. Antrim BT56 8JQ
Northern Ireland
Tel: 44-28-7082-2311
www.royalportrushgolfclub.com

SEAPOINT GOLF CLUB
Termonfeckin, Co. Louth
Tel: 353-41-982-2333
www.globalgolf.com/seapoint

STRANDHILL GOLF CLUB
Strandhill, Co. Sligo
Tel: 353-71-68725
www.strandhillgc.com

TRALEE GOLF CLUB
Barrow, Co. Kerry
Tel: 353-66-713-6379
www.traleegolfclub.com

TRAMORE GOLF CLUB
Newtown Hill, Tramore
Co. Waterford
Tel: 353-51-386170
www.tramoregolfclub.com

WATERFORD CASTLE HOTEL
& GOLF CLUB
The Island, Waterford, Co. Waterford
Tel: 353-51-878203
www.waterfordcastle.com

WATERVILLE GOLF LINKS
Waterville, Co. Kerry
Tel: 353-66-947-4102
www.watervillegolflinks.ie

WESTPORT GOLF CLUB
Carrowholly, Westport, Co. Mayo
Tel: 353-98-28262
http://homepage.eircom.net/~west
portgolf/

Hotels in Ireland

ABERDEEN ARMS
Lahinch, Co. Clare
Tel: 353-65-708-1100
www.a1tourism.com/ireland/
lahinch-aberdeen-arms.html

**ADARE MANOR HOTEL &
GOLF RESORT**
Adare, Co. Limerick
Tel: 353-61-396 566
www.adaremanor.ie

AHERNE'S SEAFOOD BAR
163 N. Main Street
Youghal, Co. Cork
Tel: 353-24-92424
www.ahernes.com

ALBANY HOUSE
Harcourt Street, Dublin 2
Tel: 353-1-475-1092
www.holidaycityeurope.com/al-
bany-house-dublin/index.htm

AN TINTEAN GUEST HOUSE
Doonbeg, Co. Clare
Tel: 353-65-905-5036
www.a1tourism.com/ireland/
doonbeg.html

HOTEL ARD NA SIDHE
Caragh Lake, Killorglin, Co. Kerry
Tel: 353-66-976-9105
www.killarneyhotels.ie

ARDTARA COUNTRY HOUSE
8 Gorteade Road
Upperlands, Co. Londonderry
BT46 5SA, Northern Ireland
Tel: 44-28-7964-4490
www.ardtara.com

ASHFORD CASTLE
Cong, Co. Mayo
Tel: 353-94-954-6003
www.ashford.ie

ATLANTIC HOTEL
Lahinch, Co. Clare
Tel: 353-65-708 1049
www.loguehotelgroup.com/atlantic

BALLINACURRA HOUSE
Kinsale, Co. Cork
Tel: 353-21-477 9040
www.ballinacurra.com

BALLYLIFFIN HOTEL
Ballyliffin, Co. Donegal
Tel: 353-77-76106
www.ballyliffinhotel.com

BALLYMALOE HOUSE
Shanagary, Co. Cork
Tel: 353-21-4652 531
www.ballymaloe.ie

BERKELEY COURT HOTEL
Lansdowne Road
Ballsbridge, Dublin
Tel: 353-1-661711

BOYNE VALLEY HOTEL
Stameen, Drogheda, Co. Louth
Tel: 353-41-983 7737
www.boyne-valley-hotel.ie

BROOK MANOR LODGE
Fenit Road, Tralee, Co. Kerry
Tel: 353-66-712-0406
www.brookmanorlodge.com

BRUCKLESS HOUSE
Bruckless, Co. Donegal
Tel: 353-74-973-7071
www.brucklesshouse.com

BUSHMILLS INN
9 Dunluce Road
Bushmills, Co. Antrim
BT57 8GQ, Northern Ireland
Tel: 44-28-2073-3000
www.bushmillsinn.com

BUTLER ARMS HOTEL
Waterville, Co. Kerry
Tel: 353-66-947-4144
www.butlerarms.com

CARAGH LODGE
Caragh Lake, Co. Kerry
Tel: 353-66-976-9115
www.caraghlodge.com

CASHEL HOUSE HOTEL
Cashel, Co. Galway
Tel: 353-95-31001
www.cashel-house-hotel.com

CHESTER BEATTY INN
Ashford, Co. Wicklow
Tel: 353-404-40206
www.hotelchesterbeatty.ie

COOPERSHILL HOUSE
Rivertown, Co. Sligo
Tel: 353-71-916-5108
www.coopershill.com

CROAGHROSS GUEST HOUSE
Portsalon, Co. Donegal
Tel: 353-74-915-9548
www.croaghross.com

CROMLEACH LODGE
Castlebaldwin, Co. Sligo
Tel: 353-71-916-5455
www.cromleach.com

DOONBEG GOLF CLUB
Doonbeg, Co. Clare
Tel: 353-65-905-5246
www.doonbeggolfclub.com

DROMOLAND CASTLE
HOTEL & COUNTRY ESTATE
Newmarket-on-Fergus, Co. Clare
Tel: 353-61-368144
www.dromoland.ie

DRUIDS GLEN MARRIOTT
HOTEL
Newtownmountkennedy
Co. Wicklow
Tel: 353-1-287-0800
http://marriott.com/property/propertypage/DUBGS

DUNRAVEN ARMS HOTEL
Adare Co. Limerick
Tel: 353-61-396633
www.dunravenhotel.com

ENNISCOE HOUSE
Castlehill Ballina, Co. Mayo
Tel: 353-96-31112
www.enniscoe.com

HOTEL EUROPE
Killarney, Co. Kerry
Tel: 353-64-7130
www.killarneyhotels.ie

THE FITZWILLIAM
41 Fitzwilliam St., Dublin 2
Tel: 353-1-662-5155
www.fitzwilliam-hotel.com

FOUR SEASONS HOTEL
DUBLIN
Simmonscourt Road
Ballsbridge, Dublin 4
Tel: 353-1-665-4000
www.fourseasons.com

GLASSDRUMMAN LODGE
Mill Road
Annalong, Co. Down
BT34 4RH, Northern Ireland
Tel: 44-28-4376-8451
www.glassdrummanlodge.com

GLASSON GOLF HOTEL &
COUNTRY CLUB
Glasson, Athlone, Co. Westmeath
Tel: 353-90-648-5120
www.glassongolf.ie

GLENVIEW HOTEL
Glen O'The Downs, Co. Wicklow
Tel: 353-1-287-3399
www.glenviewhotel.com

GLIN CASTLE
Glin, Co. Limerick
Tel: 353-68-34173
www.glincastle.com

GREAT SOUTHERN HOTEL
Killarney, Co. Kerry
Tel: 353-1-214-4800
www.greatsouthernhotels.com

GREGANS CASTLE HOTEL
The Burren, Co. Clare
Tel: 353-65-707-7005
www.gregans.ie

GRESHAM HOTEL
Upper O'Connell Street, Dublin 1
Tel: 353-1-874-6881
www.gresham-hotel-dublin.com

HARVEY'S POINT COUNTRY
HOTEL
Lough Eske, Donegal Town
Co. Donegal
Tel: 353-74-972-2208
www.harveyspoint.com

HIGHFIELD HOUSE
Termonfeckin, Co. Louth
Tel: 353-41-982-2172

KILDARE HOTEL &
COUNTRY CLUB
Straffan, Co. Kildare
Tel: 353-1601-7200
www.kclub.ie

KILLARNEY GOLF &
FISHING CLUB
Killarney, Co. Kerry
Tel: 353-64-31034
www.killarney-golf.com

KILLEEN HOUSE
Killarney, Co. Kerry
Tel: 353-64-31711
www.killeenhousehotel.com

KING SITRIC FISH RESTAURANT
AND ACCOMMODATION
East Pier, Howth, Co. Dublin
Tel: 353-1-832-5235
www.kingsitric.ie

LINKS LODGE
Doonbeg, Co. Clare
Tel: 353-65-905-5600
www.irishprogolftours.com/
linkslodgedoonbeg.asp

LISCANNOR HOTEL
Liscannor, Co. Clare
Tel: 353-65-708-6000
http://www.hotelclub.net/hotel.
reservations/Logues_Liscannor_
Hotel.htm

LOTAMORE HOUSE
Tivoli, Co. Clare
Tel: 353-21-482-2344
www.lotamorehouse.com

MARINE LINKS HOTEL
Golf Links Road
Ballybunion, Co. Kerry
Tel: 353-68-27522
www.marinelinkshotel.com

MEADOWLANDS HOTEL
Oakpark, Tralee, Co. Kerry
Tel: 353-66-718-0444
www.meadowlandshotel.com

MERRION HOTEL
Merrion St., Dublin 2
Tel: 353-1-603-0600
www.merrionhotel.com

MOUNT JULIET
Thomastown, Co. Kilkenny
Tel: 353-56-77-73000
www.mountjuliet.com

MOY HOUSE
Lahinch, Co. Clare
Tel: 353-65-708-2800
www.moyhouse.com

THE MUSTARD SEED AT
ECHO LODGE
Ballingary, Co. Limerick
Tel: 353-69-68508
www.mustardseed.ie

OLD BANK HOUSE
Kinsale, Co. Cork
Tel: 353-21-477-4075
www.oldbankhousekinsale.com

PERRYVILLE HOUSE
Kinsale, Co. Cork
Tel: 353-21-477-2731
www.perryvillehouse.com

PORTAFERRY HOTEL
Portaferry, Co. Down
Tel: 44-28-427-28231
http://www.portaferryhotel.com

PORTMARNOCK HOTEL
AND GOLF LINKS
Strand Road, Portmarnock
Co. Dublin
Tel: 353-1-846-0611
www.portmarnock.com

RATHMULLAN HOUSE
Rathmullan, Co. Donegal
Tel: 353-74-915-8188
www.rathmullanhouse.com

ROCK GLEN HOTEL
Clifden, Connemara
Co. Galway
Tel: 353-95-21737
www.westirelandholidays.com/gal-
way/rockglen.htm